Backpack Trekker: A 60's Flashback

by
Beatlick Joe Speer

BEATLICK PRESS
ALBUQUERQUE, NM

Backpack Trekker: A 60's Flashback

*This book is dedicated to Pamela Adams Hirst
better known as "Beatlick Pamela."*

Acknowledgements:

Thank you to all the many people who came together to help
bring this book to life:

Editing:
Gary Brower
Debbie Coy
Carol Moscrip
Susan Schmidt
Elaine Schwartz
Jon VerPloegh

Technical advisor:
Gary Brower

Photos:
Jim Gay,
Michael White
Pamela Adams Hirst

Underwriters:
Terry Alvarez
Deborah Coy
Michael Elliott
Jeffrey Grauer
Dale Jensen
Dana Kemp
Steve Klinger
John Knoll
Kathy Meyer
Carol Moscrip
   Celso & Mary Pacheco
   Danny & Maggie Perea

Julie Phillips
Teresa Phillips
Maria Salazar
Barb Shaffer
Mona Silkwood
Paul Sivertsen
Larry Stocker
Rita Nosper Stenicka
Deborah Victory
Judy Wells
   James Michael Wisniewski, wZ

Book Design:
Pamela Adams Hirst

www.beatlickpress.com
www.beatlick.com

Beatlick Joe Speer

FOREWORD

After a long journey *(la jornada es larga y muy difícil)* on the back roads of intellectual outlaws, a path paved with articles, letters, e-mails, books and papers, piles of papers, papers ejected by machines with machine minds, with psyches composed of human waste (nobody writes anymore; we only press buttons that generate papers), there beneath the piles and piles, a gem broke through the clutter: a genuine human thought.

I turn to page 200 and wonder at the miracle of knowledge, vision and genius (pity the genius for she is a lonely soul and he that embraces her must never let go). A poet who was once a beauty queen said:

> We must teach our readers to read anew. Where
> is she now, this illusive beauty queen? Where is
> her muse? Where is the new in the daily news?

Zen Jazz is everywhere ... and so is Beatlick Joe Speer. His name will be entered in the register of worthy travelers (as will his queen and companion). A rare creature of scholarly devotion ... an article of faith ... a testament to the art of creation itself ... a singular being ... A1... a feast of all saints and blessed wise ones: Castenada ... Joyce ... Yeats ... Ferlinghetti ... Ginsberg ... Dylan ... Camus ... Jimi, Janis, John & Morrison ... Dostoevsky ... Robeson ... Kessey, Kennedy & King ... Gabriel García Márquez' "100 Years of Solitude" ... Dante's journey to the underworld ... the last tour of the Magic Bus ... Marilyn & Joe ... Timothy Leary ... Whitey & the Mick ... the voices of east Harlem ... viva la raza: César Chàvez, Che & the labor movement ...

Whatever happened to Abbie Hoffman? He died by his own deed and there lies a story.

Joe Speer lives and dies on the pages of his tributary ... memoir ... social commentary ...

Fear not for he will rise again & again & again ....

Jack Random, Modesto, CA

Backpack Trekker: A 60's Flashback

AUTHOR'S NOTE:

This book was written with the idea to chronicle hitchhiking as a means of transportation, when it was in its prime.

"Thumbin' a ride" was popular far beyond the hippie counterculture, but as the practice became more dangerous it went out of vogue. Mainstream society took on the trappings of the hippie generation without experiencing the deep spiritual connection and oneness that I found in my treks around North America during that era.

Looking for that campsite at the end of each day kept one close to the Earth. It was a simpler time.

The hitchhiker was not looked upon as a freak of nature; the uplifted thumb was a legitimate signal that someone was in need.

People were less insulated and more generous back then, trusting and willing to pick up a stranger. Our goals were simpler back then, too... finding the next ride, the next town, the next festival.

Beatlick Joe Speer

TREK 1

*In the cold winter of 1961 Bob
Dylan arrived in New York City.*

The decade started badly for me. Albert Camus died in an auto smash early in 1960. Cars kill people every day. There should be a warning with every bill of sale.

"Caution, driving this machine may cause severe injury or death."

Getting high and writing were activities William S. Burroughs engaged in while living in Tangier, Morocco. Allen Ginsberg wrote to Neal Cassady, "The Revolution has begun!"

The 1960's had an auspicious beginning with John F. Kennedy as front man for the media. America had finished with a two-term general, maintaining its tradition of rewarding military heroes with the presidency. Mr. PT 109 followed George Washington, Andrew Jackson, Zachary Taylor, U.S. Grant and Dwight Eisenhower into the Commander-and-Chief chair. Kennedy endeared himself to poets by inviting Robert Frost to the inauguration.

The New York Yankees lost the 1960 October contest to Pittsburgh in a seven-game slug fest. I had an emotional investment in the series. When Bill Mazeroski hit a home run in the bottom of the ninth inning, the center of my universe imploded. The Yanks won two more championships before their dynasty took a nosedive at the hands of their old rivals from Brooklyn, now relocated to Los Angeles.

Backpack Trekker: A 60's Flashback

I lost interest in baseball after that. The game continues with new players and new records, but I shifted my attention to literature and cinema. "Lawrence of Arabia" in 1962 sandblasted my imagination with a large-screen experience. I was content to watch and read about life. Movies and books provided the natural medium. I did not have to act, react, or respond to human stimuli. I did not have to judge or be judged. I was happy to sit alone in a dark room and watch. I was content to sit and hold a dictionary.

But in the summer of 1969, there was such turmoil in America that I felt compelled to propel myself into the mix. My mother María encouraged me to follow my bright spirit and would support me with her resources and love. I opted to travel with no money and discover the world beyond the pale of my hometown. I loaded my backpack with dried fruit, books, rain gear, tent and oatmeal. Mother gave me a sack of pre-cooked dry pinto beans and her blessing and drove me to the outskirts of town. I promised one special letter to her for every ten pages I wrote. Five minutes after she dropped me off, I hitched a ride and was headed west.

TREK 2

In 1962 Rachel Carson wrote and published "Silent Spring", calling attention to pesticides and pollutants, helping to launch the environmental movement.

Berkeley, California, was named for an Irish philosopher. Like the thinker's mind, it was a hub of activity. Even if you were a schmo from Pie Town, New Mexico, never heard of Berkeley, and you were dropped on Telegraph Avenue, you would immediately snap to the fact that Berkeley was a ferocity of expression.

The community confronted the process of higher education with a dispute over People's Park. Folks in Berkeley had taken unused land and turned it into a recreational area. When Reagan got wind of it, he sent in the National Guard. Confrontation of enforcement squads with badges, billy clubs, shotguns and tear gas did a job on clearing the streets. Some people protested by breaking windows late at night on university property. It only took one hit with a brick at point-blank range. This simple action brought results. Next day with the broken glass, it was impossible to conduct classes.

Beatlick Joe Speer

They replaced the windows, but an encore performance of rocks brought the conflict back to the professors' podiums. They boarded up the windows. Instead of cracking a textbook, many students walked up and down Telegraph Avenue. The smell of repression was in the air.

People's Park had been fenced off as the university reclaimed its property from the community. The official point of view was that an empty lot couldn't be transformed into a gathering place for unlicensed conga drums.

Berkeley was a haven for transient traffic. If a peripatetic poet needed a place to flop, someone would take them home. They could telegraph the message and linger for the most propitious offer. One evening a host took me to his flat across the bay in San Francisco. He lived near the Presidio. Next morning I walked from there to Golden Gate Park to watch kites trace patterns in a skittish sky.

My afternoon was spent in pursuit of literature. Ferlinghetti already had the door open at the City Lights Bookstore. He sold postcards of Marcel Proust and poetry of André Breton. I stood in a protracted line for a free noon meal, wandered the streets where the earth quaked in 1906, and smelled traces of Jack London in North Beach where Columbus cuts a diagonal avenue.

I rose with a clear horizon and open schedule, bought used books at Cody's on Telegraph Avenue and felt different energies from time and space converging in recollected harmony.

TREK 3

In 1960 "La Dolce Vita" *presents a panorama of Italy's upper classes shown in a series of Fellini episodes.*

One energy from another time and space that manifested in the 1960's for young English-speaking reconnoiterers was Herman Hesse. He died in 1962, but he became a posthumous literary hero with his novels "Demian", "Der Steppenwolf", "Siddhartha", "Narziss und Goldmund" and others. His books were carried in backpacks across America and Europe. They were traded, sold and resold in used bookstores. They were discussed in hobo camps by firelight and around academic tables.

Access to books enables people to add to or circumvent the standard indoctrination of public school. The public library is avaluable resource. It was in a library, roving the shelves, that I discovered Arthur Schopenhauer.

"The world is my idea," he began his book. Arthur was a crusty curmudgeon but he taught me to think for myself.

Traditional values do not necessitate belief. I had the will to formulate my own explanation of experience. I could choose not to marry or not to vote. I could consider clocks, calendars, religion as attempts by people to establish order. I did not have to take as gospel the legislative or pontifical dictums.

I could wander the desolate area near the Big Bend and collect stones for unknown lapidaries. I could thumb my nose at the commercialism of every aspect of life. I could turn off the television when the President spoke to the union. An earthquake or exploding volcano was serious, but the pronouncements of government were often fleeting or erroneous.

"The world is my will." It was my will to travel. I wanted to saturate my consciousness with memory. Even though the term "transient" carried a derogatory tinge, I wanted to decamp daily and live outside the jurisdiction of authority. I wanted to breathe beyond the cycle of monthly payments to the various life support systems.

The rationale of government is to control. I wanted to get beyond the gubernatorial grip because I saw no peaceable captain for Spaceship Earth. I felt time moving, and as my friend Zen Jazz said I was going backwards at the speed of light. I walked sometimes and my feet didn't even touch the ground. But my time had expired. It was time for me to go.

TREK 4

The Cheekwood Mansion in Nashville, Tennessee, was originally the estate and gardens of the Cheek family, founders of Maxwell House Coffee. In 1960 Cheekwood became a Museum of Art and Botanical Garden.

The Newport Folk Festival celebrated its second birthday in 1960. Joan Baez was there singing. At the end of the decade she was pregnant and still singing. The festivals were gathering places for spirits of like ilk. The coffee house was another point of confluence. The java connection atmosphere was a vital haven for poetry. Ragged people with little money could catch a rampageous buzz. Couples from the banquet in evening dress could saunter in and dally with the rabble.

I got into a confabulation with a traveler from Canada. He had a maple leaf tattooed on his thumb knuckle. We talked for so long that we downed ten cups of coffee. With a caffeine glow on we decided to find a bar and balance out our chemicals. We finished off at the beach shouting mythological epitaphs at the sea. "Store your bones in Davy Jones locker. Rest in peace in Neptune's water closet. May Horus the peregrine fulcrum fly you on high. May you be paid per diem for dealing mushrooms and conducting light shows at the temple of Edfu."

I worked as a bone collector for the Grim Reaper. The bugger paid me by the pound. He wanted no flesh on the bones. Get your fleshy flush in life. When the cloaked scimitar cuts off your dreams, your bones will be dried in the August sun.

An overview of the civil rights problem was exemplified when Cassius Clay returned home from the Rome Olympic Games with gold in his pocket. But that wasn't enough to sit at a lunch counter and order coffee. In Nashville students from Fisk University counter-poised the situation by counting on community support. People boycotted downtown stores and business suffered. The students took their argument to Mayor Ben West and he acquiesced to the winds of change.

People had reason to be indignant. Festivals and coffee mills provided outlets to rankle the spleen. Phil Ochs and Bob Dylan made statements unteachable in school. At open-mics people could exchange ideas and information.

My brother Paul found his salvation through music. He went from playing classical violin to folk guitar. He played Donovan, Gordon Lightfoot, Buck Owens and then made up his own tunes.

Sometimes he played instrumental compositions to the rhythm of a campfire near the hot springs in the Jemez Mountains. His notes floated toward dissipation and amalgamation with the air. He set us spiritually free with his sound and we soared with the falcon of imagination.

TREK 5

In 1961 President Kennedy established the Peace Corps.

One of my favorite teachers was for my high school English college prep class. He was a kind of idiot savant. I was inspired by his finesse with language. Every period was peppered with grandiloquent interlocution. At the end of every class I had a laundry list of new words to look up in the unabridged dictionary.

There was a curious discrepancy between his linguistic luster and his daily life. First of all he was transportationally challenged because he did not have a driver's license. He rode a bicycle to school, or on rainy days his wife dropped him off at the entrance. Often his manner of dress presented a laughable spectacle with different colored socks, crooked tie and vest with buttons in the wrong hole. To approach him outside of class was to encounter a timorous wallflower. But when class began he was a *cognoscente* with coherent contemplative composure. I saw his name in a literary journal for having won a $10,000 prize for a book of poetry. He never mentioned it in class so I asked him about it. He acknowledged being the recipient of the prestigious award, but did not elaborate or even crack a celebratory smile.

I never defended myself when bullied or insulted, but I took up arms one time as a student when two of my classmates made fun of our English teacher. I didn't want to go to the office for scuffling on the school yard, so I waited until we were on neutral territory before I took them to task. I called them ignoramuses and dunderheads.

People of their ilk always resort to force to prove their point of view. As a member of the karate club I was prepared. So when the first punch approached, I blocked it and retaliated. I greeted the other duffer with a back kick. While they were splayed out on the ground, I told them never to speak disparagingly about our teacher.

The three of us became good friends after that and formed a book club. We dug a clubhouse near the apple orchard. It was a five-foot trench that led to a kiva. We covered the top with boards and dirt. A person could walk near and not even know about our secret entrance to the underground.

It was after dark one night when we got into a loud discussion in our hole about a short story by Robert Graves. It concerned a slacker matador who requested squint-eyed and underweight bulls. As the bull careened past he stabbed the animal in the side. An *espantaneo* leaped into the ring with a neckerchief and played the bull better than the matador.

A neighbor passed by and heard our voices, but could not see anyone. An investigation was made and our hideout discovered. Our parents condemned the hideout and we were forced to

shovel dirt into our trench. To deal with my depression after the collapse of our clubhouse, I wrote a poem.

When all the world's languages commingle
and create one expanded verbal medium
tariffs will become parasites extinguishable
with chemical solutions
inspiration will be purchasable metaphor
like tunnels underground
my ploy to inspire the infinite abstraction
is to fill your ears with the warm liquid of poetry.

TREK 6

In 1960 Anne Sexton published her first book of poetry, "To Bedlam and Part Way Back".

My writing started as journal jottings in public school. Some classes were boring, so I surreptitiously opened my special notebook and allowed my inner life to trickle into the light of day. The blank pages became the gymnasium of my mind. I built word chains that linked sentence to sentence. Sketches grew to short stories. "Art is process, not product," Zen Jazz said.

At the time I dabbled with the nomenclature of verse, Zen was reading Ted Berrigan. Zen served as my mentor by suggesting titles. We took trips together and I was the first to hear many of his well-crafted poems.

On one journey we hitchhiked Route 66 from Albuquerque to the Pacific Ocean. Zen wanted to peel an orange on the beach as he watched the sun go down like a mythological cheeseburger.

I gave up speaking for the duration of that trip. I said one word, and only because I felt it was necessary to our survival as artists. We had been riding in the back of a truck. We stopped at a gas station and Zen got out to stretch. Being an amicable man Zen could engage anyone in pleasant conversation. He started to bandy words with a cigar-smoking driver in a white convertible. Suddenly Zen had made arrangements for a better ride. We were seated in the car and were offered a cold drink when I realized that Zen did not have his shoulder bag. It contained prime incense of pure magnolia, ginseng tea, a guide book to Amsterdam, poems about rain rhythms on catalpa leaves and making

the choice between the muse and earth woman. It also included an ounce of dried mushrooms we planned to utilize in an idyllic setting like Sequoia National Park.

The truck was departing. I shouted, "Purse!"

Zen bolted and ran after the truck to retrieve his bag. He returned smiling like a Buddha. His enthusiasm led to a screed about reinventing the world. He wanted to capture a jazz note at a spontaneous recording at an Ornette Coleman session. He wanted to concentrate so keenly that he could hear an Italian tomato slowly ripen on the vine.

Zen accepted a cigar proffered by the driver, sipped on his cold beverage, and off we drove toward California.

TREK 7

In 1962 jazz musician Dexter Gordon moved to Europe.

I will stick to the structure of my book. Each trek is a separate entity, but taken with the whole, constitutes a part of a single tale. I will adhere to the stringent conditions of my plot, unlike Laurence Sterne, who in "The Life and Opinions of Tristram Shandy, Gentleman", constructed a book of digressions:

> ... Digressions, incontestable the sunshine; they are the life, the soul of reading! – Take them out of this book, for instance – and you might as well take the book along with them ...

So wrote Sterne in his 1760 story where the main character does not appear until late in his own book. It's like not having a birthday until you are fifty.

The cold winds of Russian literature blew through my midmorning reveries. I thought of the dichotomy in Raskolnikov's nature in "Crime and Punishment", his potential for kindness, a bright man who risks his life to save children from death by fire, and his willingness to engage in violent acts. Penury forces him to sell books to a harsh old woman. Hatred builds for the woman because she gives him a pittance for his beloved books. A theory develops in his isolated mind that he is a superior man and accordingly above the law. The decision to kill the woman is justified because he will rid the world of scum. This rationalization for

murder combined with the notion of a perfect crime leads him to enter the woman's apartment armed with an ax. He cracks her skull and is in the process of stealing her money when another woman enters and witnesses his bloody hands. In order to conceal his crime he kills the second woman. This murder of an innocent disturbs his conscious. The police inspector knows Raskolnikov's the killer but there is no evidence. Raskolnikov gives his *lucre* to a family so they can bury their father. Within that family is a young woman who works as a prostitute. He falls in love with her and confesses his horrid sin. For further atonement he confesses to the police. His punishment is detention in a Siberian work camp.

A stern digression has ruptured my story. These pages focus on the 1960's. The geometrical plot lines circle their prolongations in the summer of 1969 where I thumb my way west. I waited for the death of money and the birth of freedom.

Legalize freedom.

TREK 8

In 1960 the United States imposed an embargo on exports to Cuba covering all commodities except medical supplies and certain food products.

Querida María,

I talked to a film buff who touted 1939 as the high-water mark for cinema. "Gone With the Wind" and the "Wizard of Oz" are at the top of the list. Many talented people were actively contributing to the production line and had multiple credits to their name. Thomas Mitchell was in six movies. James Stewart starred in five. With an abundance of talent contributing to numerous projects, the creativity is multiplied exponentially. Betty Davis copes with a brain tumor in "Dark Victory". Claudette Colbert lives in the wilderness in upstate New York in "Drums Along the Mohawk". Marlene Dietrich plays a sexy saloon singer in "Destry Rides Again". Robert Donat is a shy schoolmaster in "Goodbye Mr. Chips". Charles Laughton is a deformed bell ringer in "The Hunchback of Notre Dame". In "Of Mice and Men" we take a trip to the Salinas Valley in California. The list goes on.

I beg to differ and offer 1969 as the best year for cinema, especially on the international level. The cinematic parameters are expanded. I'll give you seven examples: blacks, sex, homosexuality, violence, counter culture, independent films and the international scene.

In 1939 the best roles for African Americans involved servitude to the whites. Hattie McDaniel and Butterfly McQueen are servants in "Gone With the Wind". In 1969 we have an Academy Award winner, Sidney Poitier, in a film called "The Lost Man". The photographer/director Gordon Parks adapted his own novel "The Learning Tree", to film. "Putney Swope" offers a black executive.

D.H. Lawrence's novel is given a full-bodied treatment in the adapted film "Women In Love", involving sensuality between men. In 1939 homosexuality is not on the agenda. But in 1969 this alternative is broached with films like "Midnight Cowboy" and "Staircase".

People are killed in "Stagecoach", but violence is taken to another realm in "The Wild Bunch". In 1939 Hollywood is in bed with the tobacco industry. The only films about pot in the 1930's demonize it and make the plant illegal. In 1969 couples smoke pot in "Bob & Carol & Ted & Alice". In 1969 the independents have a chance. Dennis Hopper and Peter Fonda spend $400,000 on "Easy Rider" and reap more than $16 million at the box office. Peter Sellers goes counterculture. Andy Warhol makes "Blue Movie/Fuck". I don't know where Andy shows his films except at The Factory. I also feel in 1969 the international scene is more cranked up. In 1939 Spain has a military dictator after a brutal civil war. Many European countries surrender to Nazi occupation. The age of the dictator is in full swing in Russia, Italy and Japan. Filmmaker/director Michael Powell is busy in England, but with German hostility I think most of the resources go to the war effort.

In conclusion I feel in 1969 the variety and number of great titles expands and develops film making more than the apex of the studio system. I'm in San Francisco now and there is a theater showing "Pull My Daisy". I want to arrive early to find the place and buy a ticket.

Love, Joe

TREK 9

"Cien Sonetos de Amor" by Pablo Neruda first appeared in Spanish in 1960.

Beatlick Joe Speer

I was a member in good standing of the underground. If I said this in London or Paris, one might think I had a predilection to dally in the Metro.

The underground I refer to was a group of people united by a common cause. For example, there was the French underground that resisted the Nazi occupation. There were the bohemian students who supported the international film series at my university. The specific group for which I kept my credentials up to date was the small press and coffeehouse poetry readings. Our cause was freedom of speech and sharing our feelings.

As a member of the underground I've read in some unique venues: against a brick wall near the Public Library in Denver; in the back seat of a '64 Buick while driving over the Golden Gate Bridge to Tamalpais to disperse the ashes of a dead friend; down in the quai in Paris while waiting for a late train out of Gare d'Austerlitz; in Parque Güell in Barcelona after feeding the pigeons; in a second-class compartment going down the boot of Italy; on the deck of a crowded boat from Brindisi to Corfu and in bookstores and coffee houses that hosted open-mic nights.

As a genuine member of the underground I moved from town to town without fanfare. I carried no membership card and was not in a state of disquietude over deadlines. I transported literature and was always prepared to participate. I was more interested in the climax of "The Magic Mountain" than I was in De Gaulle requesting the removal of NATO forces from France.

Poets often exchanged cryptic messages in the form of titles or first lines. "April is the cruelest month" replanted the listener in the wasteland of imagination. "What we see is determined to a large extent by what we hear" was a reminder of the invisible generation where Brion Gysin suggested we turn off the sound on the television set and substitute an arbitrary sound track. He said the alternative sound would determine the interpretation of the visual. Certain words and phrases stir undercurrents of passion, and inspiration flows like serum from the headwaters of a sacred source.

The goal was to rise up out of the underground into the light of day. The ambition was to direct one's passion to gain acceptance, respect and earn a livelihood. Membership in the underground was a connection to the creative process. Attendance at the venues was not required, but unless a poet was incarcerated or in a coma from a brain tumor, he or she tried to get on the sign-up list.

Backpack Trekker: A 60's Flashback

In 1960 the birth control pill was approved by the FDA. In 1963 it was put on the market, and by 1965 it was the leading method of birth control for women.

In 1960 Sylvia Plath wrote "Sleep in the Mojave Desert". She delineated poetically the perfect feel of aridness. The poem reminded me of how we waited in Needles under a bridge along the Colorado River, waiting for the explosive heat of the cannonball sun to bury itself in the purple twilight.

We spent the light hours swimming in the river. We got out long enough to dry off in the parched air, the dangerous air, waiting for the cool of dark to make that mad dash across the straight road.

Zen Jazz and I camped along the river near the highway. We started a large bonfire at night and kept a cache of iced beer. Fellow travelers who gave up working their thumbs were attracted by our camp. They wandered in, dropped their luggage and accepted the beer, which loosed their tongues. We had ten people engaged in multiple conversations.

There was one man in his sixties who hobbled the open road on crutches. He had been hitching across America since 1940. He said he knew Neal Cassady from skid row hotels on Larimer Street in Denver. He had five children scattered around but did not see any of them.

There was another man who was a former student of Meharry Medical College in Nashville. He had been arrested for sit-in activity in 1960. He focused on changing two sets of attitudes: the white segregationists and the black population that accepted backdoor treatment. He was grateful to the community for not spending money downtown during the sit-ins.

"Did you graduate from Meharry?" I asked.

"No," he replied. "I transferred over to American Baptist College. I'm a minister."

And he preached us a sermon about freedom and how you have to accept the consequences for your actions. He preached and moved about like a prizefighter. "And yes, I honor my ancestors," he added.

He said he loved his grandmother for teaching him about flowers and how to make bread. He loved his mother for demonstrating the power of faith. He loved his wife for making him cry the first time he looked at her naked body. He loved his daughter for carrying that beauty into the future. His words took us all to a higher place and got everybody on their feet.

Another man distributed petitions to legalize hemp farming in his state of Kentucky. He pointed out how many people die every year from tobacco, alcohol and legal drugs, while zero deaths occur from pot overdoses. I signed even though I did not have an address at the time.

Everybody had a good time and everybody had a story. The beer supply dried up at sunrise. We slept away the day and drove across the desert the next night.

TREK 11

> In 1969 civil rights activist James Forman demanded that American religious institutions pay $500 million in reparations for black slavery.

Zen Jazz and I slept on the beach embraced by oceanic mist. The morning found us with sand in our sleeping bags. We broke camp and searched for coffee. We found an early working-man's restaurant, dropped our packs and used the restroom to wash up. A good breakfast provides the philosophical base for a successful daytime experience.

We talked about *"Le Spleen de Paris"* by Baudelaire. Charles has a story about a man who shouts "all ready" when all his companions say "finally." The man is sad about his separation from the seductive sea, from its terrifying simplicity. After days in a boat on the vat of the sea, land comes into sight. All eyes turn toward the shore with its sounds, ceremonies, its magnificent promises exuding amorous murmurs. All turn expectantly except the man.

"I'm like that man," I told Zen. "When my classmates donned the school colors of bright hues, I wore black. When carloads embarked for the homecoming game, I went to the library. While couples decked out for the prom, I wrote postcards to Podunk."

"You're always contrary and captious," Zen commented.

"I want to rebel against the dictates of nature," I continued, "start a mutant strain, go beyond the subculture to the subhuman. I have a need to contravene with contumacy."

Zen was not a practitioner of denial. He lived a modified epicurean lifestyle with moderation dependent on availability and cost of stimulus.

After breakfast we started a promenade along the beach. We inquired of sunbathers about local entertainment prospects. Before lunch time we drank beer with two women in their parked car. We had a festive frolic on Venice Beach. By late afternoon my girlfriend split to attend some self-improvement seminar. Zen's sweetheart invited us to her apartment. She and Zen shared the boudoir and I got the couch. We stayed there ten days until Zen suddenly decided to decamp for Hawaii.

On the afternoon he departed, her husband turned up. She had not so much as mentioned her hubby. He arrived with a revolver and stacks of greenbacks he had just robbed from a store.

I began to feel uneasy about crashing there so I told them there was someone I had to see in Eureka. He gave me a dollar to help defray my transportation expenses.

That night I was back on the beach.

TREK 12

In 1969 "The Forsyte Saga" began airing on the BBC - public broadcasting network.

Praise the Lord – not Lord Jesus – Lord Buckley! High Lord of the Hip! He died in 1960. "The bad jazz that a cat blows wails long after he's cut out," he said and his words still echo in the funky environs of the Phantom Gallery in Portland, Oregon.

I first arrived in Portland on the back of a flatbed truck. The driver was going to Olympia. I was on my way to Canada, but I wanted to visit Portland. So I knocked on the back window and signaled that I wanted to descend. He stopped on the shoulder of Interstate 5 and I ventured into downtown via an exit ramp.

I had heard of Powell's Bookstore and I was anxious to peruse the shelves. With my open non-judgmental vision, fantastic mysterious circumstances accelerated my *joie de vivre.*

Before stopping to rest my shoulders from the weight of my rucksack, I stared at one eye at an intersection and waited for the green light to empower my next move. It was in this state of suspended activity that I heard a mellifluous voice.

A tall woman with wavy black hair asked, "Are you a ramblin' man?" She was obviously the recipient of the rich inheritance of many generations of feminine pulchritude. She was so audaciously friendly and open that I thought for a moment she might be a streetwalker selecting a trick. Her face was full of sunshine. I didn't care if she was a lexicographer or a collector of kopecks, I was ready to parley lickety split.

"I just blew into town," I said. "I'm looking for a place to pick the wind out of my teeth." She suggested a corner tavern where we drank beer and discussed Anne Waldman. Instead of ordering another round I asked if she had any peculiar anatomical features we might discuss in private.

She said she had the words "Poets are Psychic Legislators" tattooed on her thigh.

I told her I was ready to enact some new legislation. "Let's convene the pursuit of beauty."

Walking to her apartment, we saw a flatbed truck drive by with a coffin in back. A man who looked like Lord Buckley sat up in the coffin and announced that he was performing at a club that evening. Portland contained all the ingredients of a joyful life. I could have stayed there forever, but I was on my way to Canada.

TREK 13

In the 1967 film "The Two of Us", Michel Simon plays a cantankerous, anti-Semite who unknowingly cares for a young Jewish boy.

Seattle was the next expanse of urbanization on the map. Seattle offered escape by public ferry across Puget Sound to Bremerton and beyond to the Olympic Mountains peaked in white hoods. A rain forest further to the west overlapped with the poetry of waves slapping land against the Pacific Coast Area of Olympic National Park. The park was a reserve where trees were allowed to grow.

History documents the decimation of indigenous peoples, the enslavement of black populations, but there are few witnesses to testify to the atrocities committed against trees. Arborescent beings do not defend themselves as they are converted into pulp for disposable chopsticks, newspaper or wood moldings.

There is no trail of tears for trees. There is no saga of roots for trees. There is no holocaust to remember the trees that have burned in fires caused by flicked cigarette butts.

I pitched my tent within earshot of the ocean. Day and night the sound of waves filled my mind. I ate oatmeal for breakfast, trail mix for lunch and boiled crab legs for dinner. As I recited so-liloquies from "Hamlet", I saw the ghosts of time past stalk the misty debris on shore.

When the foodstuff supply ran low, I returned to Seattle. From Seattle I hitched to Canada. The border officials did not grant me entrance because I had no car and no money. I explained to them that I had traveled to Venice Beach with Zen Jazz and then up the coast with extended layovers on the way. The guardians of the line were not impressed with my peregrinations.

One of the natural lines in nature is the timber line, a point in elevation where trees cannot grow. Marcel Proust describes a line beyond which good books exist:

> ... A good book is something special, something incalcu-lable, and is made up not of the sum of all previous mas-terpieces but of something which the most thorough as-similation of every one of them would not enable him to discover, since it exists not in their sum but beyond it ...

Lines on the road separate traffic traveling in different direc-tions. Lines on the hand reveal information through palmistry. Lines in sports indicate when the ball is out of bounds or in play. There are lines in the world that are natural or necessary, but lines separating people and restricting their movement is inop-portune when on a spiritual pilgrimage.

I returned to Seattle and the public library to study maps. I discovered a trail in the North Cascades with no border guards. All I had to do was hike a hundred miles through the mountains. No questions asked.

TREK 14

In 1969 Vanessa Redgrave dances for director
Ken Russell in the movie "Isadora".

Free thought. Free travel. Can the concept of living for free coexist with capitalism? Does one system have to squelch an-other in order to feel righteous and invulnerable? I say let all the systems tick-tick-tick like a myriad of metronomes set on different rhythms.

August was an active month throughout the 60's from the

Beatlick Joe Speer

Gulf of Tonkin incidents readying Congress to "take all necessary measures," to the Atlantic City convention in 1964, to the numerous pop festivals. On August 31, 1969, there were simultaneous festivals in Texas, Washington, Louisiana and the Isle of Wight in England. The balladeer from Minnesota, Bob Dylan, was the last act on Sunday night at the Isle of Wight. The Band backed him up while Beatles watched from the front row. He finished the decade off "beneath the diamond sky with one hand waving free silhouetted by the sea ..."

I met a man at an on-ramp near Bakersfield. He predicted that the freeway would not always be free. He claimed that access would be denied unless one drove a GMC or other product from the auto industry. The by-thumb travelers did not buy petroleum on a regular basis or tickle the palm of the Motor Vehicle Department and auto insurance companies with legal tender. I agreed it was expedient to maintain continental expressways, but we should support other forms of travel such as bicycles, equestrians, motor scooters and walking.

I knew a man in Questa, New Mexico, who did not ride in cars even as a passenger. He did not own property, but he secured permission from people to plant gardens on their land. Traveling by shank's mare with implements of husbandry was how he shared his gift as horticulturist. The patrons were reimbursed at harvest time.

The traveler in Bakersfield said the good times for hitchhikers would eventually end as the government realized this form of travel did not contribute to the coffers of capitalism. He predicted hitching would become against the law so police could arrest and fine the freeloaders. As Hearst used his newspapers to demean pot, the media would spread horror stories of rape and murder by demented hitchhikers.

A woman with three children picked us both up and drove us fifty miles until she turned into her driveway. It was a good time to be free.

TREK 15

In the 1969 movie "Death of a Gunfighter" a western town, courting eastern investors and bankers, seeks a way to kill their ex-gunslinger sheriff Richard Widmark.

Backpack Trekker: A 60's Flashback

I got a ride to the trailhead from a family who had a home-made camper on the back of their truck. They couldn't wait to rev their generator and watch "Gunsmoke" on a small black-and-white set. The asphalt disappeared into dirt road which ended at a parking lot. No cars were permitted beyond a pole pine railing. After a slow intake of air I plunged into the wilderness.

There were a few hikers at first into the heart of nowhere, then only trees. I hiked twenty miles a day for three days with pine needles for a bed and a small fire at night to engender friendly spirits.

At sunset on the third day, I came upon an empty cabin. A wooden bridge crossed a stream. The door was unlocked. A gunny sack hung from the ceiling, tied with a rope and dangled over a beam. I found a manuscript on the shelf entitled "Journey to the Heartland". I read from page 19:

... I lost sight of the road but was still going north, my head beating, going from a walk to a slow trot. I had to hurry because she might get impatient and leave. Why should she wait? I meant to tell her but never got the words out. "I love you," I should have whispered in her ear or shouted from the roof top. Faster and faster my head bursting with every step, I ran past piles of rocks and came upon a wooden fence. I jumped head first, closing my eyes to a panorama of infinite space and un-proclaimed emotions with nothing to stop my falling for-ever and continuously falling ...

There was an oil lamp so I struck a match and stayed up late into the night. Darkness in the forest often means sleep and rise early. But the magic of light extended my creativity through the dark hours. I wrote a letter to María and listened to the wind swirl like a corkscrew around the chimney.

I woke next morning to the sound of an osprey reciting from Diane DiPrima's "Memoirs of a Beatnik". Lowering the bag from the ceiling, I made myself a stack of flapjacks and a pot of coffee. A thank-you note was the last task in appreciation of the colorful cabin and the influence of perfect harmony.

It was with a sense of recalcitrant sadness that I left. It was such a serene spot and I knew it was a one-time experience. I kept turning around for a last view, hoping to infix the vision in my mind to give me strength in more erosive times.

Beatlick Joe Speer

In 1969 President Nixon gave a freedom medal to Duke Ellington.

I came out of the wilderness at Hope, British Columbia. Transcontinental Highway 1 runs from Vancouver to New Brunswick and passes through Hope. On this artery, hitchhiking was as easy as unfolding a road map.

It was distressing to see trash along the highway, so to pitch in, I picked up pop bottles along the roadside, which could be redeemed for the deposit. I had twenty bottles in a paper sack when a new hard-top white Cadillac pulled over. As I walked up to it with curious trepidation, tinted glass came down smooth.

"Hello," I said, "I'm on my way to Banff."

"My wife suggested I pick you up," said a man about sixty with a shaved face and short hair.

"Sure would appreciate a ride," I said.

"Well, get in," he ordered. "But fling that goddamn sack."

"No problem," I responded. My load vanished like a loose feather in the wind. His wife and I had sustained eye contact. She seemed to intuit my innermost thoughts. She asked me for a quote that might distract her from the passing landscapes. I wanted to impress her so I recited a Zen Jazz poem called "The Gospel According to Jazz Riff":

When Jesus found out that Mary Magdalene was
a prostitute he hocked his carpenter tools.
What the hell, he thought, I don't have that
much time to live, and if I'm gonna be known as
the God of Love I might as well live up to my reputation.
Hell, I think I really do love Mary Magdalene.
You know, when I think about it, Hell
I realize I love everybody.

The old man showed disinterest. He wanted to know what I was doing in Canada while America needed young men to fight in Vietnam.

"I'm rooting for the National Liberation Front, sir," I said. "We watched democracy get crushed in Spain during their civil war, why should we be sucked into the imbroglio of a minuscule Asian county?"

I noticed his wife waving and making faces at me behind his back. I broke off as she interrupted to explain that he was a retired general from the army.

"You're joking of course," he said.

"Actually sir," I commented, not wanting to alienate my host and be dishonorably discharged from a cushy ride, "as soon as I arrive back in the good old USA, I plan to report to the induction center immediately. I can't wait to sign up."

TREK 17

In 1969 "Butch Cassidy and the Sundance Kid" provides a perfect chemistry for Paul Newman and Robert Redford as outlaws seeing the dust of an oncoming posse.

I shared the road for three days with General Douglas and his wife Patti. He served in the Pacific campaign after Pearl Harbor. They lived in Florida and traveled in the summer on his pension. After twenty years of marriage Patti was bored but still enjoyed her pampered comfort. Without her to egg on the General, he never would have picked me up.

I reciprocated the favor by trying to amuse her. She emanated the smiling face of drama when she was happy. At other times she looked like a woman waiting for a city bus on a humid day. She had curly hair and a trim figure.

When people share time together, they soon have to eat. This factor brought out the economic imbalance in our relationship. The best I could offer was trail mix and water for dinner or oatmeal and raisins for breakfast.

The General took his wife to the best restaurants. I couldn't hang with them and tried to beg off, but Patti insisted I accompany them. She loved to sip champagne, savor good food and talk about psychoanalytical literature. Her militaristic hubby was lavish on her entertainment. Serving as her personal raconteur, I benefited from her life style.

One night she slipped me a fifty-dollar bill and told me to suggest a certain cafe in Revelstoke that she read about in a travel guide. The General was surprised when I rose out of the economic underbelly. To diffract his questioning mind, I assured him the money was earmarked to buy my mother a get-well gift. She was in the hospital undergoing treatment for a condition she contracted while working as a riveter in a shipyard during WWII.

To show my gratitude for their cordial company, I wanted to treat them to a meal. The bill came to $32 and I left an extravagant tip. Patti had an extra good time that night because she put one over on the General.

Back at the motel while the General was watching TV, I told her a story about a friend who had been busted for possession of less than an ounce of reefer. He showed up for his trial with stars and stripes sewn across his buttocks. The judge dismissed the marijuana change, but sentenced him to time in jail for defacement of the flag.

I may criticize you today, but I will love you tomorrow.

TREK 18

In a 1969 interview, Lawrence Ferlinghetti announced Allen Ginsberg's 1968 royalties from City Lights Bookstore amounted to about $10,000.

1922 was a stellar year for literature. Marcel Proust died and Jack Kerouac was born. Alfred Stieglitz took an enigmatic portrait of Georgia O'Keeffe in 1922 that readied the art world for pink tulip vaginas.

Every ride ends. The ride either goes straight while you turn or the ride turns and you go straight. The general dropped me off at Lake Louise. He and Patti headed to Calgary and another four -star restaurant.

Saying goodbye to Patti was like leaving Paris in the spring. She savvied my circumstances and slipped me some greenbacks on the sly. I remember her sitting contentedly after an extravagant meal, waiting for her husband to pick up the check.

I hiked into Lake Louise, camped overnight, and then hitched north on 93 to Jasper. It was a great ride through the mountains. I had a meal in Jasper and turned around to hitch back down to Banff. Keep it simple and keep it moving.

I read from Charles Bukowski's "The Days Run Away Like Wild Horses Over the Hills", published in 1969, another pinnacle year for creative production. I did a riff of one of his poems called "A Poem is a City":

A poem is a city divided against itself. A poem is a gathering of voices that ride naked through the streets. A poem is the pusillanimous horde routed by widespread fecundity. A poem is a three-year warranty on your toothbrush. A poem is a red balloon that chases a child over cobble-stone streets.

As I walked along creating a lavender allegory, a man stopped and offered me a ride. He spoke incessantly about the spaghetti westerns. By the time he dropped me off I had composed a poem that resulted from our meeting:

A man with no name rode into town
looking for a fistful of dollars
he became embroiled in a local feud
when he needed a few dollars more
his gun slid out of the holster
smooth like a child's dream
the bullets resounded a Morse code of death
an erudite undertaker made requisition for coffin nails.

The man enjoyed my little tribute to Leone and offered to pay me for a written copy. I sold him exclusive rights for ten dollars. We parted friends as he let me out in Banff. Then I continued my previous rant. A poem is an independent film festival carving out a sinking creek. A poem is a friend who always sends postcards from exotic places.

TREK 19

In 1969 "The Wild Bunch" actors used squibs, innovative explosives, to simulate bullets striking.

I arrived in Banff at twilight. The resort town contains a small college surrounded by Canadian Rockies. I took up residence under a stairwell in the almost empty dormitory. At first I stretched out on my Mexican poncho and slept like a yellow birch leaf in a juniper pine forest. After two days I discovered an open door and relocated to my own room. I visited the university during the musty session between summer and fall. There was one student living there, a proctor named Ludwig. He studied oboe and German philosophers. We met in the WC. His roll of TP had been stripped so I underhanded him a generous wad. We became friends and on his suggestion, I entered the listening room.

Beatlick Joe Speer

I looked like a student with post-baccalaureate credits in dream time, and I had Ludwig's blessing, so the attendants never asked for my ID. The plays of Shakespeare were my main focus, following along in the text as if Elizabethan English was a foreign idiom. Sometimes poetry smacks of Sanskrit declaimed backwards, incomprehensible to the mind because the spirit/heart uses words to connect with another spirit/heart.

I spent a few hours hiking in the mountains with water in a goatskin and my mom's pre-cooked dry pinto beans that my saliva resuscitated.

Ludwig invited me to his room at night to drink German beer and listen to Wagner. He enunciated the ideas of Hegal and Heidegger. I delved into Buddhism with a smattering of Samuel Beckett for non-liturgical chaos. I wrote a poem for Ludwig called "Beethoven in Banff":

the fallible fatherland
where music forms crystalline notes
auspicious school daze
with students in *absentia*
fishing over a hole in the ice and arguing about Quebecois
the frontier is still open for mental travelers
my dorm friend is guide to the adamant night
Ludwig is a bigwig
a *bijou*
thanks for not reporting me to the authorities
given enough fermentation
even the slime will rise to the top.

When official students arrived to claim their rooms, I said goodbye to Ludwig and checked out.

TREK 20

In 1968 Howard England began excavations of Fort Zachary Taylor, Key West, Florida, which represented the largest collection of Civil War cannons in the U.S.

Carl Jung thought himself out of existence in 1961. His pages still reveal how the mind can revel in revving excogitation. On a college campus a bevy of sorority sisters set up a table in the

Backpack Trekker: A 60's Flashback

student union building to disseminate anti-war material. They knew how to attract an audience with music and their pretty smiling faces working the crowd. Their presentation was enough to inveigle the most stalwart hawk into requesting more information.

I avoided religious pamphleteers and Islamic agents giving away translations of the Koran. But any event that included free rock-and-roll was worth a browse. I had time to groove on the tonal intricacy of an electric guitar lead. Even a disheveled panhandler would toss his beggar cup and sway to the beat. Bicyclists would dismount and walk through to absorb the vibes. Perhaps a wavy-haired whirling dervish female would cause spectators to forget their agenda as she became one with the music.

There was a man who set up a table next to the "Students for a Democratic Society" booth. He wanted to raise travel funds to visit the museum in Cairo. He was an Egyptologist who took notes in hieroglyphics. He believed in future life through resurrection of the body. Mummification was the key to eternity. Ten thousand years later a spirit would rejoin its body and rejuvenate it back to serviceable condition. The man's name was Josef and he had visions of a book of the dead opening up. He saw a sarcophagus lid move and was worried that King Mena would have a fiscal problem upon waking. He might owe millenniums of back rent.

Josef had a hollowed-out scarab for contributions and business cards of potential sponsors. Before making a salutary dropping, I asked him a question.

"Will you fly directly into Cairo?"

"No way," he replied. "I will stay a week in Venezia reading about Anubis, the jackal-headed god, and Osiris, the god who died and was restored to life. Then I'll take a boat to Athens and walk around the Parthenon while meditating on Isis and how she found the pieces of her husband, that had been scattered in various places, and put them together and revived him. Then I'll ship to Alexandria and take a train to Cairo. I'll find me a room on the top floor of a hotel and look down altruistically on the present day usurpers of the ancient land."

I wished him luck and gave him my mother's address where he could send me a postcard. A year later I got a letter postmarked Egypt. It contained an image of Horus on papyrus paper. Also included was a photo of Josef standing near a statue of Ramses.

Beatlick Joe Speer

In 1969 Frenchman Jean-Pierre Melville directs "Army of Shadows" about the French resistance against the Nazi occupation.

Alcatraz locked its doors as a federal prison in 1963. Criminals escaped by digging through the wall with spoons. Inmates were shipped out to other slammers. The following is a reenactment of a new arrival's orientation chat:

GUARD: You are in Alcatraz because you break society's rules. The only thing you will break here is your heart thinking of those go-go clubs just across the water. While here we owe you three things: food, a bed and a uniform. We have an exercise yard. You have access to it if you follow the rules.

We have a library with many novels by Charles Dickens and poems by Emily Dickinson. You can check out books if you follow the rules.

We have two showers at the end of the hall, but you can lick yourself clean like a cat if you don't follow the rules.

All prisoners eat at the same time. While you are out of your cell there will be a gun on you until you are locked back into the cell. It takes six seconds for a guard to bolt a bullet into the chamber and raise the rifle. When you hear that metallic click, you better freeze.

At Alcatraz we don't answer questions. That is all.

For inmates who were extra recalcitrant there was a special detention center in D Block. The treatment unit was reserved for inmates who broke the regulations. Two heavy steel doors. Total darkness. Bedding issued only at night. Normal stay: three to seven days.

Through cold choppy waters, it was about one mile from the super lockup to Fisherman's Wharf. Prisoners knew the restaurants, bookstores and bars open in that North Beach area were beyond their reach. They could hear the sounds of life against the invective of their freedom, but they could not see Telegraph Hill or the Embarcadero.

The Rock was a very hard place.

Backpack Trekker: A 60's Flashback

On August 19, 1969, Bob Dylan's seven-year manage-
ment contract with Albert Grossman expired.

After Banff I scurried to Calgary. Hitchhikers were made to
feel very undesirable in Calgary, as if they might introduce a ma-
lignant malady just by elevating a thumb within the city limits.
Signs forbidding hitchhiking were more prominent than billboards. I trudged along the highway, pretending as if I was on a
benefit walk, and every mile was another C note to help children
with cystic fibrosis. I came upon a car parked by the side of the
road. It was empty. I removed my backpack, lifted up the hood of
the car and stood next to it with my thumb out. Within three minutes I had a ride with a man going south to Waterton Park.

"Having car trouble?" he asked as I stashed my pack in his
backseat.

"No," I replied. "No trouble."

"What about your car back there?"

"It's not my car. I just paused beside it to catch my breath."

His name was Campbell and he was a specialist in cosmol-
ogy. He claimed to have existed for eons as vaporish mist, then
was transformed into a crystal. Buried in the earth for one hundred thousand years, he was transmogrified into a bark beetle.
Living for thousands of years under the bark of trees, he died and
was reborn as a root-eating rodent. After thousands of years as a
rodent, a new death led to reincarnation as a human being. He
had lived through a thousand faces and was ready to die to enter
his next phase.

He offered me cans of Canadian beer. I drank and he talked
as we drove down to Waterton Glacier International Peace Park.
When he let me out, I was smiling extravagantly and had a glorious buzz.

The park ranger warned of bears in the back country. The
wildlife did not commiserate with the human need for a wilderness experience. Bears saw backpackers as ineffable intruders,
a fetid memory of being hunted. Yet I had no fear. I felt insulated
with my protective barley glow.

As I hiked a trail, I heard the voice of Zen Jazz echo in a
dead-end arroyo creating a riff influenced by Campbell's cosmo-
graphical comments. What have I ever lost by dying? Going To
The Sun Highway cuts through the big sky of Montana. Bear

tracks the darkening horizon. The mauve whistle of wings over my head. A black curtain of rain behind Lake McDonald. A shadow of a shadow creates a perfect replica. My body relaxes, near tears, on igneous rocks. Out here alone in the mountains, I feel someone watching me, some invisible one. My mailbox opens to the sky. Who will insert a *billet-doux*?

TREK 23

In the 1969 film "The Chairman", an American scientist is sent to Red China with a micro-sized bomb planted in his brain.

While camping in the wilderness, one forgets about earning a living or the pursuit of a career. We can focus, while watching the flickering flames of a campfire, on the symmetrical rhythm of nature. I heard music from invisible instruments and songs that did not emanate from a human larynx. Elfin forest dancers manifested the joy of eternity.

The vacuum of night must be filled by the imagination of the beholder. The wayfarer sleeps on the belly of Mother Earth, prepared to be waylaid by any contingency. Capitalism is not iridescent while one is foraging for sustenance among wild berry groves.

I feel primeval hiking the mountain trails, safe among the trees. I feel robust in nature, whereas in urban areas, I feel like Dostoevsky's underground man:

... I am a sick man. No, I am not a pleasant man at all. I believe there is something wrong with my liver. However, I don't know a damn thing about my liver; neither do I know whether there is anything really wrong with me ...

In LA or Mexico City I am a spiteful man. In nature I follow the eight-fold path and extricate myself from delusion, desire and hostility. In the city I feel as if some humiliation awaits me like the mock firing squad Dostoevsky faced in 1849.

I left Going to the Sun Highway between Saint Mary and West Glacier and headed for Great Falls. There is a museum with the work of Charles M. Russell. Four stars and thumbs up for an artist who captured a way of life with his work. Charlie agglomerated man and animal sharing the vastness of the last frontier. His art is a documentation of the trail drivers, bucking broncos and barroom brawls.

This Montana terrain provided the background for John Ford's last film in 1964, "Cheyenne Autumn", tracing the tortuous last days of a western Plains tribe. Also in 1964 a film from Italy gave the flagging genre new impetus. "A Fistful of Dollars" emanated a new trajectory with the laconic hero and the rowdy gun.

From Great Falls I fell onto Custer Battlefield National Monument where in 1876 the Bull charged. To transcend the killing fields I marched into the Sawtooth Mountains to release myself from historical attachments. The poison in the spilled blood has congealed into the sugar of solidarity. After communing with nature I entered a restaurant and ordered a moose burger.

TREK 24

In 1965 Jean-Luc Godard took an irreverent journey to the mysterious "Alphaville". It was a French film with a cockeyed fusion of science fiction and surrealist poetry.

Yellowstone was the first and biggest National Park set aside for the enjoyment of all people. It is an explosion of the bizarre in nature: geysers, hot springs, bubbling paint pots and grizzly sights. In the campground I met a couple named Zachary and Scooter. They sang Peter La Farge songs around a blazing fire. After the melodious modulations Zachary played some easy jazz guitar along with a narration I offered up in an immutable voice:

I was deep into a sluggish slumber, slipping on high-wire antics. I fell off the wire and cracked my cranium, then entered into antediluvian dream time. An anthropoid ape accosted me at the water hole. It wanted to rob my collection of sharks' teeth.

"Take a chill pill, dude," I yelled, "we are relatives."

The ape picked up a tyrannosaur thigh bone and tried to conk me. I ran with the speed of seven winds, but the ape was on my heels. I threw a tooth down and it grew into a briar patch. I tossed another tooth behind me and it changed into a carnival hall of mirrors. The ape became infatuated with its own image and I escaped into another dimension.

I then found myself in the panhandle of Golden Gate Park. The Diggers provided free meals at the same time every day. The Grateful Dead turned on their amps and created a mellow scene. The Jefferson Airplane was scheduled to fly in on an impalpable breeze. Someone rolled a six-foot joint using pages from "The Marihuana Papers".

They propped it up with three mic stands and people lined up to hit on it. The ashes were collected and mixed into the sand at the children's playground. A scantily clad dancer importuned me to penetrate the core of her being. She wanted to do it in front of the stage. There was no space except to lift her high on my forearm as she said,

"Fill 'er up!"

Jerry liked my rhythm and invited us onto the stage to jam with the Dead.

Zachary started to chant "Hari Krishna Hari Hari Mari Juana Mari Mari Juana Mari Krishna Juana." He chanted for thirty minutes and passed out. I noticed his stash near a rock. I figured he wouldn't care, and so I rolled myself a doobie and enjoyed it while walking improvident circles in the campground. It was a dark flashlight night. An occasional electric overhead of lightning made the landscape clear. The thunder created an avalanche of sound down the canyon.

TREK 25

Rocky Marciano died in a plane crash in 1969.

The couple in the magic bus were up early despite the fact that they were celebrants at the all night hootenanny. When I smelled the coffee perk, my brain did the hula-hula. Scooter saw my eyes sensuous with caffeine objectivism and poured a cup.

"Thank you," I said. "You are very kind."

"We want you lucid," said Zachary. "We want to continue our discussion from where we left off last night before you began dancing around the fire naked. Do you really think the world was created when Kali masturbated on a lotus?"

I did not recall cavorting in the buff or discussing the goddess of creation and destruction. But I picked up the thread of conversation with a superfluous response.

Backpack Trekker: A 60's Flashback

"I can maintain many belief systems as long as I don't knock on doors and try to convince strangers of inanities such as the idea that Satan and his cohorts are in control of the world. If God can exist forever, why can't the elements of creation and destruction be eternal? Our idea of God is an anthropomorphic projection. The Hopi theory of creation is as practicable as Genesis."

Zachary and Scooter blinked. Both were from Ann Arbor, but had been living in Nepal for a year. He was a woodcarver and they made a living selling his work in parks or coffeehouses. They set out a few examples of his art while he worked on a new one, usually a likeness of someone in the room. Scooter played Scott Joplin rags on a small keyboard. When Zachary sold a piece, she shifted into Mozart. If he sold two pieces, she played Ravel. If he didn't sell anything, she changed into a minidress and sold herself. They could hustle a dollar in good times and bad.

Zachary began to fry potatoes he had boiled the night before. My nostrils flared with receptivity.

"Finish your coffee," Zachary said, "and we'll move to the next level." He handed me a cold Canadian beer.

TREK 26

In 1969 the Department of Defense set up four computer network nodes on university campuses, creating the Advanced Research Projects Agency Network.

Zachary and Scooter arose on our third day in Yellowstone National Park. They had an acute need to line their pockets with wherewithal. They required a large crowd to sell their products. I suggested we drive to the most visited site in the park – Old Faithful – and set up shop in the parking lot. Scooter was concerned we might look freakish and attract the authorities. I assured her that the subculture was large enough that while traveling we often encounter members of our own philosophical species. With like minds we cut through the religious posturing that amounts to sanctimonious Sunday ceremonies while the rest of the week is commerce as usual.

We parked next to a painted-up school bus playing T-Bone Walker on their sound system. Zachary immediately pulled out a table and set out his samples. In no time there were several customers checking out his cuddly sculpture. A slender man dressed in white cotton wanted to trade Guatemalan clay pipes for Zachary's art. Zachary said he could not put clay pipes into his gas tank. The man in cotton was loquacious but pinched for money. Scooter said he was welcome to chat or discuss the early development of piano roll music, but could he please stand to one side.

I helped create interest by walking throughout the parking lot to divert geyser bustle over to the magic bus. I pointed to the colorful bus tandem, visible from a half-mile away, and informed visitors of the bargain sale of hand-crafted wood carvings.

"Yes, sir," I encouraged one family man, "there is magic happening down there. Maybe you will find a unique gift to take home. Maybe a Slavic fortune teller with a magnified heart will reveal the secret of the pine tree."

Zachary unloaded eighty percent of his stock. When the park ranger arrived to investigate the hubbub, we departed with unceremonious haste. We drove to a store for provisions and returned to the campground with the exhilarative feeling that work was over for the day.

Then a rabbit crossed the road and reminded me of my first hunting experience. I had a .22 rifle and was poised like a sniper. When a rabbit appeared, I squeezed off a shot. The critter flipped and the ears went horizontal. I ran up excited and flush with success. The rabbit was bleeding and twitching. The joy of my accomplishment dissipated with the realization I had destroyed life. I had come onto its home ground and waited with malicious intent. I felt ashamed and, before the rabbit expired, vowed never to take up arms again.

Zachary understood my point of view but held an opposite notion. "Guns are necessary. Take for example when the Nazi army invaded Russia in June of 1941 in Operation Barbarosa. The Russians kept retreating. They figured it was a big country with plenty of room to back up. But when they reached Stalingrad, Joe Stalin instigated a no-retreat policy.

"If Russian soldiers returned to their lines after an attack, they were shot by their own troops. They also ran troops at the German position just so they would shoot and use up ammunition. German supplies ran short as fall turned into winter and many nights of sub-zero temperatures. Whole battalions of Russians would disappear, but the siege along the Volga and Don Rivers continued as reinforcements came down from Siberia and all over Russia. Stalin was not going to allow his namesake to be taken.

"The city was in rubble after bombardments and artillery and block-to-block fighting. In late November the Russians began a counter offensive. They encircled the German army and forced them to surrender in early February. Ninety-thousand Nazi soldiers gave up. It was because Stalin took up arms that they protected Mother Russia and changed the direction of the Second World War."

I appreciated his opinion. Not involved in national security, I had no intention of traveling with a gun in my backpack.

TREK 27

*In 1969 Margaret Atwood's "The Edible Woman"
reveals the life of a young woman whose struc-
tured and consumer-driven life alters drastically.*

When I was a student, the majestic peaks of the Grand Tetons made me wish I could fill my dorm room with rocks. I didn't want imported beer bottles, or old Christmas cards or calendar girls straddling motorcycles on my shelf. I wanted to adorn my study area with rock formations. But I settled for books and LP's because they were easier to move at the end of the semester. The best plan was to visit the rocks in their own habitat.

I encountered the wonderment of random rocks as I hiked a trail to Lake Solitude. It was in this remote locale that I met a Buddhist monk.

The monk had been there for seven days. He spoke English as well as seven other languages. Our minds closed ranks on the third day as rain pelted the rocks. It turned out that we both wrote poems so we created a piece alternating lines:

You and I were in a dream together
asleep under a rhododendron leaf
protesting second-hand smoke
a retired poet injected you with a free-will serum
desert winds were born from your wound
and activated the machinery of fraudulence
as the infernal blue buzz crawled through the rubbish
of our collective DNA
through the canebrake of verbiage

from a parallel universe smoky hallucinations
under a yellow back porch bug light
prefigured thoughts to reinvent the world

After spending time with him, I felt like we were fast friends. He informed me that he could not survive for extended periods on the lowlands. He traveled from one mountain range to another. He had camped in the Alps, the Himalayas, and was then touring the Northern Rockies. His important work took place in dream time.

Waking hours for him were given over to the mundane functions of the body. He created poems in his sleep and used the soft light of early morning and late afternoon to transcribe their significance.

He had escaped the Chinese occupation of Tibet. For many years he lectured to the Western World about the importance of Tibetan culture. He was content to live alone but felt a heavy calling to a troubled land.

The last time I saw him was on the evening news. He was in Vietnam. He sat down in the open in a public place and poured gas over his body. He set himself on fire to show us the unmitigated horror. The quartz Buddha of peace burst into flames.

TREK 28

> In the "Bowler and the Bunnet", Sean Connery directs a documentary on the decline of ship building along the River Clyde.

In the 1960's the sculptor Dan Flavin created installations of fluorescent tubes, arranging these banal objects into mystically glowing shrines of light. The 1960's had an impact on me not only because of the outburst of creativity, but because of the passing of many talented people: Richard Wright, Ernest Hemingway, E.E. Cummings, William Faulkner, Robert Frost, Sylvia Plath, William Carlos Williams, William Somerset Maugham, T.S. Elliot, Dorothy Parker, Langston Hughes, Carl Sandburg, John Steinbeck and Carl Jung, all departed our world.

I became intimate with them through of their writings. I carried their books around in the side pocket of my backpack for easy access. I opened them up while waiting for a ride on a lonely stretch of highway, sitting in my tent catching the waning light of the sun, drinking coffee late at night at a restaurant counter.

People can write me off for things I do or don't do, but books are constantly available to be touched. Books never disallow me a chance to finger through their pages.

> "It's very hard to be dead and you try to make up for lost time till slowly you start to get whiffs of eternity. But the living are wrong in the sharp distinctions they make."
> *-Maria Rilke*

Another kind of death is the end of a relationship. For instance when Carl Jung separated from Sigmund Freud. Jung regarded Freud as an older more mature, experienced person and Freud saw Jung as his successor.

This was embarrassing to Jung because he could not sacrifice his intellectual independence. His aim was to investigate truth. He was not concerned with matters of personal prestige. Freud wanted to make a dogma of his sexual theories. His sexual libido took over the place of God.

The year 1909 was decisive in their relationship. They traveled together on a seven-week trip to America. They were together every day and analyzed each other's dreams. Freud had a dream which Jung studied, but he wanted more details to make a complete interpretation.

Freud responded with a comment that he could not risk his authority. That comment burned into Jung's memory and foreshadowed the end of their relationship. Jung decided that Freud had a neurosis. Freud had said that everybody is neurotic and we must practice tolerance.

Jung was not inclined to content himself with that view. Jung eventually wrote a book that he knew would alienate him from Freud.

I also experienced the death of a relationship. While in school I chummed around with a fellow who had a sense of humor and seemed to have an open mind. However, one day while riding the bus, he made some slurs against black people. I was not into denigrating other races even under the pretext of comic relief. He usually made me laugh with his wit, but I did not respond to his jokes with jigaboo punch lines. I could not continue in a friendship with someone who demeaned other people. Maybe I could have been honest and protested his belittling posture.

Beatlick Joe Speer

But just as Freud would not have changed his point of view to accommodate Jung, I doubted my erstwhile friend would alter his prejudice because it offended me. I simply stopped talking to him.

There are no serial killers among my heroes who died, no dictators, no war mongers, no child molesters, no cigarette manufacturers or makers of plutonium. Even though these people have departed the earth, their words continue to exercise an influence on my studious nature.

I reconnect with them every time I pick up one of their books. "The Outsider", "The Enormous Room", "Go Down Moses", "Letter from Birmingham Jail", "Visions of Cody" and others are friends whose recurrent reappearance allow me to commune with the dead and to share that experience with the living.

Books are like angels moving between the living and the dead.

TREK 29

In 1967 Dr. Martin Luther King, Jr. delivered a speech against the war in Vietnam. He called the United States "the greatest purveyor of violence in the world today" and called on young men not to respond to draft calls.

Joni Mitchell sang "Woodstock" at the Big Sur Folk Festival in 1969. I stayed in a walk-in campground at Big Sur and avoided the person at the entrance booth by walking in through a service road with a locked gate. It was after dark when the headlights appeared and I was mixing pot with mint leaves for a super joint. I covered the makings with a copy of "The Tropic of Cancer".

It was the park ranger named Andy. He collected my fee and pointed his flashlight into the darkness. Four pairs of eyes appeared, silver-gray guard hairs tipped with black, four ravenous foragers of the night. I shouted a few lines at them from "Troilus and Cressida":

No space of earth shall sunder our two hates. I'll hunt thee like a wicked conscience still, that mouldeth goblins swift as frenzy's thoughts.

The raccoons halted slightly but did not fully retreat until I hurled a sizable stone in their direction.

Backpack Trekker: A 60's Flashback

Andy told me about a weekly reading at a local inn. It was happening that night. He offered to give me a ride into town after he made the rounds of the campground. At the reading I met Stephen Sanders. He was a geologic consultant who was employed pumping gas. In good weather he lived in a tent. In winter he moved into a friend's camper.

The hostess of the open-mic was glad to see me because it was a slow night and I added new life to the event. She invited Stephen and me to a walk-up bungalow in Palo Colorado Canyon. We sat around a lacquered pine table, listened to Miles Davis, and told stories.

I told about hitchhiking in Oxnard, California. Written on the back of a road sign in bold letters was, "Two people died here of starvation."

I had been in one spot for three hours when a tractor trailer dropped off two young women. One of them shook her ass noticeably and in five minutes they had a ride.

Stephen said he used to hitch with a large red gas can. He had sliced the can in half, put hinges and hasp on it and carried his belongings in it. To see him on the road a driver might think he was only going to the next gas station. He traveled from Key West to Vancouver with his red luggage, and the price of that gas can is the only money he ever spent to support the oil industry.

TREK 30

In 1969's "American Revolution 2" the Black Panthers and the Young Patriots realize that class, more than race, was the determining factor governing how they were treated by law enforcement.

Eleanor Roosevelt died in 1962. In 1939 Mrs. Roosevelt came to the aid of Marian Anderson who was denied access to Constitution Hall in Washington, D.C. by the Daughters of the American Revolution. The First Lady used her power to arrange a concert for Anderson on the steps of the Lincoln Memorial for 75,000 people.

Benito Gordon and I sat together on the bus ride home from school. We expounded on the merits of Octavio Paz, reading him in Spanish and English simultaneously. We had such a rackety *tête-a-tête* that two chicks sat behind us and began to echo our words. They wanted to cut in on the action so we paired off.

We decided instantaneously to double date. Benito said he could borrow his brother's car and pick us all up. Brenda, Benito's first choice, wanted to attend a sock hop in the gym. Kathy, the girl I was going to make the scene with, wanted to see a double feature at the drive-in.

I wanted to coax some 21-year-old to buy us beer and hike around the extinct volcano to discuss the modernist movement in 20th-century literature. Benito didn't care what we did so long as he drove.

We wrote our choices on pieces of paper and threw them into a shoe box, along with three fantastical alternatives. Benito picked one. We ended up going to the roller rink, which was great fun because none of us were proficient, and we fell all over each other. We got down and dirty.

When the rink closed, I suggested we go drink coffee and kick around the cantos of Ezra Pound. Kathy nixed that idea. She suggested we go to the ice cream parlor.

We had double-decker, chocolate-dipped cones, and Benito told a story about being attacked by vicious pygmies and how they had their way with him in a sleazy motel.

It was a successful social outing, but did not have any carry-over value because I stopped riding the bus in order to join the Judo Club after school. I wanted to throw other people's weight around.

The techniques of the martial arts reminded me of Robinson Jeffers, who also died in 1962, I was filled with:

... bright power, dark peace; fierce consciousness
joined with final disinterestedness ... "

TREK 31

The 1969 film "De Sade" *featured Keir Dullea as Sade and John Huston as his libertine uncle, Abbe de Sade. Roger Corman was listed as an uncredited director.*

The university I attended did not offer a class on the Harlem Renaissance. It wasn't until I met a man named LeRoi Jones Johnson that I learned there was more going on in the 1920's than the Fatty Arbuckle manslaughter trial or the funeral cortege of anarchists Sacco and Vanzetti.

Backpack Trekker: A 60's Flashback

Mr. Johnson was 65-years-old when I met him hitchhiking out of Jackson, Wyoming. He had a bad leg so he used a gimp stick to maneuver around.

We found ourselves sharing the same piece of ground near sunset. No rides in sight so we gave the highway a rest and enjoyed the changing of the light.

Mr. Johnson lived as a Harlemite near Lenox Avenue and 143rd Street. He told me about a magazine called "Fire", edited by Wallace Thurman.

It was one of his favorites because it was produced by and devoted to Harlem writers. As the sun burned the far horizon he lamented how a conflagration destroyed most of the copies of "Fire" in the basement where they were stored.

We started a fire to warm ourselves and I made some cowboy coffee. Mr. Johnson pulled a flask of brandy out and the spirit interrupted our discourse on the 1920's "niggerati" for an acappella version of "Lift Every Voice and Sing".

Mr. Johnson had no bedding so I loaned him my sleeping bag. I tended the fire most of the night, drinking coffee and writing in my journal.

When Mr. Johnson woke at sunrise, a hot cup awaited him. I asked how he made money during the 20's. He was a bootlegger during Prohibition. Federal agents raided a speakeasy while he was there to collect money.

The place was shut down but reopened in a few days just a few doors from its old location. Word-of-mouth brought back the faithful in no time.

Lacking industrial education, he and two accomplices robbed a bank. He was apprehended at a rooming house where Arna Bontemps lived. His generosity betrayed him.

It was Christmas time and he passed out crisp one-hundred-dollar bills to people on his block. It attracted attention and the police were notified.

They asked some questions and tracked him down. He was apprehended with piles of money on his bed.

Too many years in the penitentiary gave him a distaste for indoor life. He lived outside year round under the grace of a blushing sky. The last image I have of him is getting into a car headed south for warmer weather.

His day became my night and I fell asleep near the ashes.

❧

Beatlick Joe Speer

The 1969 book "Naked Came the Stranger" by a fictitious Penelope Ashe was the literary hoax of the year – collaboratively written by a group of journalists who proved that a badly-written book with plenty of sex would sell.

I've mentioned writers who died during the 60's, such as poet André Breton and biologist Rachel Carson. This trek is devoted to journalist Susan Avery who was born in 1960. Instead of reaching into the past, I will extend into the future beyond the decade which serves as the demarcation of these pages.

"Time," she writes in her journal 14 years after the death of Neal Cassady, "is the truly independent variable. We are all functions of time. It passes no matter what we do. Our job is to stay active so the time won't pass us by and make us feel useless."

The more I travel in time and space, the vastitude of distance squelches my ego and the smaller I become. However, much I add to my experience and knowledge, the more difficult it is for me to satisfy the persistent desire for more and more that strives toward complete knowledge.

"I'm living in a world," Susan writes, "where there is too much to learn, and if I feel bad for not knowing everything, I'll go crazy."

The eventual frustration of this desire and the futility of it when confronted with eternity, makes me want to stop, to select and study a single small object until I encompass all of it.

"I can't let myself be constantly cut down for my lack of knowledge," Susan writes. "In the long run, the most important thing to know is the difference between good and bad.

"In the good lies honesty, cooperation, love and all the perfection we strive for. In the bad we find selfishness, deceit, pain and all the hateful destruction we want to avoid.

"In the middle, between the two we have doubt, confusion, apathy and all the dangerous traps we so easily get caught in."

We have an inborn drive for more that has moved us from the Stone to the Nuclear Age. Is there a shut-off valve for experience? Is there a time when we can lock ourselves in a room and not desire more of anything?

"I must stop worrying about my image," Susan writes, "and start working on what makes me good."

In the novel "Orlando", Virginia Woolf examines the concept of time. Her main character lives from Elizabethan times into the

20th century. A person 38-years-old can have hundreds of years of experience while an older person may be one of the walking dead. How alive someone is may depend on their mental vivacity or their imaginative elasticity. A staid woolgatherer maybe in the final stages of intellectual *rigor mortis*.

TREK 33

In 1969 the film "If It's Tuesday, This Must Be Belgium" presents a fast-paced comedy about Americans on vacation in Europe.

Devils Tower in Wyoming is one of the sacred rocks of North America. Why is this rock that rises abruptly from its base and looms 1,267 feet above the Belle Fourche River called Devils Tower? It could be God's Penis or Thor's Thumb.

The Indians have their legends as to how the rock was formed. A hunting party took refuge on top of a knoll as a grizzly bear clawed the surrounding area in a futile attempt to devour the warriors. When the bear relinquished its carnivorous quest, the Indians were left atop the rocky tower to starve.

The prairie dogs have their own version of how the tower was created. According to them, an ancient race of stalwart Neophytes dug a huge hole in the ground to bury their plates of ore. They collected their excrement and packed it over the plates until it hardened like a sedimentary rock. After centuries of shit piling higher, the monolith was visible from miles around.

The arrival of the first prairie dogs into the area brought extensive digging. They dug until they found the plates and scratched them horrendously. When the plates were later discovered by a sun-baked wanderer and deciphered, the rodents cuneiform was put into a book and a religious sect established.

I camped out for two days near the sacrosanct stone, walking clockwise around its base and visiting with a few of the ninety plus bird species that have been sighted at this national monument.

The solemn stone collected heat during the day and slowly released it at night. Laying hands on the rock at night, I received images from the Paleozoic era.

I became an absorber of rock vibrations, picking up instantaneous geomorphic communications from Half Dome in Yosemite,

Ship Rock in New Mexico, Arches in Utah, Ayers Rock in Australia and the brooding sentinels of stone on Easter Island.

I was at the rock bottom of Devils Tower, using it as an antenna. The coyotes howled their nocturnal pronouncements. The prairie dogs scraped under the earth. All seemed serene and yet all was in flux around the great stone.

I felt the tower tremble. It blasted off the earth like a rocket ship, leaving me on the rim of a vast crater. I fell asleep and awoke at dawn near Meteor Crater in Arizona.

TREK 34

By 1967 world sales of Tolkien's books reached three million copies in nine languages.

In 1964 U.S. presidential candidate Lyndon Baines Johnson of Texas won a landslide victory over Senator Barry M. Goldwater of Arizona. Goldwater was waterlogged with eagerness to escalate the Vietnam War. His defeat did not deter the warmongers because Johnson soon announced a vast increase in U.S. aid to South Vietnam. The Free Speech Movement in Berkeley motivated the students to occupy Sproul Hall at the University of California. This action led to mass arrests of sit-in demonstrators.

Race riots blotted Harlem and Philadelphia as President Johnson called for "total victory" in his other war, the "War on Poverty". A G.I. Joe doll was introduced for boys as a toy, and a bar in San Francisco introduced topless dancers as *haute couture* designer Rudi Geinrich's topless bathing suit encouraged women to drop their brassieres.

During all the social change, Arizona's Meteor Crater has remained steadfast. It resembles an extinct launch pad for intergalactic travelers. I walked clockwise around the rim three times, watched the sun set, then camped in the center of the depression.

On the rim I received vibrations of the world's unrest: James Hoffa nailed by Robert Kennedy; spectators killed in Lima at a soccer game; earthquake in Alaska; the Mods and Rockers at odds at a British seaside resort.

Back in the center of the bowl, however, it was calm and serene. The sound of running water was poured into a cup of forbearance blended with benevolence. I drank two cups of gleanings from a good-will receptacle and saw animated previews of Fritz the Cat.

Lying on my back, looking up at the sky, I saw Dr. Strangelove bickering with Becket. I saw the Marquis de Sade directing the inmates of an asylum. I heard Ken Kesey codify his great notion. I smelled methadone in the lunch pails of school children. I saw a soup kitchen set up in the Dorothy Chandler Pavilion where a sign-language specialist from the International Atomic Energy Agency presented papers on how to dismantle bombs.

I fell asleep with a rock for a pillow and dreamed in colors. My dreams were less vivid than my waking hallucinations so I did not record them in my journal.

From Meteor Crater I went to Walnut Canyon to search for walnuts. Instead of nuts I found painted shards. I reassembled the pieces and created a bowl. I felt the energy from the person who ate out of it 1,000 years ago. I filled the bowl with Lucky Charms cereal and enjoyed a light snack before falling into a heart of darkness, sweetened with imperishable blessings.

TREK 35

> On November 10, 1969 Sesame Street started
> filling television land with Jim Henson's muppets.

In 1965 Britain banned cigarette advertising from commercial television. U.S. bombs fell on North Vietnam as some 125,000 troops took their place in the struggle against the spread of communism.

In that same year President Johnson doubled the draft call as National Security Adviser Roslow said, "The Vietcong are going to collapse within weeks."

Anti-war rallies increased in size until the movement regurgitated itself in front of the White House. Allen Ginsberg encouraged people to use "flower power" as Malcolm X was gunned down in Harlem.

Meanwhile Congress ordered cigarette packages to be labeled – "Caution: cigarette smoking may be hazardous to your health."

Ralph Nader offered another cautionary call in his "Unsafe at Any Speed". He emphasized that driving a car may be just as hazardous to your health as war, since 51,000 Americans died in car crashes during the Vietnam War.

Beatlick Joe Speer

Poet Randall Jarrell joined the "lost world" by walking in front of a car at Chapel Hill, Andy Warhol painted soup cans, "The Odd Couple" made people laugh and Rod Steiger learned to feel in "The Pawnbroker".

In San Francisco Big Brother got a hold on its Company and soon added Janis Joplin to the band. Meanwhile the miniskirt appeared in London.

I stopped in Flagstaff long enough to visit the public library and read an interview with Anne Waldman and her radical presence. "Poetry is still here," she says, "even as we move into stranger technologies."

I met a Japanese woman named Nokiki at a Laundromat. She said she was writing a research paper on the music of Lionel Hampton. I picked up on her vibes as she studied the number of times Akira Kurosawa's movie plots had been pirated by the international community.

She wanted to make a documentary of Kurosawa's career and use Hampton's music with it. Nokiki was a unique mixture of creative impulses and I wanted to see more of her.

"Do you want to go down?" I asked her, "down to the bottom of the Grand Canyon."

I thought it best to be forthright with her. Women are like editors, they either accept you or put you to one side while they check out other possibilities. I forced her to make an editorial decision to accept or reject. Point Sublime and the Bright Angel Trail awaited.

A wonderful experience was just ninety miles away, and I offered my services as her guide back through the layers of time.

She looked into my face and accepted. I felt like an acceptance notice to a major publication had arrived in the mail. She had a rented car so we loaded up with supplies and headed out toward the Kaibab Plateau.

Down, down we hiked to the Colorado River, down to "the uncontrollable mystery on the bestial floor" as Yeats wrote. Down to the singing rapids.

Nokiki said she hoped to see The Beatles, but I informed her that they were giving their last public concert in Candlestick Park. At that very moment, while The Beatles sang for the Bay Area, we hiked through the layers of time into the Grand Canyon.

I asked Nokiki to tell me about "Mothra".

☯

Backpack Trekker: A 60's Flashback

> *"Charro!" was Elvis Presley's twenty-ninth movie*
> *and the only one in which he did not sing.*

In 1966 Charles DeGaulle requested removal of NATO forces from France. The "Quotations of Chairman Mao" appeared. In the middle of the decade, in the middle of the country, Truman Capote described the temper of the time with his book "In Cold Blood".

The temples of Abu Simbel in Egypt were moved to save them from the rising waters caused by the Aswan Dam. Lenny Bruce was found dead of a drug overdose in Hollywood.

Nokiki and I were half-dead as well. Our trip down the canyon had been so exhausting and hot that we collapsed on our sleeping bags devoid of levity. I was most amenable to sleep, but soon felt things falling on my face. I was too footsore to even open my eyes. Slimy sludge continued to drop from above. It was not until the outer world impinged on me like a rodent chewing my toes off that I regained consciousness enough to open my eyelids and realized that worms were crawling and excoriating my skin.

I yelled like Elizabeth Taylor in "Who's Afraid of Virginia Woolf?" and ran to the river. I fell face down into the rapid current and washed the vermin from my face.

When I returned from the river, Nokiki had started a fire and was cooking noodles with squash. We sang "Strangers in the Night" and smiled at each other with moist eyelids. We were beat with decrepitude yet exhilarated. She acted as if it was a malfeasance to impart any information about herself, but I importuned for a retrospection of her life. Her mother was a survivor of the August Hiroshima blast. She read Isaac Asimov for recreation and preferred robots to people.

> *"La Femme Infidele" is a 1969 film so calmly and*
> *thoughtfully perverse it can have only been directed by*
> *Claude Chabrol of the French New Wave.*

In 1967 obituary notices went out for Woody Guthrie, André Malraux, Carson McCullers and Elmer Rice. Muhammad Ali was indicted for refusing induction into the military. Martin Luther King, Jr. led an anti-Vietnam War march in New York. Thurgood Marshall was appointed to the Supremes while Bonnie and Clyde were riddled with bullets in Arthur Penn's movie.

While Nokiko and I were camping in the Grand Canyon, we met a man named Hubert Bon Mot from Haiti. He was tall with an afro and called himself a "Poet from Hell". His credo was that poetry should attack the complacent listener.

He was not into verbal flanking maneuvers. He believed in direct confrontation like a rebel charge across an open field in broad daylight. Poetry, he insisted, should unsettle the listeners and threaten them. He wanted them to take up arms to protect the kindergarten that represented their world view.

He was not interested in winning contests or publishing in small press magazines. A successful poet was someone who could rankle the audience to the point of violence. His idea of a grand success was to deliver harangues to 20,000 people in Madison Square Garden and set them off rioting into the streets.

His daytime discourse was insipid compared to what oozed out of him after dark. When Nokiko started a fire to cook her rice and veggies, Hubert turned into a veritable fiend. He burned a Che Guevara poster ... wanted to dress Pope Paul VI up like an Arab and place him on the front lines in the Six-Day War ... wanted Albert H. de Salvo as Secretary of Defense ... wanted a Black Power conference held in the White House ... wanted nuclear-powered kitchen appliances ... wanted to run the entire Green Bay Packer football team along with coach Vince Lombardi through a meat grinder and feed the offal to the dolphins.

Nokiko and I were of the same imperturbable ilk. She came from a stoical Buddhist background that taught suffering is caused by desire. My undemonstrative demeanor was evinced because I was unimpressed by ranting commentary from a man with a cognomen like Bon Mot. Hubert became frustrated that he could not anger us and out of frustration he jumped into the fire. His spirit dissipated into the night.

TREK 38

On January of 1968 "Rowan & Martin's Laugh-In" filled the TV room in the lobby of the men's dorm at the state university.

Backpack Trekker: A 60's Flashback

Hiking out of the Grand Canyon, passing layers of affluent color and geologic time, was an intoxicant for dreams. Resting in the shade, dozing with fatigue, knowing that many upward miles were still to be traversed, dreams came to me as a release from the drudgery. Dreams supplanted news broadcasts of the Tet Offensive.

In 1968 North Vietnam endured the bombs. The frustration of U.S. troops was reflected in the My Lai massacre. In Mexico City police opened fire on student demonstrators. The charismatic Robert Kennedy was gunned down after winning the California primary. Martin Luther King, Jr., who represented truth outside of public office, stopped long enough on the motel balcony for an assassin to get a bead on him.

Police bloodily dampened the Festival of Life at the Democratic Convention in Chicago. Richard Nixon, who waited like a goat for someone to leave the greenhouse door open to the White House, won the election by a narrow margin with his secret plan to end the Vietnam War.

My dreams sheltered me from it all. Dreams transport us to other realms, swirl us into a space odyssey and shift us into a yellow submarine. Removing the weight of my backpack from my shoulders, I dreamed of electric Kool-Aid acid tests, nights of the living dead, and Volkswagen beetles driving blue highways. My soul was on ice as I read a "Blue Book" for the planet of the apes. I felt like a lion in winter eating Rosemary's baby. I could dispense with writing completely if I could photograph my dreams. If I could laminate my fantasies, I would not submit to underground magazines or the "L.A. Free Press." If I could solidify my dreams, I wouldn't need the "Berkeley Barb."

As we trudged out of time, a phantasmagoria of esoteric reverie interpolated reality. I dreamt to forget my sore feet; to replace my sweaty T-shirt with a cool silk robe; to replace the rocky trail with a shady harem. We dreamt of peace where people did not estrange themselves from the estuary of time and color, where violence did not rectify the misanthrope, and attained our goals from diligent perseverance.

Nokiko and I reached the rim of the canyon and saw a bus load of clean tourists taking group pictures. We treated ourselves to a restaurant meal and a motel. Candles and incense were a prelude to mutual foot massages. We had gone down so we could climb back up. We blended our dreams and strengthened our resolve to return to our mutual endeavors with renewed vigor.

Beatlick Joe Speer

In September of 1969 Phil Dona-
hue started his daytime talk show.

In 1969 Mickey Mantle retired from baseball. Also in 1969 the bottom rose to the top when the New York Mets beat the Baltimore Orioles four games to one. Casey Stengel, who managed the Yankees in 1960, had an influence on the once laughable Mets. A guy named Joe Namath flew the New York Jets like a Montana wind past the Colts in Super Bowl III.

Ho Chi Minh died at age 79. The body of Mary Jo Kopechne was found in a 1967 Oldsmobile sedan down in eight feet of water. Man walked on the moon in 1969 as hundreds of thousands of demonstrators massed in D.C. to demand a moratorium on the war in Vietnam. Chicago police attacked Black Panther headquarters with Thompson submachine guns.

They attacked the sleeping Panthers and killed Fred Hampton and Mark Clark. "Penthouse" magazine began publication as "The Saturday Evening Post" called it quits.

One event ended as another took its place. Muddy Waters was the last act at the 1960 Newport Folk Festival. Jimi Hendrix finished it off at the 1969 Woodstock Music and Art Fair. Lysergic acid diethylamide was consumed more than vitamin C.

In films "Midnight Cowboy" learned to earn money in an urban environment and the "Easy Rider" should have stayed in New Orleans. Director Sergio Leone brought the Italian western to John Ford's country with "Once Upon a Time in the West", and in the Big Apple, performers in "Oh! Calcutta!" tossed their clothes off Broadway.

Down south Hurricane Camille ripped the Gulf Coast. Out west California's Supreme Court ruled that the state's anti-abortion law was unconstitutional. On the medical front a study revealed that monosodium glutamate caused brain damage in mice.

On the literary scene of 1969 John Berryman won the National Book Award for Poetry with "His Toy, His Dream". It was a book of dream songs, one per page, each separate and numbered. In "1939" he wrote:

... The knowing books opened themselves in vain.

Backpack Trekker: A 60's Flashback

One of the top commercials from 1969 was called "Uncle Max's Funeral." A rich man died and as his loved ones drive to the cemetery, we hear a voice reading the will. To his wife Rose, who spent money like there was no tomorrow, he left $100 and a calendar. To his business partner whose motto was spend, spend, spend, he left nothing, nothing, nothing. To his sons who spent every dime on fancy cars and fast women, he left $50 in dimes. To his nephew Harold, who knew how to economize and said it sure paid to own a VW, Max left his entire fortune of one-hundred-billion dollars. After the limos passed, Harold brought up the rear of the procession in his VW bug. He wiped away a tear then smiled inadvertently.

TREK 40

> *In the 1969 film "The Candyman" a drug peddler in Mexico City plots to kidnap the child of an American movie star.*

After I read "The Razor's Edge" by Somerset Maugham, I wanted to be like Larry and travel, read esoteric books, work a variety of jobs to collect experience and visit worldwide archaeo-logical sites.

I wanted all my time to be close to the sacred places of the earth. Unlike Larry, however, who had an unidentified continuous source of income mailed to him wherever he wandered in Europe or India, I earned money on work-study programs and resort lo-cations. A desk clerk in the Colorado mountains during the sum-mer at a dude ranch was a cool place to receive tips and wages.

A daily cash flow is like having access to a natural spring. The click of a cash register reverberates like the solo piano of Willie "The Lion" Smith. I had to grubstake my peregrinations with temporary jobs.

I met an ex-con who was at loggerheads with the entrenched economic system. He insisted the money game created by the governments of the world was another way to control people.

"Money has a transient value," he went on as saliva beaded up at the corners of his mouth. "The Continental Congress bills can't buy air tickets. The paper issued by the Confederacy won't buy a round during happy hour at the corner bar. An escudo has no merit in Russia. The peso won't exchange for a hamburger in Flagstaff."

He suggested, since we devote more time earning money than in worship to the divine, that we genuflect and pray at the government mints.

From Flagstaff I headed down 89 to Sedona and over to Tuzigoot. I camped out for three days near the ancient site of stone walls. I felt lucky to live in the open and not plugged into the fizgig of electricity and house payments. Every morning was a *"tabula rasa"* and evenings spent by a camp fire.

One night a law enforcement agent walked into my camp. He had seen my flames distant in the dark and came to inform me of the rules. No fires. He wrote me a ticket. As he asked me questions, I told him my name was Loomis Pound and that I was born in Alaska to parents who worked at a free-health clinic treating natives for syphilis and gonorrhea.

The agent insisted I douse the fire, but I refused to use my drinking water, so I pissed on it and watched it die slow, imperceptibly like the ruins at Tuzigoot melting back into the earth.

I crawled into my sleeping bag and read a chapter of "The Brothers Karamazov" with a flashlight, gradually dissolving into the embrace of Mother Earth.

TREK 41

The New Orleans Jazz & Heritage
Festival started in 1969.

I met Carrington in the campground one morning. He was foraging recently vacated sites for castoff food or trashcan condiments. Having served time in Vietnam, he had been drummed out of the army for refusing to follow orders. He lived on the fringes of society, having struck a deal with the park ranger to clean the campground which exempted him from the nightly fee. A camouflaged tent was his residence and he was seldom seen except as a vague, distant figure moving through the bush.

We connected at the rest room. I brushed my teeth while he filled a water jug. I liked his vibration, so I invited him to my campsite where he recounted parts of his military experience. Three days after his tour of duty started, he began the countdown toward the expiration of his time. The consensus with all the members of his platoon was that if they didn't attack the Vietcong, then Charlie wouldn't fire on them.

Backpack Trekker: A 60's Flashback

They had piled their rifles up like tepee poles under which they built campfires at night. Mortars were discarded. They eked out a false truce until a new second lieutenant arrived to reactivate their morale.

This lieutenant was a lifer who came to authorize the forces of right action. It took days of pestering and guilt-laden ramifications before the men inserted live ammo into their weapons and marched once again on patrol.

They walked onto a mine field. Three men were killed and Carrington's best friend sustained the loss of a limb. He survived unscathed, but very angry. To give vent to his violent surge of reaction, Carrington entered the lieutenant's tent late one night with a burning cigarette between his lips and a Chinese bayonet in his hand. He stabbed him in the throat with the Chi Com blade and within ten minutes fell into a dreamless sleep in his own cot.

Carrington was not sent to jail for murder. They never found out about that. He was imprisoned at LBJ (Long Binh Jail) for refusing to obey orders. A dishonorable discharge brought him back to the States with a feeling of guilt. Not able to work or meld with women, he lived on the outside as a collaborator with the serpent in the undoing of man.

Some nights he expressed himself to twilight emptiness on the harmonica, blowing his sound to no official ear. His sound permeated my tent like the music of Blood, Sweat, and Tears and his gifts of found food adorned the picnic table. He gathered the wood and I lit the crumpled newspaper. The flames for him were not used for heat or light, but for reconciliation with memory.

Like Chief Joseph, Carrington would fight no more.

TREK 42

WMOT jazz radio station started in Murfreesboro, Tennessee, in 1969.

Carrington often felt like an eight ball with a stripe, like contaminated water nobody wants to drink. His war experience alienated him even more from people. Sports sustained him in his solitude. He lived day to day on a regimen of foraging for food and basketball scores. On the off season he savored old newspaper clippings. His favorite team was the Boston Celtics. One night around the campfire he recounted a few anecdotes from the Celtic dynasty.

"The Celtics won the championship in '57 and '59. The great rivalry between Wilt Chamberlain and Bill Russell began on November of 1959. Wilt was the first seven-footer in the NBA. He had an unstoppable fallaway jumper. To set the tone for the new decade, Bill blocked Wilt's first shot and Boston won the game. Boston defeated the big warrior every year they met in the playoffs except in '67. Red Auerbach retired his victory cigar, and that year Russell became coach/player. As he made the adjustment Chamberlain and company overpowered them," he said.

"In '69 Wilt was awarded a million-dollar contract with the Lakers. The Celtics were aging and it looked like LA was a shoo-in for the championship. With Wilt down low, Elgin Baylor at forward, and Jerry West at guard, the smart bets were on the Lakers. It all came down to a seventh game in the Forum. Jack Kent Cooke, the club owner, was so sure of victory that he had balloons in the ceiling ready to drop in celebration.

Late in the game Wilt claimed an injury and took himself out of the game. I think the Mafia offered him some tax-free money to tip the game toward the Celtics. Wilt also attempted thirteen free throws and only made four.

The game ended with Wilt on the bench because the coach was too angry to let him back in. The Celtics won by one basket. After winning, Number 6 quietly quit," Carrington finished his harangue.

He read from "Sports Illustrated" where Russell talked about the beauty of men coordinating their efforts to achieve a common goal. The players would alternately subordinate or assert themselves towards teamwork in action. Bill lost his competitive urges. He could not participate in something he didn't care about.

Bill Russell would play no more.

TREK 43

In 1969 Francois Truffaut's "Stolen Kisses" picks up the hero of "The 400 Blows" ten years later and follows his adventures around Paris as a hotel night clerk.

I knew a mailman who compared registration for the draft to a daft impulse, said it was like a white cracker in a Cadillac driving through the Watts riots in 1965. He equated it to being down on your uppers and sending a change of address to your creditors.

Credit goes to the dissenting voices of the Vietnam War. They encountered armed resistance from pursuing teenage draft dodgers across state lines to utilizing assassination as a political tool, the profiteers of war were adamantine and profligate.

Especially unyielding was J. Edgar Hoover, director of the FBI since 1924. As he approached the age of compulsory retirement, JFK had no intention of extending the old man's scurvy influence. Kennedy had written an executive order to take effect in January of 1964 to pull troops out of Vietnam. When LBJ was suddenly installed in the White House, he changed the law so Hoover could maintain his marriage to power. Johnson rescinded Kennedy's order and continued to expand the war until, in frustration, he threw in the towel.

Also frustrating at times was hitchhiking. Waiting on an entrance ramp for six hours as drivers ignored you was enough to make one consider buying a camel and moving to the Atlas Mountains in Morocco. Hand-written messages that proclaimed how previous hitchers expired from dehydration or overexposure to the sun were unnerving. Hitchhiking was the theater of all possibilities. A ride may offer a meal and place to slumber or the driver may try to cut off your ear to hang on the mirror.

My brother Paul and I were hitching on US 66 west. In Arizona a man named Mina picked us up. He had his family and all their possessions in a station wagon. He could not drink alcohol, but traveled with an ice chest full of tall boy malt liquor cans. He kept us supplied with beer and was invigorated to watch us leave the state of Arizona and slowly enter the state of inebriation.

Paul engaged in a lengthy talkfest with Mina's nine-year-old son. The boy had constructed a rocket ship to carry his family and pet gerbils into space.

He read that the earth would be destroyed to make room for an intergalactic by-pass. He didn't want to depend on the infinite probability factor in order to be saved. His name was Edgar and he wanted to be in control.

TREK 44

In 1969 Anne Sexton wrote "In Celebration of My Uterus":
Everyone in me is a bird/I am beating all my wings

Beatlick Joe Speer

Anne presented her work publicly, smoking cigs and wearing a long dress. She celebrated womanhood. The IUD and pill protected woman from unwanted pregnancy.

The sexual revolution took couples from kissing good night on the front porch to culminating a new relationship with carnal knowledge. It was not unusual to meet someone at a party, engage in a splendiferous *tête-a-tête*, and retire to the boudoir to disrobe and commingle body fluids. People tried to take relationships to indefatigable heights without base camps and arduous climbing. With alcohol to invigorate and music to activate the sweat glands, people turned up the volume on Credence Clearwater Revival, The Doors, The Rolling Stones and danced their primitive spontaneous movements. Revelers pushed the furniture back and their bumptious bodies filled the night with dauntless action.

Little Eddie, a post-graduate friend of mine at the university, was especially active. He notched up sexual encounters like a gunfighter in a range war. We worked together. I had a facility for meeting girls. I'd start a smooth chat then introduce Eddie with glowing details on his scientific achievements. He'd take over and close the deal. If the combination was successful he'd disappear and return with a smile on his face. Sex for him was weekend entertainment. He thought kissing contests should replace football. He wanted to play his skin flute at every available concert.

Eddie scored lots of leg before the fun factor was undercut by the unexpected pregnancy of a girl named Sue. On her first adventurous outing into the skin trade, a sperm swam into her egg like a panzer division rolling into Hitler's last territorial demand. Her eyes were closed like she was in a dentist's chair. She didn't even have an orgasm. At seventeen she felt her body had betrayed her. Eddie offered to pay for an abortion. Other than that he avoided her like she was a coughing TB victim.

She did not feel the baby should die for her mistake. She decided to have the child. Then feeling unprepared and overwhelmed by motherhood, she gave custody of the infant to her parents.

Her last date was with carbon monoxide in a closed garage.

I stopped seeing Eddie after that. The frivolity of our association had dissipated like exhaust fumes out a tailpipe.

☯

Backpack Trekker: A 60's Flashback

In 1969 Gene Siskel got a reporting
job with the "Chicago Tribune".

In 1859 John Brown was found guilty of treason and hanged. His crime was similar to that of Nat Turner in 1831. They both used extreme measures to combat slavery. Henry David Thoreau compared Brown to "the best of those who stood at Concord, Lexington, and Bunker Hill." Brown, like Turner, was unrepentant. In a farewell letter to his family he wrote:

> ... I am waiting the hour of my public murder with great composure of mind, & cheerfulness, feeling the strongest assurance that in no other possible way could I be used to so much advance in the cause of God & humanity & that nothing that either I or all my family have sacrificed or suffered will be lost.

Within a year and a half the Civil War began and the evils of slavery was purged with blood. If Brown had perpetrated his raids during the Civil War, perhaps he could have generated a larger force. If the American Revolution had failed people like Washington and Jefferson would have been hanged as traitors.

I learned to mistrust history as recorded for undiscerning minds. There is a difference between what people denounce and what they deliver. Nixon for example, was elected in 1968 on a promise to end the Vietnam War. What he actually did was change the emphasis from ground troops to bombing.

I had a friend in high school named J.D. There was always a great disparity between what he said and what he did. He talked about digging in an extinct volcano and finding a cedar chest full of gold ducats. The treasure was traded for a collection of rare copies of "Dial" magazine.

According to J.D., his summer vacations were replete with adventure: diving off the cliffs in Acapulco with a *piña colada* in his hand; looking for gold nuggets in a dead creek bed while pulling an obstreperous mule with a lariat once used by Tom Mix; walking barefoot in Haight-Ashbury with a bed roll slung over his shoulder and on the lookout for an angry fix. With a placid composure he claimed to have transcribed most of "The Ticket That Exploded" as dictated to him by Burroughs while the author was held captive by the Nova Mob. I had to keep pace with his imagination so I described my part in the construction of spacecraft Surveyor 7 that landed successfully on the moon. I recounted an epic poem written on the shore at low tide from Redwood National Park to Oregon Dunes National Recreation Area. I narrated about my interviews with park rangers and their confrontations with wolverines in jeans.

I liked J.D.'s palaver, but I separated his egregious claims from fact.

TREK 46

In the 1967 film "The Exterminating Angel" Luís Buñuel shows what happens to a chattering party of resplendent guests in a Mexico City town house after the opera. No one can leave but Buñuel never explains why.

In 1960 Zora Neale Hurston died in Florida. In 1925 she had arrived in Harlem with $1.50 and no job. She won prizes for her short stories in "Opportunity" magazine sponsored by editor Charles S. Johnson. Financed by Mrs. Osgood Mason to research folklore, Zora's books were published as the Harlem Renaissance faded out. She was a significant member of the 20's "Niggerati" who disappeared quietly into an unmarked grave as the civil rights movement loudly celebrated a rebirth of the New Negro.

I studied history to understand how events interconnect. My brother Paul was of the opinion that historical data should be destroyed. Paul said history is "a quagmire of consciousness." With a wry smile he referred to history as "quicksand to eternal progression." James Joyce called history a nightmare from which he wanted to awaken.

I got a ride with an art teacher to Montezuma Castle. Her name was Sara. We visited the well-preserved cliff dwelling and laid out a blanket for a picnic. After ingesting apple slivers, I was possessed by my brother's diabolic attitude. I suggested that all existing art be turned into a recycle center. Paint over the canvases of Claude Monet and Georgia O'Keeffe. Melt down the metal sculptures of Henry Moore and Frederic Remington. Reshape the marble of Michelangelo. Sara was smitten with odium at such an outrageous suggestion. If art eradication was possible, then she would be out of a job as an art history teacher.

Backpack Trekker: A 60's Flashback

"Then become an artist," I intoned. "Fill museums with the work of living artists. Why should art dealers make big bucks on the labor of dead painters? Let living artists get paid for their creativity."

Sara was flabbergasted at my irresponsible prattle. I detected anger in her voice rising like Mercury after sunrise in the desert. She was attractive and I didn't want to alienate her over a theoretical scenario. I retracted my statements and insisted I'd never consider scraping my reproduction of "The Little Milkmaid" by Modigliani. After she was sufficiently relaxed, I offered to massage her feet. She was compliant, but when I maneuvered up her legs she became squeamish.

"To ensure balance," I explained, "I should give you a full body massage." She did not want my fingerprints all over her.

"I am not malleable clay," she said with a devilish smile. "I do not want to be reshaped."

TREK 47

> In the 1969 film "Monte Carlo or Bust" the competitors in an international car rally travel from various points in Europe to Monte Carlo.

From Montezuma Castle I traveled to Wupatki. A family in a VW bus picked me up. The driver was an English teacher named Wallace. His wife Joan was an organizer of a commune in Orange County, California. As they stopped she made sandwiches and peeled carrots to distribute. They were accompanied by their precocious nine-year-old daughter, Tammy, and her best friend, Angel. They satiated my thirst and hunger.

Then they invited me to camp with them. The girls and I collected firewood where I discovered Tammy's ebullient imagination.

"Look," she said pointing to the ground. "Tracks of a war party."

"Are we in any danger?" I asked.

"No. I can tell from the signs that a band of warriors were double-timing it after a skirmish with union troops."

A few minutes later Angel saw a rattlesnake coiled up like a garden hose in winter. "If we remove the rattles," Tammy suggested, "we can use it as a talisman for nighttime incantations." We waited until it slithered away; then, I pinned its head down with a stick while the rest of the body flapped like a full-pressure fire hose out of control. Tammy stood on the snake's head as I moved down its body with both hands and cut off the *cascabel.*

We returned to camp with armloads of wood and our reptilian token. The girls danced around the fire chanting until Joan subdued them with chocolate cake. All was silent until Tammy suggested I tell them a story.

"I'll tell you a story," I replied. "I camped one night near Sunset Crater. I dug a fire pit with my plastic spoon and used tooth picks as fuel. A brown bear saw my flame in the distance and came to present the bare facts of its hunger. All I had was a bag of trail mix to distract it. I threw the bag at the bear, and while it was sorting the nuts from the yogurt raisins, I escaped. I moved away from the confrontation to a pay phone and started to dial the authorities. My call was interrupted by a raccoon with an emergency. The raccoon's mate had been run over by a milk truck and it wanted to summon an ambulance. I relinquished the phone. After the paramedics arrived and departed, I called a park ranger and complained about the rampaging bear. The ranger said for me to sing the chorus of any Robin Williamson song, and the bear would join in and forget about food. When I returned to my campsite, the bear and I had a songfest. It was fun but I remained pissed off because the bear had picked through my trail mix and eaten all the cashews."

TREK 48

In "Me, Natalie" Patty Duke moves to Greenwich Village and lands a job at the Topless Bottom Club.

Wallace pulled out a cigar and the three of us passed it around like a peace pipe. Whoever held the burning tobacco was toastmaster and could expound until they relinquished the cigar to someone else. Wallace puffed and threw two logs into the campfire.

"My class studies the Harlem 1920's writers," Wallace said, drawing an H in the dark with the burning ember of cigar that gave him control over us. "When word got out that life was jumping at The Cotton Club and other dance joints and gin mills in Harlem, white tourism began to pour into the jazz clubs. Rudolph Fisher was there before black came into vogue. He hung out in all-black clubs. Then he left and returned years later to walk once more through the speakeasy he used to frequent. After being seated at a table and looking up, he noticed everybody in the club except the band was white. A disconcerted feeling caused him to depart hastily." Wallace passed the cigar to his wife Joan.

"I became involved in communal living," she began, "to experiment with self-government. We had no leaders. We met once a week in a geodesic dome to assign jobs which were rotated. Many commune members practiced free love, but I followed a strict course of celibacy. I had a shrine to Mary. When sexual urges interfered, I retreated to my statue of the Blessed Mother and recited Hail Marys until my mind was clear. If I could go all week without sexual distractions, I rewarded myself by spending all of Sunday in church." She handed me the cigar.

"Since we are in a forest," I said, "I'll tell you a story about a pine tree that escaped Christmas. A young tree, six-feet tall, was cut down by the rotating teeth of a well-oiled chainsaw. It was loaded onto a flatbed truck, propped up in a fenced yard and sold. It was crammed into a station wagon with dogs, kids and grocery sacks.

"While the family prepared a corner for it, the tree escaped. It hopped to a bus stop and rode to the end of the line. An old man in a pickup culling the highway for castoff items drove the tree back to the forest. He replanted the tree with a special ceremony, reading poems from Bukowski's 'The Days Run Away Like Wild Horses Over the Hills'.

"The tree enjoyed a long and happy life and became known in the forest as the tree that escaped Christmas."

I threw the cigar stub into the fire and we bedded down for night.

TREK 49

In 1969 the U.S. Supreme Court unanimously struck down laws prohibiting private possession of obscene materials.

On my third day with the vacationing family we drove from Wupatki to Navajo National Monument. The parents relaxed in their bus while Tammy, Angel and I hiked into Keet Seel. We removed our shoes and socks and walked for miles in the stream. The heat caused us to splash each other and roll in the water.

"Geronimo rode through here once," Tammy said. "He started a Native-American revolution by leaving the reservation and adopting the concept of freedom." Even though I was older than Tammy, I spent most of the time listening to her.

"This terrain is like Jurassic times," she continued. "We are apt to see anything here. There goes a chameleon with spines of painted shards. There is a Gila monster digesting the tail of a kangaroo rat. There is a roadrunner outfoxing a coyote in a game of seven card stud."

"Look," I shouted. "An arrowhead." I picked the artifact out of the dirt.

"Let me see," Tammy insisted. "Yes, this was used by a member of the Hohokam culture. It penetrated the flank of an elk that provided meat for a family of four."

"How do you know all that?" Alice asked.

"I squeeze the arrow and concentrate. The information is stored in the stone. I tap into it the same way I can hold a crystal and gain access to millions of years of vibrations collected in it."

"If I squeeze your head, will I be privy to your past life?" I asked.

"Let's try it. Hold my head and look into the crystal."

"I not only feel every detail of your nine years on earth, but I can see clearly into your future. You will matriculate from a state university and travel to Pisa with plans to prop up the Leaning Tower with discarded bicycle tires. You will receive your first kiss near a pool in *Le Palais de Versailles, construit par ordre de Louis XIV*. No, that's not right. You will be kissed right now in the open air in front of a witness." I kissed her on the forehead.

"She has already been kissed at the skating rink," Alice remarked.

"Shut up," Tammy said. "Or I'll squeeze your head and submit my findings to an abnormal psychology journal."

TREK 50

The 1969 Japanese film "The Green Slime" featured funky looking aliens running amuck on a space station.

Alone again ... circulating my memories ... sure was fun ... monkeyshines with the family on vacation ... spontaneous theater with jovial friends ... got to feel safe ... snakes that shed miracles ... cigars that burn for hours ... a story that picks up two days later exactly where it left off ... you never know how far your imagination will travel until you dare to embark ... no agent ... no road signs ... just make it up as you look into someone's eyes ... the bear ate the expensive nuts ... left me the birdseed ... I started to sing Neil Young songs ... the bear was too old to appreciate Young ... it returned to hibernation ... I could continue the story but no audience ... my mind is bootless with no one to tax it ... after a wonderful connection with an energetic person, I feel disjunctive ... traveling between my ears ... alone, alone ... remembering my classmates who want to secure their future with investments ... make a mark in the dark ... leave their prints on the sands of history ... write, publish, sing, make moolah ... how can one live a full life and leave no traces ... no input into history ... no material for biography ... have your work transported to other continents, but remain unknown like B. Traven ... to disappear at sea with no fanfare like Hart Crane ... to desist with loneliness like the long-distance runner ... how to vie for national attention and still remain anonymous ... I entered the bear's lair ... it was dead as a ducat ... a punched out meal ticket ... I clapped my hands and sang Richie Haven songs ... the bear did not move ... ignored my artistic expression ... I set its tail on fire and watched its eyes pop open ... "Fire" ... like copies of "Ulysses" on fire in 1922 ... like copies of "Fire" on fire in a basement ... Wallace Thurman going into debt ... what good is information if we have no one to share it with? ... what use is imagination with no one to ply it on? ... can humor exist without the sound of laughter? ... the bear didn't respond favorably to the heat ... it ran out and began clawing the bark off a tree ... here comes a VW ... focus on a ride ... the next lift will give me something I need ... damn ... the VW drove by like I was a squashed bug ... I may have to create an imaginary friend to eat dinner with ... maybe I can conjure up H.L. Mencken to share oatmeal with me ... we can smoke a cigar and talk about the American language ... here comes a truck ... I'll ride in the back ... pull it over ... maybe I should cross the road and try my luck in the other direction ... hell's a poppin' keep on walkin' ...

TREK 51

In 1969 "The Lost Man" Sidney Poitier leads a group of black militants in robbing a factory in order to provide money for some civil rights organizations.

Beatlick Joe Speer

I got a ride with a British gentleman in a rent-a-car. He was bored driving the open vastness of the southwest and needed some diverting dialogue. He was well-heeled and headed for Las Vegas, a city of dreams where spending is the order of the day. A mixed drink was on the dashboard and smooth jazz was coming through the speakers. His name was Jonathan and I sensed a financial windfall if I could connect with him. He wanted to bet on the number of cars that would pass us in the next hour. I didn't have any wherewithal to wager so he loaned me $50. After the first bet he doubled the ante and bet on how many bugs would smash against the windshield. Then he covered up the odometer and we bet every five minutes on how many miles we had traveled. It wasn't long before he won all his money back. Then he fabricated a new game. He said if I could name a dozen writers who used a pen name, he would stake me to a full day of gambling in Las Vegas.

"That's easy," I said and began to list names. I pronounced the *nom de plume* first, then the real name:

André Malraux aka Emile Solomon Wilhelm Herzog
Mark Twain aka Samuel Langhorne Clemens
Oscar Wilde aka Fingal O'Flahertie Wills
Saki aka Hector Hugh Munro
O. Henry aka William Sidney Porter
Pablo Neruda aka Neftalí Ricardo Reyes Basoalto
George Sand aka Lucie Aurore Dupin Dudevant
George Eliot aka Mary Ann Evans
Gabriela Mistral aka Lucila Godoy Alcayaga
Stendhal aka Marie Henri Beyle
Emily Bronte aka Ellis Bell
George Orwell aka Eric Arthur Blair

When I answered his behest with unhesitating alacrity, he stepped on the gas with fear and loathing. In Nevada the gas stations contain slot machines in the restrooms. When I went in to relieve myself, I discovered Jonathan with one hand on his penis and one hand on a lever playing the slots.

Special concessions allow Nevada to earn money in special ways. Without gambling, prostitution and boxing since 1910, when Jack Johnson defeated Jim Jeffries, who was persuaded to come out of retirement, the state would only be useful as a nuclear test site.

Backpack Trekker: A 60's Flashback

In 1969 a huge oil slick contaminates the coast of Santa Barbara, California.

Jonathan called room service and had breakfast in bed. I went downstairs to the restaurant and ordered a "Gamblers Special". After he was properly attired, he took me to a barbershop, a haberdashery and a bank where he put $20,000 cash into my pocket. I warmed up on one-armed bandits, then moved to a blackjack table. Jonathan stood next to me staunch and pensive. He communicated to me through subtle signals whether I should take a hit or stand pat. I increased my roll and we moved to the roulette wheel. We moved to the crap table, and when it was my turn to toss the bones, I cajoled a lady spectator to blow sweet fortune on the dice. I had a winning streak until a pair of snake eyes took me out of the game.

At noon we broke for lunch. We ordered steak, baked potato and salad. There was a slot machine near our table. Jonathan bet on how many times the machine would pay off during the course of our meal. Whenever I bet against him, he seemed to have an edge on me. He had an uncanny, inexplicable touch for winning. It was like losing was not an option. After the meal we retired to the lounge for a drink. He removed an ice cube from his glass, placed it on the counter and bet on how long it would take to melt. Most of the bets were abstract and random, but some of them were psychically personal set ups. For example, he was willing to bet $400 that I would not pour ice water on the head of a stranger. Even though I had the chance to control the outcome of the bet, I did not bet because I knew I would lose. I did not bet with him after that.

That afternoon we played Keno and more roulette. We never stayed too long at any one location. Keep it simple and keep it moving was Jonathan's philosophy. By five o'clock we returned to the room and counted our winnings. We had over $60,000. Jonathan took $50,000 and gave me the rest. Then he packed his overnight bag and left because he had an appointment in Hong Kong and had to be at the LA airport for a flight. I could have stayed in the room as he had paid for three nights, but I had a queasy feeling and decided to move to the Starlite Motel.

As I waited for the elevator to rise from the ground floor, four men dressed in suits gathered in front of the room I just vacated.

They knocked, and when no one answered, they used a pass key to enter. As they disappeared into the room, the elevator door opened and I departed the building.

TREK 53

Octavio Paz resigned from foreign service when the Mexican army crushed an anti-government movement and killed more than 300 students in 1968.

I checked into the Starlite Motel under the name of Alexander Pope. I had plenty of money but no desire to gamble. I walked in and out of casinos, watching inveterate gamesters bivouacked in front of slot machines. I bought a newspaper to scan the entertainment. Elvis Presley was making his first live appearance in eight years at the Las Vegas International Hotel in July of 1969. He starred in 33 movies but in '69 he had a change of habit. With Priscilla he discovered the trouble with girls.

I was not a devoted Elvis fan. I'd just as soon listen to the Almanac singers belting out "Away Rio" or "Blow the Man Down". I did go to the hotel to swim in the vibrations. It is wonderful to feel the commonality of joy and excitement in an audience having a good time. I left the area wanting to dance on the sidewalk under the luminescence of Fremont Street.

Back in my room with no inclination to sleep, I called an escort service listed in the newspaper. I requested a vanilla girl with a penchant for D.H. Lawrence. About thirty minutes later there was a knock on my door. I looked out the window to make sure it wasn't a hotel dick or a pair of Mormons.

My guest had arrived. I swung the door open and invited her inside. She had a coy smile and a copy of "Women in Love". I helped remove her outer covering. She wore a one-piece mini dress. I gave her a hundred-dollar-bill to establish rapport and assure her of my intentions to do business.

"Consider that a retainer," I said. I locked the door. She pulled her dress off over her head in one easy motion. No underclothes. After I joined her in the state of nakedness, she examined my equipment. She even washed my mojo down over the sink. Her suggestion was to discharge between her breasts. We bumped together with only the bathroom light on. I entered her gully through the bramble patch. I stroked her to the point of ejaculatory inevitability, then pulled out to reposition my artillery.

She compressed her mammary against my cannon and I shot a load onto her chest. We showered together and dried each other off with towels. She dressed in a moment and I gave her another two bills from my wad. We kissed. I let her out and watched her walk to a parked car. The dome light came on as she opened the door. There was a dark man in the driver's seat. She closed the door and they drove away.

TREK 54

In 1968 Volkswagen sold over 568,000 cars in the United States.

I hired a car and driver to visit Hoover Dam. Whenever I think of Hoover I think of J. Edgar. Any black intellectual who appeared in America during his reign came under investigation from Marcus Garvey in the 1920's, to Richard Wright in the 40's to Dr. King in the 60's.

It's a short jaunt from Las Vegas to that imposing yet profane defilement erected to dam the life blood of the Colorado River. I ordered the chauffeur to pick up every hitchhiker en route. We had five passengers when we arrived at our destination. We toured the bowels of the concrete structure singing, "Let me take you down."

After the tour we drove to a restaurant and I told everyone to order anything on the menu. It was my treat. The conversation was random and hectic, a maelstrom of catch phrases: Girls say yes to boys who say no ... Tune in. Turn on. Drop Out ... A teenage inductee could be arrested for refusing to kill and be imprisoned with men who were locked up because they killed ... Hell no. We won't go ... What if they gave a war and nobody came ... Caution, police are armed and dangerous ... Make love not war ... Power to the people ... Don't trust anyone over 30 ... Split wood not atoms ...

"Do we have any streakers?" I asked. A man named Flash said he had been arrested three times for streaking – once during a production of "Dutchman" by LeRoi Jones, once for running up and down the aisles while "The Sand Pebbles" was playing the scene where Jake Holman was activating the engine room of the ship and once while Ravi Shankar was jamming a raga at the

Monterey Pop Festival. He streaked during a production of "Hair" but the audience thought he was part of the cast.

We separated outside the restaurant. I had the driver drop me off at Las Vegas Airport. I paid him and bought a one-way ticket to Mexico City.

TREK 55

In 1969 four-hundred students at Harvard University seize buildings as part of a campus-wide strike.

I enjoy long flights while looking out the window at rivers and empty ball parks. When the clouds blocked the view at 30,000 feet I read "Uncle Tom's Children" by Richard Wright. It is right to say he left a rich mark on literature. He introduced a new element into American fiction. He created a tension from the possibility of random violence. H.L. Mencken taught him how to use words as weapons.

In the story "Big Boy Leaves Home" three Negro men go skinny dipping in a lake. There are no signs of trouble until a white man appears with a rifle. He kills two of the men but Big Boy manages to kill the white man. Later, while trying to secure a hiding place, he beats a snake to death with a stick. From a hideout he watches a friend get burned with hot tar and gas. He strangles a barking dog that sniffs him out and threatens to disclose his presence. Big Boy is pursued by the vigilante committee but he escapes to the north.

Richard Wright escaped to Paris in 1946. In 1953 with the publication of his novel "The Outsider", he culminated the work of the Harlem Renaissance and joined forces with French existentialism. Wright died in Paris in 1960 and his ashes are interred at *Père Lachaise*. He shares the cemetery with other exiles such as Oscar Wilde and Jim Morrison.

The stewardess asked if I wanted a drink. Her skin was the color of a cooked pinto bean so I assumed she was a *Latina*. I replied in Spanish that I wanted a beer. She popped the cap on a Corona and we bantered back and forth in Spanish. She complimented me on my accent and asked where I learned to speak *Español*. I explained that I read Antonio Machado. My father served in Spain during their civil war. He accompanied Machado into southern France and was at his bedside when the poet died in exile in 1939.

Backpack Trekker: A 60's Flashback

She asked if I was familiar with Federico García Lorca. I told her my mother was a student at Columbia University in 1929. My mom provided the lonely poet with a conversation partner. He gave her a hand-written poem called *"La Aurora"* which he signed "Federico". She kept it until 1936 when she showed it to a neighbor who inadvertently spilled a blotch of ketchup on it. Lorca's name was smeared blood red.

We landed and like Dean Moriarity, I crossed the street into Mexico "on soft feet."

TREK 56

> *In 1969 the Strategic Arms Limita-*
> *tion Talks are begun in Helsinki.*

Passing through Customs was easy compared to running the gauntlet of cab drivers and other representatives from the cultural welcoming committee. I moved rapidly to out-distance these touristic predators. I bought a map and hunkered down with a cup of coffee to study my next move. First on my list was Teotihuacán with its pyramids to the sun and moon. The Aztecs were settled there when Hernando Cortés arrived. After checking my pack and changing money, I interviewed three cabbies before selecting one with a knowledge of Mesoamerica.

"Yo quiero subir hasta encima del pirámide," I told the driver.

"Será buen ejercicio," he replied. He drove me to the archeological zone. I paid and thanked him with a tip.

"Si estuviera usted aquí en tres horas puedo usar sus servicios como chófer otra vez. Si no, pués gracias y vaya con Dios."

"Ándale," he said. *"Disfruta las ruinas."*

In quicker than jig-time, jewelry vendors surrounded me. They showed me bracelets made of silver and precious stones. I bought several and when word got out that top *peso* for hand-crafted goods was paid, there were suddenly ten salesmen dogging my heels. When I refused to purchase any more, the prices went down. I tossed a fistful of *pesos* onto the ground and escaped down the *Avenida de los Muertos.*

From the top of the pyramid I had a splendid view of the plumed serpent shedding its skin; the eagle with extended talons; the sacrificial blade seeking to quell a heartbeat; William telling the police that an apple threatened to crush the cranium of his wife; Quetzalcoatl planting macaw feathers along the floating gardens; the kiss of boredom seducing me into a tomb of gargoyles; snake heads and creatures frozen in stone.

At the appointed time my taxi appeared and we returned to the central part of *Distrito Federal*, a sprawling matrix of traffic, noise, the resolution of political polemics with bullets, murals by Rivera, over 7,000 feet with a mild climate. He dropped me at the *Zócalo* and I entered the cathedral to pray and give thanks for my good fortune.

TREK 57

Andrew Wyeth first saw his model Helga Testorf in 1969.
She was selling homemade bread during the May Fair.

I spent a day in Chapultepec Park, looking at the Aztec calendar and other artifacts in the National Museum of Anthropology. At the castle I met a man from Santiago, Chile. He was an undocumented worker depleted of cash. His dream was to cross into the USA and procure a job in the fruit industry.

"Mucho trabajo y poco dinero," I told him.

"No hay remedio," he said. *"Uno tiene que sudar por su pan de cada día."* His name was José Pérez. I took him to a *taquería*. Over *tacos* and *Dos Equis* he recounted his adventures since leaving his homeland.

He started out with a wife and her three children. They ran out of money in Guayaquil, Ecuador. She worked as a prostitute until they had enough to fly to Panama City. A businessman from Uruguay befriended them. They needed more money to pass through customs. The man gave them enough money to facilitate crossing the border. He even paid their bus fare to Tegucigalpa, Honduras. They lived outdoors for awhile, until José landed a job cooking chicken in a restaurant. They moved into a dingy rooming house, replete with roaches and bedbugs. During their stay a neighbor girl was kidnapped and sold to a couple in Toronto, Canada.

The fortitude of the mother wore thin and, after an argument with José about the dismal life of her children, she called her family in Chile to wire money for returning home. José worked another six months to earn money to continue his trip to *El Norte*. In Guatemala City he worked unloading trucks. He entered Mexico illegally and was living in a hotel, two weeks behind in his rent, with a promise to pay up if a bearded man would appear with feathers. I had a beard and a hawk feather in my hat, so I fulfilled the prophecy.

After taking care of his bill at the hotel, the next item on José's agenda was to arrive in California. He wanted to pray at the Mission San Juan Capistrano, especially on March 19 when the swallows return on Saint Joseph's Day.

I had no experience smuggling aliens across the border. Maybe I could hire a *coyote*. At any rate, I had the time and money and decided to help José complete his dream.

Follow that dream. Go north in the summer. Listen to Beethoven in the fall. Bach in the winter will keep the room warm. Haydn in the spring will help the flowers glow. Follow the Grateful Dead and the Summer of '69 will inflate the earth with helium.

TREK 58

> *In the 1969 film "That Cold Day in the Park", Robert Altman directs a psycho-thriller about a spinster who imprisons a boy and supplies him with his every need.*

I would have enjoyed a trip to Cuernavaca to see Malinalco and the temples and sculpture hewn from living rock or visit Cholula to see the pyramid of Quetzalcoatl, the largest ancient structure in the new world. But I relinquished my sightseeing to accommodate José and his trek northward. We took a train to Mazatlán, crossed the Gulf of California by ferry to La Paz, then traveled up Baja by bus to Tijuana. We could have crossed the border west of El Paso and walked over the desert, but I wasn't into reenacting a Geronimo survival expedition, eating cactus, traveling at night and sleeping during the day to avoid the blazing sun of July. The Border Patrol was spread pretty thin over that desolate area, but I knew they had checkpoints on the highways north of the border, and two men on foot hitchhiking seemed like a risky business. I calculated a plan to rent a fishing boat on the coast and have the captain set us ashore south of San Diego.

The question was should we move at night or during the day? I thought of the Poe story "The Purloined Letter". In this account of a stolen letter a person hid a much sought document in a "filigree card-rack of paste-board". It was so obvious it escaped detection. So I hired a large boat with deep-sea fishing gear and we embarked at midday. Captain Méndez was at the controls.

José was below deck and I was seatbelted to a chair with a fishing pole hung over the side.

A Coast Guard boat came to check us out. In response to their questions I told them I was a political science major at UCLA staying with relatives in San Clemente for the summer. I wanted to catch a marlin and have a taxidermist stuff it.

They did not board us. No grappling hooks. We waited until the coast was clear and had *el capitán* drop us where we could swim to shore.

The only other close call we had was walking along a street as two police approached from the opposite direction. I told José to nod his head understandingly while I described in a loud voice how the Bruins were going to miss Lew Alcindor. But I anticipated Coach John Wooden would construct another winning combination. The officers eyed us but did not hinder our passage.

"Rowe and Wicks will carry them to another championship," I said. José kept nodding and we walked into the land of the free.

TREK 59

> *In 1969 Federico Fellini made his strangest film with "Fellini Satyricon".*

No significant historical period can be surgically separated from what preceded it. The tumultuous 1960's didn't suddenly start with a crowd of merrymakers standing in Times Square at midnight in 1960. Prefatory events from 1955 included Rosa Parks refusing to give up her seat; seeking to qualify blacks to voters rights activist Lamar D. Smith being shot in front of the a courthouse in Mississippi; Allen Ginsberg reading "Howl" to a gallery of literary characters all atwitter with expectation; James the Dean of rebels criticizing his parents; Bill Haley rocking around the clock and Jean Genet looking down from his balcony.

In 1956 Ingmar Bergman broke "The Seventh Seal". John F. Kennedy recounted his "Profiles in Courage". Elvis recorded "Love Me Tender", "Hound Dog" and "Heartbreak Hotel". Johnny made cash with "I Walk the Line" and "Folsom Prison Blues".

In 1957 Jack Kerouac continued the beat with "On the Road". He emerged as spokesman for the subterranean culture while chronicling his travels across North America. He was a low-budget gadabout who shared Mezz Mezzrow's interest in jazz and pot. His novel served as a handbook for the flower power generation. Two other titles of equal merit included *"Piedra de Sol"* by Octavio Paz and *"Doktor Zhivago"* by Boris Pasternak. Eugene O'Neill washed his family laundry posthumously in "Long Day's Journey into Night". David Lean directed his first on-location epic with "The Bridge on the River Kwai".

In 1958 Orson Wells directed and acted in "Touch of Evil". Lawrence Ferlinghetti lit up our mental midway with "Coney Island of the Mind". John Kenneth Galbraith took a close look at "The Affluent Society".

In 1959 DeGaulle was proclaimed President of France. Fidel Castro became premier of Cuba. Federico Fellini directed *"La Dolce Vita"*. William Burroughs gave America an upset stomach with "Naked Lunch".

Berkeley students protested everything. The administration tried to discourage them from thinking about off-campus issues, but students were concerned about free speech and civil rights.

They attended teach-ins not listed in the catalogue. The Vietnam Day Committee planned events to protest the war. They demonstrated against the dismissal of classmates and the abolition of campus organizations. They wanted a voice in the program. They wanted freedom of speech.

I did not arrive in Berkeley until the end of the decade. But when I saw the entrance to the university I was consumed by the commotion and played "ducks and drakes" with my leisure time. Pundits argued about the usefulness of Don Quixote's community service as he and Sancho rode across Spain on their adventures of knight-errantry. I got involved in the defense of a homeless man in the student union building. The man was asleep in a chair when campus security tapped him on the foot and ordered him to move along.

"Leave him alone," shouted a student. "He isn't bothering anyone."

Many other voices suddenly chimed in to protest the bum's rush treatment. I found myself joining in, "Let him be. He is resting his eyes between exams."

Faced with a roomful of hostile voices, the security agent backed down.

☯

Beatlick Joe Speer

TREK 60

In the 1969 film "John and Mary", a couple meet in a bar, have sex, then ask each other's name.

Jorge Louis Borges, Aristotle Onassis, and Helen Hayes turned 60 years old in 1960. A U-2 US supersonic plane was shot down over Russia and Washington admitted duplicity. Premier Khrushchev retaliated by bank-rolling Fidel Castro.

The Monroe Doctrine was reaffirmed to prevent the cancer of communism from entering the body of the Western Hemisphere. In tandem with the Civil Rights Movement, European colonies in Africa gained independence. Cyprus disengaged from British control.

As Kennedy entered the White House the connection between government and the public was strong. This bond disintegrated at the end of the decade as Nixon watched a football game on television while hundreds of thousands of demonstrators in D.C. demanded a moratorium on the Vietnam War.

As southern senators filibustered to block civil rights legislation, I served time in the public schools and played little league in the summer while Chubby Checker sang "The Twist". The coach had me bat cleanup because of my ability to hit the ball over the outfielder's head. A base hit was inconsequential because I had my eyes on the horizon.

In one game we were up against a fire ball pitcher. He threw a smoker and had a curve ball that flew straight at you then suddenly broke over the middle of the plate. It was the bottom of the sixth inning, two outs, and we trailed by two runs.

Our catcher had already put his equipment on in preparation for taking to the field. The next man up walked and the third place hitter reached base on an infield bobble. I selected a piece of lumber with Hank Aaron's name on it and dug in at the batter's box. Our catcher followed me to the plate. He removed his protective gear knowing that I would deliver in the clutch.

The pitcher was off with his control as he ran the count to three balls and one strike. Their coach signaled for an intentional base on balls even though that would load the bases. The catcher who followed me was a weak hitter. Their strategy was to avoid a possible long ball and pick up the final out with the catcher to end the inning. I decided to swing. When the pitcher lobbed the ball on the outside I stepped across the plate like

Roberto Clemente and smashed it over the head of the right fielder.

TREK 61

In February of 1969 Woodstock promoters John Roberts and Joel Rosenman meet their financial backers Michael Lang and Artie Kornfeld.

The Bay of Pigs invasion of Cuba proved to be an embarrassment for the Kennedy administration. CIA-trained exiles were repelled by Castro's forces. In 1961 the Berlin Wall was erected from August 15 to 17 to halt the exodus of East Berliners to the West.

Roger Maris took advantage of the short distance down the right field line in Yankee Stadium to pull past Babe Ruth's season home run record. The Peace Corps was established for Americans to serve in undeveloped countries. Diana Ross and friends were supreme in Motown. John Hammond hammered down a contract for Bob Dylan with Columbia Records. James Baldwin continued "The Invisible Man" theme with a collection of essays called "Nobody Knows My Name". Joseph Heller created a surreal comedy with "Catch-22", the story of a bomber group in a big war.

The most fun time of my school days back then was when the final bell sounded and we students scrambled for the bus. I usually sat in the front because in the back were concentrated obstreperous pranksters. They wielded pea shooters to pelt people from behind. Sometimes fisticuffs broke out. I viewed testosterone tussles as crude behavior, something I'd rather see in choreographed gang fights like in "West Side Story".

A girl fight, however, that was an event to raise your eyebrows. One afternoon a couple of *chicana* chicks got into a shoving match. The bus driver chilled them out, but they agreed to continue the fracas off the bus. I rode past my stop and got off with the two combatants. I wasn't the only person interested in the outcome. A boisterous group of fans followed them to a ditch bank and cheered as they pulled hair, scratched, slapped and called each other vile expletives. The girl receiving the worst treatment employed a secret weapon. She tore the clothes off her opponent. When the teats were exposed the upper hand shifted. What made girl fights exciting was this potential to disrobe each other. It wasn't a trial of strength. It was a process of humiliation through verbal abuse and nudity.

The loser finally covered herself with shreds of torn blouse and ran off.

TREK 62

The Cuyahoga River burned in 1969 due to pollution from the iron industry.

In 1962 the Cuban Missile Crisis provided tension with a possible shoot out in the Caribbean Sea. We have a steadfast settlement at Guantanamo even though Castro turned off the electricity. The super gunfighters cut a deal - Moscow agreed to withdraw atomic warheads from Cuba and the U.S. removed rockets from Turkey. James Meredith enrolled at the University of Mississippi with a federal guard ensuring his safety. John Glenn made first earth orbits for the U.S. in Friendship 7.

Ken Kesey examined life in the mental ward via "One Flew Over the Cuckoo's Nest". Edward Albee asked, "Who's Afraid of Virginia Woolf?" William Faulkner published his last book "The Reivers", then his spirit passed out of this realm.

Wal-Mart and K-Mart opened for business. Philip Morris introduced "Marlboro Country" to promote its filter cigarette. Tab-opening cans made soft drinks and beer more accessible. Aluminum chains grew.

Films included John Frankenheimer's "The Manchurian Candidate", "Ride the High Country" by Sam Peckinpah, Akira Kurosawa's "Yojimbo", Luis Buñuel's "The Exterminating Angel", Robert Mulligan's "To Kill a Mockingbird" and Robert Aldrich's "What Ever Happened to Baby Jane?"

A film with Tom Courtenay called "The Loneliness of the Long Distance Runner" had a short run in our town. I was a speedster in the 50 and 100-yard dash. In this movie Tom trains hard, runs the race, arrives at the finish line first; then stops, allowing his competition to catch up and cross the line ahead of him. Tom had a gripe with the administration which influenced his behavior. I liked his non-cooperation against any captious force.

I was the fastest runner in my class. They wanted me to represent our school at an inter-city track meet. I wasn't enthralled by the competitive aspect and the long-distance runner came to my mind as we lined up. I had no reason to be anticollaborationist but I wanted to prove that I was the fastest without winning.

Hands down. Head up. Go. Ahead of the pack all the way, until near the finish line and I veered off - stage left. That was my last time at a track, except to run laps for fun.

Which way to the coffeehouse?

<u>TREK 63</u>

In 1969 N. Scott Momaday writes
his novel "House Made of Dawn".

On November 22 of 1963 the world was saddened by the death of C.S. Lewis. Lee Harvey Oswald, a Marine Corps veteran, was arrested, charged with killing patrolman J.D. Tippit. Two days later Oswald was shot by Jack Ruby while moving to safer quarters. Britain's war minister Lord John Profumo was charged with making love to call girl Christine Keeler. President of South Vietnam Ngo Dinh Diem was killed. The U.S. federal budget was nearly $100 billion, almost half of which went to military appropriations. NAACP leader Medgar Evers was murdered. Valium, synthesized by chemist Leo Sternback, was approved by the FDA. Supreme Court ruled the Lord's Prayer or Bible verses unconstitutional in public schools. Emergency "hot line" linked Washington and Moscow.

The Beatles wanted to hold your hand. Alfred Hitchcock became an ornithologist. Sylvia Plath put a bell jar over herself at thirty one.

A pharmacist friend named Owlsey borrowed the idea of pheromones to concoct a love potion to aid couples in mutual attraction. It was a lotion to kindle desire. He developed pheromones for humans and mixed it with a perfumed attractant guaranteed to make a match before last call for alcohol. I never tried to use it, but one night it was used on me.

I was at a party using a new touch-tone telephone, inviting a girl to rendezvous before the beer was gone. She agreed to join me and I was reciting a love poem softly into her ear when someone touched my hand. Even before I saw who the hand belonged to, I was struck with an overpowering desire to copulate. I hung the phone up without an explanation. I left the party blindly with this person without speaking. I remember having a good time until the potion wore off. Then I discovered my mate was a life-size cardboard cutout of Betty Boop. Someone had tricked me. Someone had doused her with Owlsey's romantic oil and I lost control of my breathing. I started heaving. While I was running full throttle, the mastermind of this plot burst in on us and took our picture. I didn't care about being caught in this awkward situation. The potion was so strong that all I wanted was to satiate myself with Betty Boop.

TREK 64

> The first public showing of the Zapruder film, shot during JFK's assassination, was in 1969 when New Orleans District Attorney Jim Garrison used it in his unsuccessful prosecution of Clay Shaw.

In 1964 Nelson Mandela was sentenced to life imprisonment for subversion against apartheid laws in South Africa. The 24th Amendment made U.S. poll taxes unconstitutional. President Johnson signed an Economic Opportunity Act in August. Australia signed a contract to supply Japan with iron ore. The expansion in the Japanese steel industry made Japan an industrial superpower. U.S. gasoline cost 30.3 cents a gallon. Jimmy Hoffa brought U.S. truckers into a single Teamsters Union. He hoped to unite railway, airline and shipping to teamsters, but Attorney General Kennedy wanted him in stir and Jimmy was found guilty of jury tampering. The U.S. Department of Agriculture activated the food stamp program. Films included: "Mary Poppins", "Woman in the Dunes" and "Zorba the Greek".

Young men were not as willing to participate in war as were their fathers in the 1940's. Rather than serve in Vietnam some potential soldiers fled to Canada. Others employed psychological stratagems to avoid military duty. One man bathed in bubble bath, then sealed up his ass with peanut butter. While standing naked at his physical examination, he nonchalantly used his fingers to dig this brown substance from his rear and licked them clean. Another man with long hair applied lipstick and rouge and dressed in a womanly fashion. He marked "homosexual" in big letters on his paperwork. The draft board never called him back.

Early draft calls had an easier time hoodwinking the Selective Service. As the killing fields needed more men, they couldn't be so selective. The draft realized some inductees resorted to deceit and the army tightened their scrutiny. Some young men resorted to more desperate measures. One man cut off his big toe. Another man cut off his trigger finger. Some men accepted jail terms rather than be put into a war they thought was wrong. Some took draft dodging further by organizing resistance, producing fake draft cards and providing hiding places for men on the lam.

The Vietnam War became unpopular to the point that the veterans who fought there marched in protest and threw their medals at the Lincoln Memorial.

TREK 65

In 1969 the mysterious writer B. Traven dies.

Despite draft evasion, anti-war rallies and teach-in broadcasts, by 1965 some 125,000 U.S. troops were in Vietnam. Indonesia withdrew from the United Nations and a massacre of communists began. Gambia gained freedom after 122 years of British rule. Prime Minister Ian Smith declared Rhodesian independence from Britain. Hundreds of civil rights demonstrators were arrested in Selma, Alabama, over voter registration issues. The Voting Rights Act became law on August 10. Race riots in Watts destroyed $40 million worth of property. U.S. university enrollments grew because of draft deferrals for college students.

Books included "The Psychedelic Reader" by Harvard professor Timothy Leary and "The Autobiography of Malcolm X" by Alex Haley. Films included "The Shop on Main Street" with Josef Kroner and "A Thousand Clowns" with Jason Robards, Jr.

I had a high school teacher who never taught us anything. He took roll on the first day of class and that was the last time he said anything to us. After that he sat silently at his desk and stared into oblivion. He resembled a man in a terminal stage of prostate cancer, like he had been injected with morphine. The class sat where they wanted, talked, laughed, got bored, waited for the bell to ring. I was curious about the old codger so at the end of every class I asked him questions like: What were the ideological differences between Booker T. Washington and W.E.B. Dubois? When did Anaïs Nin first write of Henry Miller? Who got the bucks together to send Henry to Europe in 1930? For how many years did the grave of Edgar Allan Poe remain wholly unmarked? Did he travel in ships like Alex Haley? Did he read "Everything That Rises Must Converge" by Flannery O'Connor and what was her rare disease? Was he repulsed by Polanski's "Repulsion"? Did he think the Stones made the Beatles sound like choir boys?

He always answered my questions calmly and at length. He was a library of information. On the last day of class I asked him what I would be doing in the summer of 1969. In 1965 he could not know about my movements in the future. He did, however, give me detailed accounts of me hitchhiking around America, a trip to Mexico and me attending a music and arts festival in August.

It wasn't until 1969 that I realized he was correct.

TREK 66

In 1969 Howard Sackler won the Pulitzer for his novel "The Great White Hope".

In 1966 Hanoi was bombed intensively. By year's end 389,000 U.S. troops were in South Vietnam. The National Organization for Women was founded. The first black U.S. senator was elected from Massachusetts. "Star Trek" began on NBC with William Shatner as Captain James T. Kirk and Leonard Nimoy as Mr. Spook. It ran for 78 episodes. Freddie Laker founded Laker Skytrain, a low-cost passenger service from England to America. Houston built the Astrodome.

Books included "Quotations of Chairman Mao".

Films included "Andrei Rublev" by Andrei Tarkovsky. It was about a 15th-century Russian icon painter. Paul Scofield made himself into "A Man for All Seasons". Michael Caine got together with Shelly Winters in "Alfie".

I flew Laker Airways several times between New York and London. Passengers were hip to the fact that no refreshments were served. As important as a boarding pass was a bottle of wine, quart of beer, fruit, bread and cheese.

On my first flight with Laker, after take off and the green light was given to remove seatbelts, we had a party. People fed each other and passed bottles around. I went to the rest room to arm myself with a disposable cup. It was like Mardi Gras without the parades or doubloons. People who traveled with Laker became faithful customers. The airline started with two planes so they could only haul a limited number of people. This involved getting on a waiting list and putting your departure on hold for a day or more because there were no reservations. It was first-come, first-served.

A fellow traveler invited me to his home in Long Island. We had breakfast in Hell's Kitchen, saw a double feature on 42nd Street, attended a poetry reading at Saint Marks in the Bowery, took a stroll around The Battery and played a game of checkers in Washington Square Park.

The Laker Skytrain flights were cheap and exciting. They were not for people in a hurry or for people who did not smile at each other. They were designed for people that found obstacles and postponement adventuresome.

TREK 67

In 1967, after Dr. Martin Luther King, Jr. was assassinated, blues guitarist Jimmy Rogers rededicated himself to his music career.

In 1967 Che Guevara was killed in Bolivia. Muhammad Ali refused induction and was arrested. H. Rap Brown of the Student Nonviolent Coordinating Committee was arrested for his suggestion: "Burn this town down."

Black Power separatist Stokely Carmichael urged blacks to arm for revolution as Thurgood Marshall was sworn in as Supreme Court Justice. Selective Service director announced that college students arrested in anti-war demonstrations would lose their draft deferments.

Christian Barnard of South Africa performed the world's first heart transplant. Rolling Stone magazine began publication. The Green Bay Packers defeated the Kansas City Chiefs in Super Bowl I. A production of "Hair" brought the counterculture into an off Broadway theater.

Books included *"Cien Años de Soledad"* by Gabriel García Márquez, "Light Around the Body" by Robert Bly and "The Debauched Hospodar" by Guillaume Apollinaire, which was first printed in America.

Films included "The Graduate", "In the Heat of the Night", "Cool Hand Luke", in which Paul Newman ate 50 eggs, and "Don't Look Back" by D.A. Pennebaker.

The Monterey Pop Festival established the prototype for the large rock gatherings. The Who contended with Jimi Hendrix for the hard-act-to-follow award. Jimi set his guitar on fire. The Who demolished their equipment. Some 50,000 people attended.

Ottis Redding left fans standing on the dock of the bay when he died in a plane crash. Monterey was the epicenter of music in '67. The ticket prices for the Festival started at $3.50.

"The Oracle" spread the word. Let's convoke a Human Be-In. Be sure and wear flowers in your hair.

I drank a beer in the alley near City Lights. Berkeley poets flung direful lingo in feckless protest at the university. I spent about two weeks in the Bay Area. What a swelling summer of love to be in the park. North America was a postcard of secret charms. I had a ticket to ride.

Beauty cleaned my retina, tapped my roots, opened my sky, provided a source of cosmic fuel to enjoy the sights and sounds dancing in the pure colorful void.

TREK 68

In 1969 Warner Brothers produced "Young Brigham" for Ramblin' Jack Elliott.

The Tet Offensive in 1968 was a show of strength for the Vietcong and North Vietnamese as they attacked many cities, including Saigon. The communists showed the world they were not ready to roll over dead.

North Korea seized the U.S.S. Pueblo. The U.S. lost its 10,000th plane over Vietnam. At My Lai village American soldiers wasted men, women and children.

Senator Eugene McCarthy made a strong showing in the New Hampshire primary. The Berrigan brothers burned 1-A classification records. The priests were sentenced to prison terms. President Johnson announced he would not run for re-election.

Senator Robert Kennedy was shot down in his bid for the presidency. The African continent, pulling back the sheet of domination, reverted to mostly black control.

The police cracked heads and pushed people around to keep the "Festival of Life" celebrants from hanging out in Grant and Lincoln Parks.

Books included "Soul on Ice" by Eldrige Cleaver, "The Electric Kool Aid Acid Test" by Tom Wolfe and "The Whole Earth Catalog".

Films included "2001: A Space Odyssey", "Night of the Living Dead", "Planet of the Apes" and "Yellow Submarine".

Neal Cassady died in 1968. He was not a professional writer like Jack or Allen. His wife Carolyn said, "Neal viewed most of his past – even if only yesterday – as a likely mistake or cause for guilt and best it be forgotten as quickly as possible." Most of Neal's writing appeared as letters to friends and lovers. Two years in San Quentin for marijuana charges did not slow him down. He drove the magic bus for the Merry Pranksters as they capered around America. The last days of Neal's active life were spent in Mexico. He collapsed on a railroad track, an appropriate symbol for his life of travel and years spent working as brakeman and conductor on the Southern Pacific Railroad. His life was an inspiration to his friends. Jack took Neal's energy and propelled it into "On the Road".

A year later Jack Kerouac followed his beloved friend into the timeless world, into the light beyond the sun.

TREK 69

> About 70,000 people paid $18 in advance to attend the Woodstock Music and Art Fair in 1969.

In 1969 600,000 U.S. and allied troops were in Vietnam without nudging any closer to victory. "Sesame Street" started on public television. "Laugh-In" was the number one show on TV. A golden spike was driven in the Trans-Australian Railway. The John Hancock Center in Chicago was completed.

Books included "Slaughterhouse Five" by Kurt Vonnegut, Jr. and "The Godfather" by Mario Puzo. Films included "If", "Medium Cool" and "They Shoot Horses, Don't They?".

The Woodstock Festival was the antithesis of the Vietnam experience. Four days in August on private property were devoted to peace and love. There were no chairs lined up in rows like soldiers standing at attention. People sat on the ground or on spread-out blankets.

The promoters were rejected from their original location and had less time to prepare for the event. They were unable to control access to the site so ticket sales became meaningless. They opted to make it a free concert. The rock rolled and so did the movie cameras. The Hog Farm from New Mexico prepared free food. Country Joe kicked it into high gear with his admonishment "There's 300,000 of you motherfuckers out there ... "

There was free first-aid for people who were hurt or freaked out. Even though the basic elements at the concert were free, there were entrepreneurs who worked the crowd selling hamburgers and drugs.

One man collected a handful of useless tickets and walked away from the festival site to encounter incoming people unaware that the concert was free. He huckstered the tickets for half-price, made some quick cash, and disappeared into the crowd.

The cleanup crew created a huge peace sign out of garbage that could be seen from the air.

The Rolling Stones, not wanting to be left out, invited several Bay Area groups and hosted a free concert on the West Coast at Altamont. The Grateful Dead was on the bill, but did not like the vibes so they did not play.

Take me home, out to the highway.

TREK 70

"Notes of a Dirty Old Man" by Charles Bukowski
was published during 1969.

The 1960's worked itself to a boil in '69. But history continues and overlaps. Just as the Harlem Renaissance spilled over into the 1930's, 1970 rounded out the decade and rolled to snake eyes on the dice. Jimi, Janis and Jim died at 27. Not since the propinquity of death knells for Keats, Byron and Shelley had the creative world suddenly lost such luminaries.

President Nixon acquiesced as the armed forces dropped more bombs, fired on sleeping Black Panthers, protesting students and prison inmates at Attica with makeshift weapons. The Indians were escorted off Alcatraz Island to end their symbolic protest.

Hitchhikers were gradually eliminated from the highways, confined to entrance ramps or arrested. The power structure did not want people traveling for free. Again the press released more horrendous accounts of hitchhikers mutilating drivers to instill fear. Between police harassment and tarnishment of image, the raised thumb was effectively cut off.

Backpack Trekker: A 60's Flashback

The overlapping years of 1969-71 were creative peaks for The Who and Joe Cocker. Both were featured in the award-winning documentary film "Woodstock" in 1970. The Who released "Tommy" in '69, recorded "Live at Leeds" in '70 and pissed on the monolith in "Who's Next" in '71.

Joe connected in '69 "With a Little Help from My Friends". He went on tour with Leon Russell and friends in '70 and flexed his muscle with "Mad Dogs and Englishmen" in '71. This was also a fertile period for Leon. He was involved in "The Concert for Bangladesh" and soon released "Carney".

However, 1969 is the termination year for this narrative. So think of Judy Garland gone over the rainbow. Think of "Woodstock Nation" written soon after the festival by Abbie Hoffman. Think of "Okie from Muskogee", "Honky Tonk Woman", "Games People Play". Think of Boris Spassky turned back in '66 by Tigran Petrosian only to emerge as the world-champ chess player later on. Think of another chapter in the government's War on Drugs with "Operation Intercept" to restrict the flow of marijuana from Mexico. That decision caused heroin sales to skyrocket because the price of marijuana climbed so high that heroin sold at a competitive price. Think of the International in Las Vegas, the world's largest resort hotel, at a cost of $60,000,000. Think of Katharine Hepburn as "Coco" Chanel, the Parisian dress designer. Jump in a deprivation tank and think.

TREK 71

In 1969 Philip Whalen created poems in the Buddhist tradition with "On Boar's Head".

In southern California again, I took my Chilean friend José to dance clubs and bars in hopes he might meet an eligible *señorita* willing to sign marriage papers. I set him up in a motel for one month and lined his pockets with enough cash to keep him afloat until a miracle materialized. We parted company; he to follow the American dream and I to hitch north on 101.

I got a ride with a Jehovah's Witness, who tried to instruct me from his watch tower perspective. He had a Bible on the dashboard and rested his right hand on it.

"This book was inspired by God," he said.

"Every religion," I replied, "claims divine inspiration from the Upanishads of Hinduism to Joseph Smith and the 'Book of Mormon'. A religion is worthless without being sanctified by a god-head. Every sacred writing is based on outlandish claims of celestial authorship. If God co-writes books, I don't believe religious texts have exclusive rights with divinity. Why can't the complete poems of Elizabeth Bishop be inspired? The holy books are literature and other genre of writing is imbued with inspiration. In 'Moby Dick', for example, the white whale rose again on the third day. In 'Ulysses', the structure of the novel is based on the trinity of the father, son, and holy spirit as manifested in Molly Bloom's reverie. But our religious polemics are fruitless because the claims of godly intervention cannot be corroborated. Dogma, like the fidelity of your spouse, has to be accepted on faith."

My lack of receptivity to his proselytizing exacerbated my host. I did not ameliorate the situation when I tried to discredit him as a witness because his information was secondhand. He hit the eject button and deposited me back on the highway.

My next ride was from a corpulent man who offered me ten dollars to watch me masturbate.

"Did you say masticate?" I asked. When he handed me color pictures of naked women, his intentions were clear.

"Hurry up and decide," he coaxed. "I have to turn soon." I figured why not get paid for something I enjoy.

"OK," I said. "But make it thirty dollars."

He agreed and we parked off the road. He asked questions about my earliest erotic fantasies. I asked for a lubricant and he gave me a melted chocolate bar. He wanted me to impregnate Mother Earth so I dug a hole in the dirt. My sperm dripped into the hole and I covered it with small stones.

"You knocked up the earth," he yelled.

This occurred near San Simeon. After receiving my wages, I made tracks up the hill to Hearst Castle.

TREK 72

In 1969 Elton John sang "Empty Sky" in a UK release. Songs included "Skyline Pigeon".

William Randolph Hearst was a newspaper mogul who used his wealth to construct a personal palace. Like Louis XIV, he was into home improvements. Journalistic jottings are like a road map through time. Ambrose Bierce was a journalist and gave occurrence to strong imaginative stories. In his seventies he cast away his books and rode into Mexico on a white horse, looking for a bullet from Pancho Villa.

Hearst created his abiding monument overlooking the Pacific Ocean. I spent several flabbergasted hours eyeballing antique furniture, rare art treasures, movie theater, swimming pool, a tennis court and everything beautiful with sunsets extended beyond breath. I thought I saw a camel and a giraffe in a cross-country race, but maybe I was hallucinating from sensory overload.

I spent the night on the beach dreaming of Versailles. I dreamed of Ambrose Bierce at 22 fighting in the War Between the States, at 72 engaging in the Mexican Revolution and charging against gunfire. He had a clean shave and wanted to be a good-looking corpse. A simple recipe for being a good soldier, says the old gringo, is to try always to get yourself killed. I dreamed of rosebuds washed out to sea while "Citizen Kane" built his warehouse to contain more art. Old man Hearst could not enjoy the camera angles in Wells' 1941 movie because the resemblance to his life was too glaring. I dreamed I saw a llama eating a banana, a chameleon in living black and white. I saw Carlos Fuentes feeding *cerveza* and tuna to a stray cat.

I awoke with the mist and walked the beach to warm up. There was a boat dry-docked for repairs. I climbed in to escape the wind. The larder was well-stocked. I cooked a can of cream-of-mushroom soup. A copy of "The Brothers Karamazov" was on the shelf.

Long novels make good road companions. An ongoing story gives me something to do while waiting for a ride or drinking coffee back home at the Frontier Restaurant. As I got to the end of a novel, I would reread chapters, before I had to consume that last sip of coffee, the last page.

The calm of the boat encouraged reflective time for writing letters. It was a perfect situation for a landlubber, grounded and dry while near the roar and splash of the ocean. I replaced Feodor with a book I just finished reading, "Don Quixote", and left two twenties as bookmarks.

Big Sur was the next rest stop. Kerouac wrote about the waves as he relaxed at Ferlinghetti's cabin. Henry Miller left his mark in the area and the air was rich with his uncompromising prose.

I sat on Bixby Bridge and watched the in and out of the surf as it chugged like grandma's washing machine.

☯

Beatlick Joe Speer

TREK 73

In the 1969 film "The Illustrated Man", a young drifter meets a tattooed man and each tattoo causes a fantastic story to unfold.

Camping in Big Sur I met a man traveling with a studded-collar husky. The man's name was Butch and he called the dog Balzac. Butch was the dog's best friend. They lived together in the open. When it rained they had a large piece of plastic tied between trees for shelter.

Balzac was the catalyst for our coming together. He stared at me one night while I filled my canteen from a spigot. The idea came to me that I should follow him. At first I thought it was my idea, but later I realized that Balzac could put thoughts into my mind.

I didn't socialize with them during the day. The light hours I spent hiking along the beach. At night Butch tended a campfire. He boiled water and we drank maté.

Butch wore a hat with a tassel that represented the Canadian Mounted Police. He sported a set of false teeth handed down from an uncle. He was loquacious and considered himself well informed. *"La Traición de Rita Hayworth"* by Manuel Puig was a novel he had just enjoyed. We had a disputation about Maya Angelou's first book. Butch insisted it was "For My People".

"Sometimes we let things slide," he said, "because it's too disruptive to call into question. But if you know it's not right, like people not given equal service, you have to take issue."

"That's not right," I said.

Butch suggested we consult Balzac: one bark for affirmative and two barks for negative. I had implicit faith in his barks to decide the issue, yet I wanted to test his sagacity. Was he a sage more for the *literati*?

"Is Maya's first book "Quicksand"? Balzac barked twice. "Is Maya's first book "For My People"? Balzac barked twice. "Is her first book "I Know Why the Caged Bird Sings"? Balzac barked once.

We accepted the judgment. When it came to the right goods, Balzac could not be moved. At the end of our soiree that night, Balzac accompanied me back to my tent.

"Will you join me on a walkabout tomorrow?" I asked him. He barked once then disappeared into the dark.

Backpack Trekker: A 60's Flashback

In 1969 the Sinking Creek Film Celebration in Nashville was founded.

The second night around the fire with the man and his dog, Butch pulled out a chunk of hash that would pop the eyes of a Moroccan dealer. He softened it over a flame then broke a piece off and crumpled it into a paper trough of tobacco. He rolled, licked and tickled its underbelly with the flame.

Balzac gnawed on a bone that Butch had salvaged from restaurant scraps. A covered pot on the coals kept our maté hot while I conducted a punctilious interview.

"So how long have you lived in Big Sur?" I asked.

"We lived here two years now," Butch replied. "Last winter a friend let us stay in a broken-down school bus. We installed a wood stove. On one side I blocked out the sun with old Fillmore West posters. I wired a set of antlers around the stovepipe on the outside. No electricity but no rent either, so we lived there until the owner sold it to a lackadaisical lapidarist who fixed it and drove off to Oregon."

"How long have you and Balzac been cheek-to-cheek?"

"I met Balzac in Golden Gate Park," Butch said. "I was wandering around aimlessly on brown acid. This knavish husky peered into my eyes and we connected. He led me to a crash pad where I fell asleep on the floor. There was an incessant flow of people so my presence was not worthy of notice.

"When I woke up from a dream about flying dogs, this dark canine was standing like a conscript of vigilance. He led me to a free meal at a soup kitchen on Turk Street. I didn't know his name, but I knew he was an eminent creature. I had to pick a name for him, so I opened the B drawer of the card catalogue in the public library and selected the very first name I saw: Balzac. He responded to the moniker as if he has Montparnasse in him.

"After learning of Balzac's special gifts, I told a man in a bar if he'd spring me to a brew my dog would answer yes or no questions with one bark or two. When he realized how accurate Balzac was with responses, he wanted to know about horse races and lottery numbers. Balzac was reticent about wager questions."

Butch earned some money working at the Nepenthe restaurant on weekends. He wanted to supplement his pocket change using Balzac's acumen. However, Balzac had an uncanny sense when he was being exploited. Whenever Butch had a cash bet on the line, Balzac would sabotage the deal every time.

The carnivore was given to commercialistic non-cooperation.

TREK 75

In the 1969 film "The Killing of Sister George", Susannah York has a nude lesbian love scene.

If I'd lived in Harlem in the 1920's, I would have attended the poetry readings hosted by Miss Ernestine Rose at the New York Public Library on 135th Street. I might have seen Casper Holstein smoking a cigar. He ran a numbers racket in Harlem. He was a successful business man who invested in the arts and donating money to "Opportunity" magazine to create contests.

As I drank coffee early one morning, ruminating on Harlem of the 1920's, Balzac appeared. The idea occurred to me that I should follow the black canine into the forest. We entered the wilderness through the postern gate. I loaded water and book into a day pack and off we trudged toward the big trees. Redwood trees are mnemonics. Any life form that lives 1,000 years has a venerable memory. He led me to a grove of trees that were 2,000-years-old.

"Can you communicate with trees?" I asked. Balzac barked once. The following story was telescoped into my mind:

The trees remember a time of pain, cuts and collapse. They remember people using their fallen branches to make fires, the smoke of the burning limbs rising up their bark and depriving them of the aura of filtered light, hundreds of years of sedentary perspicacity, life in peace and steady growth.

"Would you rather live in Istanbul?" I asked. Balzac barked twice. The thought entered my mind that Balzac could live anywhere. His purpose was to serve a species that considered two legs better than four.

But Balzac did not hesitate to serve, embracing the role of subservient. He was a spirit contained in the body of a dog, the kind of spirit that relocates when the host is toasted.

That night, around the campfire, Butch removed his false teeth and set them on a rock.

"I can make those teeth talk," he said. "Would you like to wager ten bucks on it?"

"Not really. If you need money, here," I let a twenty-dollar bill fall into his lap like a harbinger of autumn.

"Easy money," he said. "I'll bet you twenty that I can make one of these old trees uproot itself and pirouette across a meadow."

"No more bets," I said, giving him another twenty.

"What about Balzac. I'll place a bet on his behalf."

"Do you need any money, Balzac?" I asked. Balzac barked twice.

TREK 76

In the 1969 Swedish movie "The Passion of Anne", Andreas is a man struggling with this broken marriage and emotional problems when he befriends a married couple also in the midst of psychological turmoil.

Querida María,

I think dad was right. I have a dream that is leading somewhere, but there is the avarice of reality. Of late I have disappeared from reality, living in a time vacuum. No new discovery in the laboratory for pathology. I had a foreboding of the girl next door. The paucity of her mind is balanced by the depth of her emotional response to life.

She went through a love relationship, was hurt, returned the hurt, and now separated from her lover, she twitters in a state of psychic shock. She still needs someone to hug her, kiss her neck and share a movie. She says she wants a place to fit in. I want to help her, offer a simple resolution like walk around the block three times. I tell her about the healing power of haiku, not a new car or verisimilitude in journalism. Write humorous letters to your friends or send postcards even if you don't travel.

Everything that lives is seeking the light of love. People go off in a myriad of directions in pursuit of it. Some people get lost in the oligarchy of solitude. I saw a man on the street dying of loneliness. I detected it in the jittery eyes. We must open ourselves up to the power of truth and love.

We must beware of fear which serves to close us up and shut us off. We must not fear pain, for there is no growth into awareness without a burn. We must not cease to mature, for to do so leads to stagnation and the enjoyment of commercials. Love must be cultivated like a delicate flower. Only after it has blossomed and contributed its beauty to the world, will it fulfill its purpose. The seed of love contains our greatest joy but also the possibility for our most profound sorrow.

We resign ourselves to this ominous paradox and continue to seek the light. Everyone needs help, a firm handshake or improvisatory congratulations. If it wasn't for you and dad I wouldn't even be an omnivorous seeker of adventure. I'm grateful you loved each other.

And the girl next door, she needed more than luscious aphorisms. A pleasant dining experience can often redirect a mishmash of emotions. I invited her to eat, my treat.

Your son

TREK 77

> In November of 1969, 250,000 march in Washington, D.C. to protest the war.

John Kennedy started 1960 with hope and catholicizing appeal. Another John Kennedy ended the decade with the final statement of despair. John Kennedy Toole committed suicide in 1969 in New Orleans after leaving a corker of a manuscript about an hilarious character named Ignatius J. Reilly. Ignatius is a self-proclaimed commentator at odds with the 20th century. The story was published years later due to the assiduous efforts of Toole's mother who trundled the manuscript around until someone took notice. "A Confederacy of Dunces" is belatedly one of the great novels of the 1960's. It is replete with the idealistic innocence of the era depicting people engaged in the struggle while Ignatius himself is terribly disengaged.

Another extraordinary book is "The Codex Nuttall", which I discovered in a used bookstore in 1969. The tome appeared in the Dominican monastery of San Marco in Florence in 1859. It is assumed that Cortés sent it back to Spain as part of the goods confiscated from Moctezuma. The Mixtec were from the Oaxaca area further south so possibly the volume was lifted from them. Today, the original is kept in the British Museum. A facsimile of it was available to the public in 1902.

I left Big Sur and headed north to San Francisco. I got a ride with an herbalist named Herb. I knew piddling about botanical concerns. To turn the conversation didactic, I asked about edible plants of the desert.

Backpack Trekker: A 60's Flashback

"Nothing better than prickly pear syrup on buckwheat pancakes," he said. "The cactus is most common in the Southwest. The fruit is delicious but watch out for the glochidium. Skewer it on a stiletto and toast it on a flame until the intimidating spines are gone. You can peel it, bite in and expectorate the seeds or squeeze the juice through a cloth."

After he expounded on his forte, he asked me what topic I could throw light on.

"I read about the Harlem Renaissance," I replied. "I even got into a tiff with a college professor one time concerning when the period ended. I suggested the energy stopped with the riot in Harlem in 1935. Breaking windows, burning and such destructive behavior is the other end of the spectrum from creativity. The professor insisted the period continued with the books of Zora Neale Hurston. Now her books ran from "Jonah's Gourd Vine" in 1934 to her autobiography "Dust Tracks on a Road" in 1942. This last book deals with her zombie findings and voodoo in Haiti. I retorted that if Zora is the measurement for the period rolling to a halt, then why not extend it with the writings of Langston Hughes. He wrote many powerful civil rights stories in the 1950's and was active until his death in 1967."

"What kind of stories did Langston write?" asked Herb.

"One of my favorites is called 'There Ought to be a Law'. His character Simple says the government should create Game Preserves for Negroes. A fantastic idea that came from watching a short movie about how the government protects wild life. Simple's drinking friend insists that Negroes are not wild. Simple agrees but with the stipulation that Negroes need protection. The film showed how thousands of acres were put aside where the animals could not be shot. It even showed a National Park where airplanes dropped food for the deer when the snow was so deep they had nothing to eat. There are lakes with big signs up 'No Fishing - State Game Preserve.'

"But there are no signs that say 'No Lynching.' The film showed peaceful ducks in a meadow behind a 'No Hunting' sign. It showed a deer asleep and nobody said, 'Scram, you can't sleep here.'

If that deer was a black man, they would give him the bum's rush at any white hotel. Simple said there ought to be a nice place for him to hang out. There ought to be a law. He wanted to petition his Congressman to introduce a bill for Game Preserves for Negroes."

Beatlick Joe Speer

We both had a good laugh at the end of the story. Herb turned at Carmel and I got off near Tor House - a home built from stones by Robinson Jeffers and his wife.

TREK 78

In the 1969 film "Staircase", Rex Harrison and Richard Burton play a couple of gay hairdressers, who show their mutual affection by continuously sniping at each other.

The artifice of imagination went blind in the other eye. Like Milton and Joyce, the light failed. A drinking glass became more useful than an eye glass.

My friend Karl went blind at age twelve after watching his parents get murdered. There was no medical reason for his blindness. One diagnosis was that he willed himself not to see.

Portions of his inheritance arrived in the mail box every month. When he was sixteen, he installed king-sized bunk beds in his room along with wall-to-wall aquariums. I left the confines of my ascetic dorm room to attend the fetes he catered every six months. He provided exquisite cuisine and kegs of iced beer. His pleasure was perceptible as he paid friends to set it up. He served with a sincere smile.

Anyone could visit him in his bedroom, but they had to disrobe at the door and climb into one of the beds. He made up for his lack of sight with his exuberance for tactile contact.

He ascribed his happiness to Ruth, a high school drop-out girlfriend, who became his caregiver. They never cheated on each other. When they made love with someone else, they did it together. They enjoyed having fun with friends and group sex was a natural outgrowth of their conviviality.

At nineteen he decided he no longer wanted to have his name recorded as part of human history. He destroyed his high school diploma and all forms of identification.

He paid someone to break into the Bureau of Vital Statistics and burn his birth certificate.

At twenty-one he transferred his money and property into her name, Ruth Blair. He thanked her for being a helpful companion and tore his passport into individual pages, which he mailed off to friends. After the New York Mets won the 1969 World Series, he held himself underwater in the bathtub. He had a strong will.

☯

Backpack Trekker: A 60's Flashback

In 1969 Maggie Smith portrays an eccentric school-teacher in "The Prime of Miss Jean Brodie".

In the gyrations of 1960's protests, the clamorous civil rights and anti-war activists made the daily news. I felt the nefarious war on marijuana would reach a cease-fire. How can the government ostracize a plant? It didn't make any sense until, like Jack Herer, I did some research.

In the February 1938 issue of "Popular Mechanics" it states:

... American farmers are promised a new cash crop with annual value of several hundred-million dollars, all because a machine has been invented which solves a problem more than 6,000 years old. It is hemp ...

Then I understood the great haste to outlaw the plant in 1937. In that year DuPont had patented an acid to process wood pulp paper. William R. Hearst had interests in the lumber industry. He brought the word "marijuana" into common use through his newspaper chain. "Marijuana" comes from a Mexican song *"La Cucaracha"*. It is a slang term which refers to the recreational use of the plant.

Hearst, Dupont chemicals, the lumber and pharmaceutical companies did not want hemp to enter the market place. According to "High Times" magazine, "Cannabis is the crude vegetable preparation of the plants Cannabis sativa L. and Cannabis indica. The pharmacologically active components of the drug are cannabinoids, including delta-9 transtetrahydrocannabinol, cannabidiol, tetrahydrocannabivarin and perhaps 60 other cannabinoids of varying pharmacological properties."

Hemp has many uses: fabric, fuel, paper, textiles, the seeds for oil and food, foliage for medicine and relaxation. The barons of industry wanted to nip in the bud any competition from the hemp plant. As prohibition against alcohol ended, a new industry was created.

In 1937 New York state had one narcotics officer. Now look at the officious agents breaking down doors and sending up river the enemies of The Federal Bureau of Narcotics and Dangerous Drugs. Every war has victims and profiteers. The government agressively victimizes its own citizens to protect certain economic interests. As long as the War on Drugs continues, there are jobs for the duplicity of entrapment specialists, prison guards, and the analysts of kidney waste matter.

It is in the government's interest to continue the war *ad nauseam*. War is a staple part of American culture. It makes me want to find fallow bottom land and plant some insidious seeds.

TREK 80

> *In 1968 Indian filmmaker Satyajit Ray follows "The Adventures of Goupy and Bagha."*

In 1968 "Black Fire: An Anthology of Afro-American Writing" appeared. In name it is a descendant of "Fire", edited by Wallace Thurman from the 1920's, but in bulk (over 600 pages) it is more akin to "The New Negro", edited by Dr. Alain Locke.

"Black Fire" was edited by LeRoi Jones and Larry Neal. When Dr. King was assassinated, LeRoi changed his name to Amiri Baraka and moved deep within Harlem. Larry Neal worked on the "Liberator" magazine as did Claude McKay.

There is a grandiloquent link between the 1920's and the 1960's. If a rainbow was set in the 20th century, one end will be rooted in the 1920's with the other end sprouting in the 1960's.The editors of "Black Fire" understand the words of John W. Vandercook:

> ... A race is like a man. Until it uses its own talents, takes pride in its own history and loves its own memories, it can never fulfill itself completely ...

Among the writers included is a fortuitous sampling of Sun-Ra, the musician mystic. Sun-Ra transcends mundane conflict. "Some people are of this world," he said, "others are not." My natural self is not of this world, either.

From his poem "The Image Reach", Sun-Ra wrote:

> ... The happinesses I have known
> are no longer mine. I cast them to the world;
> and say "Take these,
> as you have taken all else from me.
> For I have one foot upon
> the threshold of other realms ...

Coming into San Francisco we heard on the radio a song about little boxes that all look just the same. We passed apartments painted different, but they all looked just the same. My ride dropped me off in the Mission district near 19th and Guerrero St. I walked to Twin Peaks because I was not completely ready to shed the Big Sur experience. I needed the lingering touch of nature, the aplomb of heights.

I met a blond in the park that I felt was an adjunct to my happiness. She gave me her photo. I told her I'd love to spend three hours with her: the first thirty minutes running my fingers through her hair; then thirty minutes poking my tongue between her fingers; then thirty minutes rubbing arabesque patterns on her legs. Unimpressed with my blatancy, she dumped me.

I went to North Beach and lost myself in City Lights Bookstore.

TREK 81

In 1969 "Johnny Cash: The Man, His World, His Music" offers a wonderful documentary on the man in black.

It is natural that in the vociferous Bay Area, with the high-wire velocity of Telegraph Avenue and the frivolity of San Fran, that Oakland saw the first headquarters of the Black Panther Party. Huey P. Newton and Bobby Seale created a ten-point program for self-defense. They thought black men should be exempt from military service, not be forced to defend a racist government. In '69 their Chicago headquarters was closed with a rain of bullets. It was an organization where many of the members were arrested or shot.

I loved walking up and down the hills, the nearness to brine, jumping on a crowded cable car and riding for ten blocks then sliding off before the ticket vender arrived.

There was a jazz sax player on a street corner who blew for tips. He called himself Light of Day. I listened to him blow, then offered to buy him a meal. He lived in Paris for six weeks and bankrolled his stay with bent notes in *le metro*, the sound of his horn flooding the underground tunnels. *Le parisien aime la jazz.*

San Fran was another town where he could support himself as a street musician. Some afternoons he set up on the world's most crooked street, Lombard near Russian Hill Park. The sound climbed the steep hill faster than pedestrians. One man who lived in an upper apartment tossed him cans of beer. Most residents liked the music but occasionally someone made long-distance disparaging remarks. A disheveled, disgruntled diamond cutter paid him a lump sum to go away.

After eating we attended a poetry reading. He rang a bell before and after his recitations. He burned Egyptian musk incense while chanting "ohm." He inspired everyone in the bookstore to chant with him. His voice was an instrument of modulatory treble. His saxophone was a piggy bank people dropped money into.

After the reading we walked to Fisherman's Wharf. He played the sax and I pretended to be blind. I held a tin cup like a sinister simian and recited at random from the selected poems of Ted Hughes.

Light of Day faded when the tourist crowd waned. At the stroke of midnight he packed up his horn. We split the dividends and he disappeared. I think of him at times. With the dispersion of loved ones, I hear his lugubrious sax, adding luminosity to the natural light of day.

TREK 82

In 1969 "Girl In Gold Boots" features a beautiful young girl who looks for stardom in the city and becomes a go-go dancer.

Querida María,

Love London. Went to Madame Tussaud's Wax House. Some figures bear remarkable resemblance to the original prototypes while others are poor imitations as if artists of varying talent were at work. I stood perfectly still at one point to stare at Pablo Picasso. I had on my poncho and my Australian outback hat. Someone started to stare at me. I waited to prolong the effect, then suddenly moved. The person nearly jumped out of his socks.

When I was in NYC I told you about Warren, who took me home to Long Island. Well, entering Victoria Station, who do I meet but himself and friend. They have waited several days to buy a ticket on Skytrain. There are about 1500 people lined up along different streets with makeshift shelters for protection from the rain. Warren conducted me to the end of the queue which zig -zagged a half-mile away from the station. I got my name on a list and became part of a sub group. We divided our time to serve shifts on the street to hold our spot. I elected to do the night-shift. Fortunately, I commandeered a large piece of plastic from an abandoned site and made some provision for nocturnal down-pours.

There are constant folks manning the sidewalks, moving up as their turn comes, only to have the line extended by new arri-vals. I never thought I'd be camping on the streets of London. Here we are waiting for spasmodic moves to up and away on the mechanized bird.

The event is making doleful news in the daily paper. (I guess no Jack the Ripper to flout.) All the airlines are backed up. Lon-don's Heathrow and Gatwick airports are like refugee camps. Lo-cal people taunt us with jocund gibes, "Don't play the telly too loud or the landlord will hear about it."

People pass by selling sandwiches and foam pads. "Ah! The profit motive," The guy next to me said with a few improvements on his lean-to he might be able to rent it.

The rain in London is on twenty-four hour call. If the south-west could export sunshine to the British Isles, a steady market could be established. Let Texas sell oil. Let's sell sunshine.

A lady told me Japanese products were at one time tempo-rarily banned from parts of the world market. So the Japanese renamed one of their cities Usa and continued selling their prod-ucts marked Made In USA.

Your son

TREK 83

> *In 1969 "Where Eagles Dare" dramatizes a dan-gerous mission to rescue an American soldier from a German prison.*

Back in the US I thought of Bud Powell as I walked down a hall at the Fremont Hotel and heard piano music. I booked a room in the hotel because it has a wonderful elevator ride on the side of the building that offers a splendid view toward Coit Tower.

I ran into Zen Jazz in the poetry section at City Lights Book-store. He bought a volume of Galway Kinnell. I purchased a Derek Walcott. We walked to a bar to celebrate.

"How was your trip to Hawaii?" I asked, not having seen Zen since we separated in LA.

Beatlick Joe Speer

"Great," he replied. "I met a financier who was loaded. He had been in a psychiatric hospital suffering from depression. He had earned millions of dollars during his career, but nobody knew who he was. It disturbed him that he might be forgotten so he commissioned a hack to write a book depicting him as a major cultural influence in Hawaiian history. It became a best seller. He bought his way into a major encyclopedia and funded the publication of new history books with pictures of himself and arranged for them to supplant texts in public schools as required reading. Articles were added to micro film in library archives that described him as a great humanitarian. This barrage of bogus documentation of his accomplishments led to a statue being erected in his honor. A scholarship fund was established in his name."

"That reminds me of a line from 'The Invisible Man,'" I said. "If they want to tell the world a lie, they can tell it so well that it becomes the truth."

I invited Zen Jazz to my room at the Fremont Hotel. "I had a windfall in Vegas, Zen. I'm lousy with pin money." He looked at me from across a great credibility gap. He knew I never had more than severance pay in my pocket.

"I'm not into wearing my pins down on these sidewalks," he said. I suggested we call a cab but Zen Jazz had another idea. He bid me wait near a fancy restaurant. Zen was dressed like he just strolled off an airplane. He pretended to represent Valet Parking. While the authentic attendant was occupied, a Cadillac pulled up to the curb. Zen stepped out to greet the driver. His voice had a ring of verity. "Park your car, sir?" The man handed him the car keys. Zen picked me up and off we drove.

<u>TREK 84</u>

In the 1969 movie "Paint Your Wagon", Lee Marvin and Clint Eastwood sing Lerner and Loewe numbers from the Broadway musical about two prospectors who share the same wife.

Zen drove us across the Golden Gate Bridge to Tiburon where we took a ferry to Angel Island. There was a group of people on an outing for a high school reunion.

By some curious quirk, Zen knew two of the passengers, two chronic film buffs from Berkeley. Zen met them in a cathouse in

Lanai. They all convened in a special "love service" center.

For a standard menu price they were seated at a long table and fed shrimp and fried rice. Underneath the table a zenith experience was offered which was paid for with tips, preferably twenty-dollar bills.

It was a ministration provided by an underground androgynous energy. On the ferry we engaged in a colloquy about "The Wild Bunch", directed by Sam Peckinpah. The film reflected the closing of the frontier.

An aging band of bank robbers looked for shelter. Like Geronimo they rode into Mexico. But Mexico was not far enough. South America was not far enough for Butch Cassidy and the Sundance Kid. The forces of law and order were nipping at their heels.

They had it all: money, coffee tinted *señoritas* to lick the dust off their fingers. But they could not rest easy. They could not go back and they could not go forward. Their time had expired. It was time for them to go.

They opted to shoot themselves out of time. Maybe they should have backed off. Like Malcolm X could have after Molotov cocktails burned his house; he could have taken his daughters to the Catskill Mountains instead of giving one more speech at the Audubon Ballroom. His time had expired. It was time for him to go.

Geronimo took the train east. He never returned to his homeland. Crazy Horse was dead. The buffalo herds were decimated. The Dalton Brothers had been killed trying to rob a bank. The OK Corral was closed. Their time had expired. It was time for them to go.

Zen did not want to disembark. We remained on board and created cut up poems.

We alternated lines. Zen said, "The gods are always busy reinventing themselves."

I never knew when Zen might reach a vanishing point. It was a desideratum that we commingle lines. We created a piece called "I Smell Smoke from Burning Poetry".

TREK 85

In the 1969 movie "Change of Habit", Elvis Presley plays a doctor who rocks.

Beatlick Joe Speer

"I Smell Smoke from Burning Poetry"

To give the trek direction, I pilgrimage to Mt. McKinley
we see a new world
cross the desert that does not divulge a secret
approach from the stochastic stock pile of mass destruction
rely on highway to inch up the map
of stars hatching new colors
past nude beach in southern Cal
with a horehound taste that
over Golden Gate and floating Sausalito homes
this poem dissipates
into Eureka with Streakin' Deacon
trying to evoke a climactic world since childhood
who preached a fifty-mile sermon
making it sound like a small sigh
across Columbia River and onto debris of Olympic shore
a place where you can hear
crowds brim Seattle market
an Italian tomato
professionals hook in diaphanous gowns
slowly ripen on the vine
ferry docks at fishing village
it is perhaps not me
blue mass of compacted ice
school of whales off bow
I invent heroics to assuage my mind
solitary lighthouse swings luminous arm
dead on an old moon
on to Fairbanks and McKinley by train
where suicide is a sacred act
peaks peek through clouds before descent of eternal veil
the kiss of boredom
mist and rain cover lofty heights
seduces me into a tomb
mountain is a myth, a postcard attraction
I like it here
on frozen tundra damp dark days drag on
because all sides are even
and burning poetry keeps me warm.

☯

Backpack Trekker: A 60's Flashback

*In the 1969 movie "The Madam", a lonely biker
finds employment at a house of ill repute.*

The ferry returned from Angel Island. We drove back into San
Francisco over the Golden Gate Bridge. We parked the car in
Lincoln Park and left the keys in the ignition with a note on the
dashboard, "drive it away".

Walking along the shoreline the Pacific Ocean precluded anything but wet imagery. Zen Jazz took a chapbook out of his
pocket. I thought it was a brakeman handbook but it was a chap
of poems Zen had published in Hawaii. He recited to me as the
waves moved in and out.

"Where do you get your inspiration?" I asked.

"From stones that have remained unturned for centuries;
from lizards that slither across smooth sand; from Chinese characters on a billboard near an abandoned highway; from crushed
piñon nuts; from red clay of Jemez sunset; from Rio Grande
mud; from catalpa leaves churned up in eggnog; from the shadows of past lovers; from Kansas at midnight; from the submissive
homesick blues; from discordant harp notes played from a dry
lake bed where God says the world is ours to remake ... where
do you find inspiration?"

"From looking down into a crater of a long since spent volcano," I said. "I put pen to paper when I espy a mountain range
in the distance and drive up into it where a clearing is prepared
for a tent near a stream; from hot water pouring out of the earth
and pooled with hand-laid stone; from ocean waves drowning the
time clock; the hands of time doing hand stands on a stretch of
pacific coast; numbers changing place in the order of things; from
poetry that is not influenced by the trepidation of parochialism;
from the sinuous suggestion."

"Let's go to the hotel room," I concluded.

"I can't be confined to a room right now," he said. He started
taking his clothes off and dropping them on the sand. "I need
some nostalgic embrace." He ran into the ocean naked.

"Zen!" I yelled.

"Come back." I followed him into the water until I could taste
the salt in my mouth. He could no longer hear me but I continued
to yell, "I have money. I have a room. We can have pizza delivered by a show girl from Bangkok."

Then the brazen waves compelled me to retreat back to the beach. I watched him swim into the turbid sea. His time was expired. It was time for him to go. Our burning poetry was doused with brine.

"I'll see you in Oregon," he shouted. I figured he knew what he was doing because he had a smile on his face when he finally disappeared. He had an aptitude for the wet and wild. I would see him again, but I had to wait for extrinsic events to move us along.

TREK 87

In 1969 rampaging hippos killed nine people in Zambia.

As I walked back to the Fremont Hotel I thought about Wallace Thurman. He was not included in "The New Negro" edited by Dr. Locke. Thurman saw prejudice operating from within. I compared Thurman's involvement with literature in the 1920's to Hendrix's participation in the 1960's music scene. They both entered the movements about midway and faded out as the periods dissipated. They both came from the west and traveled east to the center of their vortices. They gave it up for art while indulged in available substances.

I walked past a gas station and saw a man with a long stick measuring the level of the liquid. He examined the wet mark and licked the stick clean like it was a popsicle.

"How can you ingest a petroleum product into your body?" I asked with amazement.

"At first it made me vomit," he replied. "But then I acquired a taste for it. The value of the gas made it palpable. And the process of drilling for oil; of penetrating the earth; pumping fuel into underground holding tanks; taking a daily measurement with a long stiff device; sticking the nozzle into the aperture of a gas tank – I find the whole process exciting."

"But petroleum products pollute the air and water," I said, "and can you imagine changing the oil in your Chevrolet and pouring the dark liquid on your flower bed. How do you get the awful taste of gas out of your mouth?"

"I smoke a cigarette," he replied. "Tobacco also made me nauseous at first, but I learned to enjoy it. Somehow that burning at the tip of the cigarette so close to the gas on my lips fans my flames and sets me all atwitter." He began a hacking cough. I waved at a passing taxi. It stopped and I jumped into the back seat.

"Where to Bub?"

"Fremont Hotel please."

As we drove he asked if I wanted to buy firearms.

I said no to that and he offered me a good price on an eight-ball of cocaine. "The only snow I want to see is on top of Mt. Ranier," I said.

TREK 88

The National Mobilization Committee to End the War in Vietnam was a relatively short-lived coalition of anti-war activists formed in 1967.

I spent a couple of hours each day in the glass elevator. One day on the 19th floor two children entered. One was a small red-headed boy and the other his older sister. "Where are your parents?" I asked them.

"We gave them the slip," said the boy.

"And the onliest time we felt chicken-hearted," said the girl, "was when a lion roared like it wanted to eat us, but we changed its mind."

How did you accomplish that feat?" I asked.

"We did not use our feet. I had a brush and offered to comb its mane. The lion was real messy, so it let me climb on its back and brush out the tangles. When I got finished the lion was not so angry."

"You may have improved its appearance, but what about its hunger?"

"I gave it peanuts," said the boy.

"We changed its menu," the older sister said. "After chewing down on boiled peanuts it never wanted meat again.

"With the money the zookeepers saved on food they hired a hairdresser to come in and brush the lion's hair," she explained. "The lion attracted more visitors because it looked so spiffy."

"I wanted to bring it home," said the boy. "It could of lived in our closet. We could have watched 'Sesame Street' together. I could of polished its nails and taught it to play pick-up sticks. We could of had lots of fun, but Mom and Dad don't allow no pets in the house," she said.

After riding up and down and sharing stories with the children, their parents discovered them.

"There you are," said the mother. "You shouldn't wander off."

"Your children are safe," I said.

"They wanted to ride the elevator. You should be proud of such intelligent and beautiful offspring."

"They are naughty to scare us like that."

The mother pulled them by the ears, guiding her wayfaring brood off the elevator.

TREK 89

In the 1969 movie "The Big Cube", Lana Turner portrays an LSD dealing doctor.

I sat on the floor of the elevator at the Fremont Hotel, opened a beer and continued to ride up and down. I'd ride to the top and just hang there until someone below hit the down button.

I was thinking about history, how portions of it are totally described and analyzed while other aspects are covered up or even altered. Take for example the title fight in Havana, Cuba, 1915, between Jack Johnson and Jess Willard.

Jack had been heavyweight champ since 1908. This position carries symbolic significance and recognition. Jack was an irritant under the blanket of the power structure.

The search for a great white hope even brought James J. Jeffries out of retirement, but to no avail. What irked them even more was that Jack was bold and sassy. He enjoyed the company of white women.

They used this characteristic to attack him as he was slapped with the Man Act, transporting a woman across a state line for immoral purposes.

If a woman joined him for a joy ride she probably did it on her own volition. To escape imprisonment he fled the country.

The powers that be probably offered him some deal to take a dive in Havana. After 26 rounds Jess supposedly knocked him out. There were shouts of "fake" from the audience.

In 1919 another Jack appeared on the scene. Dempsey pounded Willard. After three rounds Jess would not come out of his corner. If the power structure had not harassed Johnson out of boxing, I think Jack would have met Jack in 1919 and that could have been the fight of the century.

The elevator door opened. I stood up to make room for a young man in a wheelchair. We started talking and he stayed on to tell me his story.

He had become paralyzed from the waist down after falling off an elevated dance floor. After months of rehabilitation he moved into a wheelchair community in San Diego. He played basketball, billiards, participated in wheelchair racing and went skiing in Colorado. They tied him to a board and he would slide down the slope.

He was in San Fran to attend a James A. Michener festival. From "Tales of the South Pacific" on he had read all of Michener's tomes. His reproductive tool was inactive but still he had three girl friends. I felt sorry for him at first, but then realized he was more active than me and I accepted him as another person on the road, doing the best he can.

TREK 90

In 1969 the movie "Take Them As They Are" follows the sexploits of three rowdy couples.

I walked to Haight Ashbury to fraternize with road warriors and other social freaks. I entered a bar that had twenty motor cycles parked in front. A group of Hell's Angels were absorbing liquids, playing pool and guffawing acrimoniously. They were hairy and scary, tattooed and imbrued with raw energy. I spoke to one of the club members who wore a sleeveless Levi jacket with Harley Davidson insignia. He wielded a knife with which he demonstrated various attack modes: upper cut to the abdomen and slash across the thorax. He honed his blade until it was so sharp he could gouge thin air.

The Angels organized after the Huns capitulated at the end of World War II. American fly boys mustered out of the service became discontent with civilian life. They attracted enough attention that Hollywood tried to cash in on their image, but Brando as the wild one was too spick and span to even approximate a distant facsimile. Angels are rough-hewn like turquoise before the impurities are separated. They don't start trouble but if you knock their cycle over or spill beer on their bare chest, you might wake up badly damaged merchandise.

Sports to them is not watching men knock each other down on the gridiron, but riding an open stretch of highway while standing atop their motorcycle. They compete by seeing who can balance the longest while riding on a course of two-by-fours or maneuvering the machine under a dangling hot dog so the girlfriend on the back can bite at it. After drinking one beer in their company, I quietly moved on.

I met two brothers and their common girlfriend in a head shop who were amiable and offered to share their stash. When I told them I had a room at the Fremont Hotel, they were very excited. They needed a place to crash.

"Well, let's go," I said, wanting to share my good fortune with someone. They collected their packs and a guitar with a rope as a strap. Their appearance was such that they might be detained in the hotel lobby so we stopped at a department store and I outfitted them with new duds. Once at the hotel I guided them to the elevator quickly and we soon arrived at the room. There was a football game on TV. Roger Staubach threw a long pass for a touchdown.

TREK 91

In the 1969 movie "Krakatoa, East of Java", the volcanoes erupt and colossal tidal waves rise from the sea.

My friends' names were Shawn, Eric and Buffy. They were small town denizens who were on the lam from home because two of them were classified 1-A. Buffy was a lover to both potential soldiers. I called room service and ordered a bottle of cognac and a large fruit platter.

"So when did you hit the road?" I asked them.

"About a week ago I received a 'Greetings from Uncle Sam'", said Shawn. "Just because I don't have the 'do-re-mi' to enroll in college doesn't mean I'll make a good target for a VC sniper. Johnson had two wars running in tandem - his war on poverty and his war in Vietnam. He used one to solve the other by drafting the lower level of the economic strata and sending them off to war."

"I lived in France," said Eric, "and I knew they had nothing but trouble when they tried to reoccupy Vietnam after World War II. Vietnam was involved in a civil war. When the U.S. had their north against south war they didn't want England to butt in or kibitz for the Confederates. It seems to me only a certain clique makes money off the conflict and the rest of us are victims of the war. How do we help them by destroying the region? Their land will be so crater-ridden they won't be able to farm. If the U.S. cannot force its rule over them I doubt any food or aid will be forthcoming."

"It irks me," I said, "how we claim to fight for freedom when we don't support freedom within our own country. Example: When two sanitation workers were killed in an accident in Memphis in '68, they had no insurance. There was nothing for their families. Working for little pay and no benefits the workers realized how stinking their situation was. They walked off the job. The only reaction they got from the mayor was that it was against the law not to work. Other people joined the struggle. The local power structure tried to restrict freedom with an injunction against the right to assemble. Dr. King got involved and saw this as a dangerous miscarriage of justice. They had to break the injunction and march. If Dr. King had to absorb the violence of the antediluvian Memphis drill sergeants, then he had to gainsay them."

Buffy Saint Marie had a galaxy of songs in her coffee house repertoire. To give us a respite from pummeling the government she broke into a song called "Piney Hills". She led us into "Mr. Tambourine Man". After holding hands and blasting into "We Shall Overcome", we heard a loud knocking on the door.

TREK 92

In the late 1960's the end of licensing requirements created a transition that transfused Times Square into an orgy of porn theaters, peep shows, and massage parlors.

"Blues for Mr. Charlie", in 1964, was made possible by the success of "A Raisin in the Sun". However, James Baldwin's "Blues" is not as good as "Raisin". Both plays deal with racism but "Raisin" traces the dynamics of a family living in tight quarters, their shortcomings and aspirations. "Blues" has no dramatic tension. We know that someone was killed, we know who is the culprit and we know the outcome of the trial. With no dramatic conflict all we have is the repugnance of a lynching. He wrote the play because Elia Kazan approached him about working in the theater. Baldwin wanted to redress the killings of Emmett Till

(1955) and Medgar Evers (1962). Baldwin's intent is commendatory but the product is lackluster.

The knocking on the door proved to be the authorities. Someone had complained about our noise. When they discovered that only one of us was registered, they asked us to quiet down. We hailed a cab in front of the hotel and we drove to a bar in the Mission district. We sat in a booth and ordered beer.

"There is a person in Berkeley who makes fake draft cards," I said. "He lives on Carleton Street but the only way to find him is through a jewelry vender on the avenue. You have to ask for a squash blossom made by a resident of Oraibi of the Hopi Land. The dealer says he doesn't sell any Indian jewelry, then gives you an address to make inquiries. You go to that address and a voice over an intercom directs you to a garage apartment. The number on the door is 4-F and there is a Jane Fonda poster of her disrobing in a film called "Barbarella". For a small fee you can have your classification adjusted."

There was a weekly on the table, which listed readings. An open-mic was soon to kick off nearby on Guerrero Street. I asked my friends if they wanted to attend. They were interested as long as I picked up the tabs. Let's go. I wanted to find out if my words were commensurate with Bay Area bards. I had a new poem I wanted to flash. We arrived at a dingy back room with loquacious local poets milling in communal anticipation.

After the reading I went to a midnight screening of "If" with Malcolm McDowall, a look at the education system in England. I was so invigorated by events that I walked across the Golden Gate Bridge that night.

TREK 93

In 1969 the movie "That Tender Touch" features a woman who breaks up with her lesbian lover and marries a man and moves to the suburbs.

Querida María,

This summer's journey of hitchhiking to L.A., British Columbia, to Alberta let-your-hair-hang-low, with no money to start with as an experiment, was prompted by the words:

"Provide neither gold, nor silver, nor brass in your purses, nor script for your journey, neither two coats, neither shoes, nor yet staves: for the workman is worthy of his meat." Matthew 10: 9

"I would not travel like that," said a man who picked me up. "I got to have my beer and pussy."

An even greater journey than miles covered was to leave behind the comforts of home and friends, to enter the unknown, to embrace the open road and to rely on faith that God will deliver us from any circumstance.

I didn't range as far afield as I had anticipated. I could have extended the experiment, but I felt it was successful enough and therefore unnecessary to perpetuate the cause. I allowed my energies to flow into other projects.

Henry David Thoreau could have resided longer at Walden, but he had worn a path to the lake, and there were many other lives to live. Each occupation we engage in should be an advancement over previous endeavors. The number of steps leading onward is limitless.

If we offer our service to the One, praying for wisdom and free tickets to the festival, our path will offer constant direction. We need not shudder at the world's iniquities until it dims our view of the sunset. If we develop patiently, we will be transformed into angels and called into service. Faith enters. We must contribute to the good of the movement.

I saw Zen Jazz and he left me with a few lines:

There is a God up here driving a snake into America's heart. The snake is wriggling, upsetting the apple cart. There is a God up here who speaks in snow. There is a God half-man, half-woman.

Your son, Joe

TREK 94

> In 1969 Dwight David Eisenhower
> passed away peacefully.

The Highlander Folk Center at Monteagle, Tennessee, was an important incubation nucleus for non-violent techniques. Dr. Martin Luther King, Jr. attended workshops. Mrs. Zilphia Horton believed in the effectiveness of song to unite people and dispel fear. When she died, Guy Carawan became musical director. He and Pete Seeger learned "We Shall Overcome" and sang it everywhere they went. It was easy to learn and harmonize on and people could add verses. Just as jazz music was "the revolt of the emotions against repression," "We Shall Overcome" was an effective tool in dealing with oppression.

I walked to Point Reyes, an uncluttered stretch of beach with only the sound of waves sliding over smooth sand, and wondered why the Civil Rights Movement occurred in the 1960's and not in the 1920's. The South and the North had to refight the Civil War, but this time for the real emancipation. The white terrorists, who could have worked as extras in "Birth of a Nation", were actively shooting and ambushing blacks or bombing churches.

Black men could have forced the issue of racism during WW I like the Irish making their statement for freedom in 1916 with the Sinn Fein Easter Rebellion in Dublin. They took over the Post Office and forced the English to regain control. Black men could have taken over the Lincoln Memorial. Instead DuBois advised participation in a war to make the world safe for democracy. They served with distinction in such units as the 369th Infantry called the "Harlem Hell Fighters".

When John F. Kennedy became the first Roman Catholic president-elect the movement had a sympathetic member within the power structure. Sit-ins began at lunch counters in Greensboro, North Carolina. Freedom riders were organized by the Congress of Racial Equality. James Meredith lived on campus at "Ole Miss" with protection from Federal guards. A bomb killed four school children at Birmingham's 16th St. Baptist Church. President Johnson appointed Thurgood Marshall to the Supreme Court. The sanitation workers walked off the job in Memphis in the last great battle of the civil rights movement. The workers won their demands but Dr. King was lost to a sniper bullet.

I wrote my name in the sand in big letters. The waves rolled in, and after several passes of its aquatic trowel, my name floated far out to sea.

TREK 95

*In the 1969 movie "The Gypsy Moths", skydivers
jump and hope that the parachutes open.*

I wanted to visit the wine country of Napa Valley. I rented a car then picked up the first hitchhiker I met. His name was

Backpack Trekker: A 60's Flashback

Pomeroy Pope. I insisted he drive while I sat in the back seat. We stopped at every winery along the route to sample the products. The wineries were generous with the samples.

In the first establishment we sat with three compatible people: two from Australia who had camped on top of Ayers Rock and a guitar player from Nashville who had featured often at Tootsie's Orchid Lounge on lower Broadway.

"I want to visit the Outback," I said, "and rent a Jeep with gas cans latched all around."

Pomeroy took out a map of Paris. He tried to retrace the steps of Henry Miller. He stood where Sylvia Beech had her bookstore, Shakespeare and Company. "I prefer French wine," he said. He took a bottle out of his bag.

"May I?" he asked the attendant. She nodded and turned away.

"Drink up that local swill," he whispered. "Let me fill your glass with this compendium of Western Civilization, direct from Bordeaux." He made sure everybody started fresh and then he proposed a toast.

"Let's drink to travel as a means of education." We clicked our glasses.

After we finished Pomeroy's bottle everyone shouted "local wine." We all tapped our glasses on the table. The silver-apronned attendant brought two more bottles. I bought a case of wine at that place.

After our party Pomeroy and I went for a walk in the orchard. There were clusters of grapes still on the vine. I chewed up handfuls and spit out the pulp.

My fingers and lips turned purple as we walked. He was obviously interested in education so I got off on Harlem which always occupied a portion of my private thoughts. I told him how Marcus Garvey came to Harlem in 1916.

"He started to lecture on a street corner where Malcolm X later got his start as a public speaker. In 1919 Garvey purchased an auditorium in Harlem and called it Liberty Hall. He conducted nightly meetings and sometimes as many as 6,000 people attended," I said.

The effect of the wine forced us to park the car on a back road. I continued talking about Garvey and how his dream was based on a flaw.

"He thought Negroes would be glad to board a steamship on his Black Star Line and travel back to Africa. But most Negroes considered America their rightful home and after helping to build it, had no desire to leave.

"His Negro World collapsed completely when he was sent to prison for two years for mail fraud. When he was released from incarceration, he was deported. In 1937 he conducted a conference for the Universal Negro Improvement Association to pass on what he had learned trying to uplift his race. He died in London in 1940 a penniless man."

When I finished my discourse on Garvey I realized Pomeroy was asleep in the front seat. I poured the contents of the bottle we had been working on down my gullet and joined him in the land of Nod.

TREK 96

In 1969 the movie "Marooned" features astronauts stranded in space.

A component for adventure is a quick mind. When Pomeroy Pope awoke he had a fantastic idea. "Let's go to Alcatraz Island," he said.

"How do we manage that?" I asked.

"I know a man who lives in Sausalito with a boat. If we grease his palm he'll take us. Maybe we can sleep in one of the cell blocks or if that is too spooky we can set up tents. The Indians have occupied the island and they are refulgent with possession and pride. Imagine, America's longest prisoners-of-war have taken over the yard. What do you say? We can carry enough food and water and arrange for my friend to pick us up."

I returned the rented car and we took a cab to his friend's house. His name was Beto; he was a potter from Saint Lucia. He made large pots big enough to hold a human being. On the outside rim of his pots were red figurines, ceremonial dancers of the Navajo tribe. On other pots he recreated Mimbres designs in black and white. Piles of buffalo femurs awaited sanding. He took the bones and inlaid them with turquoise.

His wife invited us to a meal of tofu and squash. We all held hands around the table as he recited grace, giving thanks for the food and their boat. Being sympathetic to the Native-American cause, he transported supplies and people to The Rock. After signing a petition of support for César Chàvez, we left for the marina and loaded up.

Backpack Trekker: A 60's Flashback

The ride to The Rock was exhilarating over the concordance of waves. Beto dropped us off at the dock. I saw the Bird Man of Alcatraz wave from the cell house. I heard Al Capone cough in his hospital isolation cell.

Someone held subversive thoughts of suicide. The huge incarceration unit loomed up like an amusement park. We camped in the exercise yard. At night we could hear all the sounds of the city: the cable car, traffic over the bridges, the door to City Lights Bookstore open and close. I saw tepees set up by members of the American Indian Movement near the parade ground. We had a great view of the sunset through the bay as it sank below the Golden Gate Bridge.

TREK 97

In 1969 Woody Allen made us laugh with his book titled, "100 Advanced Sexual Positions and How to Achieve Them Without Laughing".

At Alcatraz the Indians had laid out stones in circular patterns for campfires. Pomeroy and I thought about setting up in the yard, but the view was obstructed so we camped near the Warden's House that was built in 1929. Having a free place to pitch a tent in the middle of the Bay Area was an unequivocal boon. Sometimes I did not hear the outboard motors that came and went because I was in D Block – a section reserved for inmates who broke regulations. Sometimes I sat in the library and thought of Mitya Karamazov, who had been found guilty and awaited shipment to Siberia.

In the evening we enjoyed a campfire. There was not much to burn on The Rock but someone hauled wood from the mainland. We gathered around the fire to chant and sing. There was a white man they called Frankie. Rumor had it that he used to be a former resident, that his real name was Frank Morris and he reoccupied the same cell before his escape in 1962. He had long since been presumed drowned in the cold, swift waters of the bay. Some seabirds returned and lived off the scraps of the campers.

I usually stayed up past midnight. No sense rising before ten in the morning. It took the sun until then to burn through the mist. The fog was so thick some nights, I could feel the walls decay as we lay there. A salt wind moist and chilly hit my face like a Floyd Patterson fist.

Normally I carried my ID and money with me at all times. But one day I left everything in my tent while I went for a wade near the guard tower side. When I returned, my passport was still intact, but all the cash was gone. Pomeroy Pope was gone also. I wasn't aware of any boats to the island that day, so I don't know how he left. I least expected to become a con game condiment on such an isolated location, but nihilistic patterns blotted my vision. When you live outdoors exposure to the weather is inevitable. I didn't sing at all that night. The Indians asked why I was so quiet. I explained that a friend had disappeared that day without saying goodbye. It made me sad.

"Maybe he made a special trip back to the city to bring you more books. Boats don't usually dock here at night. It is too dark. But maybe he will greet you in the morning."

"Maybe so," I said.

As I prepared to bed down that night I found a key on my sleeping bag. It had a tag on it that identified it as a key to a P.O. Box in Mill Valley. I had no idea what it meant.

Beto was scheduled to retrieve me in his boat the next day at 0:900 hours. I enjoyed my last views of the tepees on Alcatraz Island. We all felt it was a matter of time before government agents arrived with guns and escorted them away.

TREK 98

In 1969 Joan Baez sang from "David's Album", in honor of her husband, David Harris, who was imprisoned because of his opposition to the draft.

Before the launch arrived to carry me off the island in the morning I got into a conversation with a man named Long Knife. He was a descendent of people killed at Wounded Knee. He complained that every battle and skirmish during the War Between the States has been turned into hallowed ground with state parks and monuments. With America's longest running war, the war against the Indians, there was little attempt to remember the many conflicts that occurred across the continent.

"What do you think about Columbus?" I asked.

"Columbus Day is not something 'skins' celebrate. It is a day recalled with bitter aftertaste. When the Pilgrims arrived the native people should have destroyed their boats and driven them back into the sea.

"My parents were rounded up as children and herded off to industrial schools. The whites cut their hair and taught them Christian myths. I did not remove the glare of white from my eyes until I lived for one year at Acoma Pueblo. I remember the nights of primal simplicity on the mesa top and the confluence of earth and sky. This was not an unsettled place before the white man landed. Even when Lewis and Clark made their trip to the great uncharted West, they received help from many tribes. As the massive migration followed, many of the same tribes lost their land."

I saw Beto's boat coming in. I lifted my backpack and moved to the dock. "Good luck to you Long Knife," I said.

"Peace."

Beto had a big cigar in his mouth.

"Let's go," he said. "I don't want to dally around here." The imperious motor conveyed us to dry land. I told Beto about our friend Pomeroy vanishing along with my money. He had not seen our mutual friend, but my story softened his heart enough for him to give me a free ride to Mill Valley.

I wanted to try out the key to the P.O. Box in Mill Valley. What relevant info could explain the heist of my cash? With the key in hand it was like Christmas morning waiting to open presents. I entered the post office and pretended to write a letter as I cased the place. Everything seemed normal. There were no FBI agents lurking around. I opened the box, removed the contents without expectation and receded outside. I walked a mile away before releasing myself to imperturbable satiation of my curiosity. I found a flute, a poem and a schedule of plays for the Shakespeare Festival in Ashland, Oregon.

TREK 99

In 1969 Katharine Graham became the publisher of the Washington Post.

Poem found in my PO Box :

to travel slowly
to masticate each day
to sail smoky slumbers on seas of night

to visit a resting mallard and a curious squirrel
to remain silent in pools of screaming swimmers
to smile hello and pass on as a virtuoso wordsmith
to back alley through propitious venues
to burrow in voluminous pages of imagined life
to open a green door and receive green approbation
to wander desireless
to fill ones space with harmony
in reflected heat of asphalt highway
on log of lakeshore beach
under bridge and dripping sky
near voodoo doll with ravenous fangs
as scholars learn and forget
I implant myself everywhere
yet when I go leave nothing behind
always leaving and forever remaining

everything returns.

It was my own poem, hand-written on yellow legal paper. I wrote it while living at home and thinking about travel. It was a piece I had discarded as cumbersome. I guess Zen Jazz thought more of it. The flute belonged to me as well.

I decided to make tracks to Oregon. Maybe Zen was there playing flute for tips on a street corner. Maybe he had two all-festival passes and was waiting for me in front of the theater. With Zen anything was possible.

TREK 100

In 1969 Nicol Williamson played Hamlet in a production directed by Tony Richardson.

Querida María,
It would be interesting to read African-American literature if there had been no color line: if Negroes had never had to ride Jim Crow buses or use "colored-only" restrooms; never were refused service or lodging; never had to be sharecroppers cheated by land owners or be denied the vote and job opportunities; or never were lynched for defiling the purity of a white woman by just looking at her ...

Backpack Trekker: A 60's Flashback

I wonder what the storylines would be. Most Negro plots were designed to address the problems of segregation and legal discrimination.

One of the novels of 1924 was "The Fire in the Flint" by Walter White. Walter was light-skinned and could pass for white, but he opted to struggle for civil rights. His story is about Dr. Kenneth Harper, a Negro who lived in the North and served in the military in Woodrow Wilson's war, a war created with propaganda slogans like "Make the World Safe for Democracy".

The American Negro had no vested interests fighting in Europe. Perhaps the government suggested better treatment for them if they joined the cause. I think it was a missed opportunity to confront the real enemy here in the South. The Negro and the Irish could have revolted at the same time. Negroes could have taken over the post office in Montgomery.

Anyway Dr. Harper returns to his home in south Georgia after World War I to see that nothing has changed since the parade for the Harlem Hellfighters.

Despite that he helps all people who need him. Some patients cannot pay him until the crops are sold. He looks like a young Sidney Poitier. He is young, helpful, wholesome.

After his sister has been raped and his brother murdered by prejudiced white men, a Caucasian family calls him in to help their dying daughter. He drives to the house and with all the resentment accumulating in him, he decides he can do nothing but let the girl die as revenge on the white race.

After a tortuous inner struggle he decides to help her live despite his bitterness. As he leaves the house he is attacked by murderous white men waiting in the dark. They exploit the fact he is in the house of a white family while the husband is away.

Also in 1924 Jessie Redmon Fauset came out with her first novel "There Is Confusion". Jessie was a rare woman of color in the 1920's who worked outside of domestic service. She was editor of "Crisis" magazine. She tried to find work as a publisher's reader or social secretary. Even though she was highly qualified nothing materialized. In the later 20's she taught French in a junior high school. The 20's did not roar for everyone.

Also in 1924 Franz Kafka died and his novel "The Trial" was published a year later, thanks to his friend Max Brod. The Nazi rise to power in 1933 was not favorable to work by a Slavic Jew.

If Kafka had lived he would have found himself in a concentration camp. "The Trial" is incredibly prophetic as it describes how a man is accused of some unknown crime. He cannot defend himself because he has not done anything wrong. The verdict ends with the execution of Joseph K.

I know the only book you read is the Bible. I feel compelled to read as much as I can from the 20's. The rainbow of 20th Century creativity spans the 20's through to the 60's.

I'm off to the Shakespeare Festival and hope to see Zen Jazz.

Love, your son

TREK 101

In 1969 the "Over the Hill Gang" made-for-TV western features Walter Brennan as a retired Texas ranger.

I mailed post cards to my dad in Albuquerque. Cards containing facts about areas I visited. He did not hanker for speculative prose or philosophical treatise. He enjoyed solid information. The youngest of eleven children, he had remained at home to tend his mother until she passed from old age. He got a job with the commissary on the Santa Fe Railroad, which entailed many hours traveling the great Southwest.

He arrived home one afternoon with a new car - a '57 Chevy. He taught me to drive this stick shift out on the West Mesa, an expanse of empty land crosshatched with dirt roads awaiting development. I could stop in the middle of the road or even run off the road without injury or annoyance to anyone.

Sometimes as I drove along he'd fire a pistol out the window at a rabbit. He provided me with invaluable driving experience and graced our Sunday table with fresh meat. Rabbit tasted like chicken and the hides we dried and sewed together for rugs. When he hit a rabbit I honked the horn and raised enough dust to make Okies dream of California.

By the time I drove on pavement I had enough experience to apply for an interstate commerce license. Dad had the patience and time to teach me better than any AAA instructor. When I was ready for the driver's test I could parallel park between two sage brush plants and change gears like a seamstress threading a needle.

Dad retired in 1960, the same year Ted Williams hit his last home run and did not tip his hat like the Babe rounding third. Mom took over working, logging long hours in her beauty salon.

Dad was available to wake us up for school, cook meals for us in the evening.

He drove us to and from events that Mom would arrange, like swimming lessons at the YMCA, band practice after school or a double feature at a movie theater downtown. He was always available to arbitrate any fist fights between me and my stuffed monkey.

Dad was always there for any questions or problems that arose. He was a staid fixture in the kitchen, where he set up his 1908 Underwood typewriter. He corresponded regularly with relatives. My Uncle Ira received a letter once a week. Dad kept a rubber ball which he squeezed every day, a technique learned from Gene Tunney.

Dad provided me with the best present I ever had, a 1966 VW bug, for which he paid cash. He laid sixteen hundred-dollar bills down on the table as the salesman's eyes bugged out.

Dad dropped out of school in the seventh grade but he helped put me through college. He was a wonderful friend and constant support. He always woke up with a smile on his face. When I decided to hitchhike instead of drive, I parked my love bug in his driveway.

TREK 102

In the 1969 movie "100 Rifles" there is interracial sex with Jim Brown and Raquel Welch.

I spent several days at a ManPower place in San Francisco. Eric Hoffer, the longshoreman philosopher, described his stints with ManPower labor pools in California. To distinguish himself from the 200 other men he used a flamboyant bandanna. When the designator of assignments looked up, he said, "You with the bandanna, let's go to work."

Following his example I surrounded my cranium with an electric Ladyland-PurpleHaze-Hendrix-style headband. When the assignor of positions looked up, "You with the headband, reading the book, let's go to work."

Conveniently located next door was a bar and packaged liquor store owned by the labor pool. They had pay phones, juke boxes and vending machines – all kinds of ways to spend your money. Much of the hard-earned cash never left the building.

Beatlick Joe Speer

When I had collected a sufficient amount of do-re-mi, I headed north to Ashland, Oregon, for the Shakespeare Festival. They were doing three of the Bard's plays.

My first night there all the tickets were sold out. So I walked out of town to find myself a campsite. I found a spot on Upper Staircase outside of a Jehovah Witness Kingdom Hall. It was a safe and comfortable place to sleep.

The next night I was staunchly ensconced in front of the theater. I experienced an incredible piece of good fortune. A man showed up wanting to unload all of his tickets at an extremely low, once-in-a-lifetime price. It seems he had experienced the distressing news that his thirteen-year-old daughter had been kidnapped by a religious cult and was being held captive in a wilderness cabin. We made a deal right there on the street. And that night I saw "Henry IV" part one.

Coming out of the theater I ran into Zen Jazz. We embraced effusively and retreated into a Waffle House for coffee.

"What brought you to the Shakespeare Festival?" I asked.

"I knew I would find you here," he said.

So I walked in during an intermission and found an empty seat for another round of entertainment. It was a fascinating play about Hotspur the revolutionist and his readiness to give Henry IV a snootful. His son Prince Hal lives a life of debauchery with recreant knaves in East Cheap taverns and bawdry houses.

"Zen," I said, " I was robbed of a large sum of money while camping on Alcatraz Island."

Zen Jazz never believed that I had a large amount of money in my pocket at any one time, but he did ask how the heist came down.

"I was beset by a dozen money-grubbing brutes," I lamented. "They tied me down and tickled my feet until I released my bankroll," I explained.

"I broke loose and sent three of them to the other side. I would have sent more of their ranks to perdition, but as I chased them they were very fleet of foot. They transformed into sharks when they hit the cold bay waters."

TREK 103

In 1969 Leonard Bernstein bowed out as New York Philharmonic conductor.

Backpack Trekker: A 60's Flashback

I showed Zen Jazz the flute found in the PO Box.

"Do you recognize this extension of the Great Spirit?" I asked. He examined the nicks on the bamboo.

"This was my instrument of choice," he said. "I played it on a trip to Mexico City. I remember leaving it in a boat at Xochimilco after proposing marriage to a girl from Chiapas. She thought I was a wealthy bibliopolist collecting rare comic books. She agreed to my proposal and I scurried her off to my hotel room. She wanted to visit the church first. I explained that in my culture it was the *dormitorio* first and then the vows. She was reluctant so I took her to the Floating Gardens and played her an extended solo on this flute. The sound of this protuberance convinced her my intentions were *bona fide* and we returned to the hotel. After pumping her full of high-quality sperm I begged off claiming I had to go exchange money. She wanted to come along but I beat it out the door."

"So you didn't legalize the relationship?" I asked.

"I couldn't," Zen regretted. "I had another woman in a different hotel. I had to scoot from the Floating Gardens to *Insurgents Norte.* But I'm delighted to see this flute again. It was given to me by a relative of Tupac Amaru. I learned to play it on the train traveling south. It was a constant companion until I left it behind."

"When I first saw it I was reminded of your dexterity with holes. How did you find your way into Henry IV?"

"I knew where to find you, so I walked into the theater during intermission and found a vacant seat. What a bunch of wastrels Prince Hal has for colleagues."

I described my sleeping accommodations on the back stairs of the Jehovah's Witness Hall. Zen had no prior arrangements for his lodgings so he joined me.

He spoke about the importance of poetry. He felt poetry should be at the center of culture. "Poets should not lurk on the fringe. Poetry is more important than the poet," he insisted. "The poetic process was the way to refine our being."

We fell asleep counting railroad tracks in a nether galaxy.

TREK 104

> In 1969 The Rolling Stones hit with
> "Honky Tonk Woman".

Beatlick Joe Speer

I gave Zen Jazz an early wake up call and we scrambled off the top staircase and down from the Jehovah's Witness Hall. We had no commitments until curtain time for the Shakespeare Festival. Zen didn't cope with algebraic equations or poetic surrealism until an elbows-on-the-table breakfast was consumed. After the second cup of coffee Zen informed me of his activities since we parted company.

"I had an appointment to meet the editor of an underground press in Seattle. I got a ride from two Swedish women touring America for six weeks. They wanted to see Lassen Peak. I told them I loved extinct volcanoes. I like being near a cone-shaped object that years ago shot a wad."

"You know, Crow," he motioned for the waitress to refill his cup, "I like to accumulate layers of dried cum on the sides of my legs. For a short spurt I averaged two orgasms a day. I let the overflow semen harden like lava. One of the women massaged my back as I made love to her friend. We camped near Lassen and they hiked around. I stayed in camp and prepared a hot meal for them to bolster their joint resolution.

"We all slept together at night. They insisted I read poetry to them before we blew out the candles. I read landscape poems:

cholla cactus with lizard resting in the shade
moonlight on adobe wall

"I saved the erotic poems for my last set. They would squirm with the worm. Camping near old volcanic heat made me want to meet every day with an upright attitude." Zen excused himself to go to the restroom. The waitress refilled my cup.

"Would you like anything else?" she asked.

"Yes. Bring me a blue corn tortilla covered with Chimayo chile power."

"Sorry sir. That is not on the menu. I can bring you a hamburger."

"Do you offer any discounts for road-kill meats?"

"No sir. We do have day-old doughnuts for half-price."

"No thanks. Just bring us the check and we will square it up with you."

Zen did not reappear. I looked in both rest rooms. There were no windows or back doors. The waitress did not see him leave. Zen Jazz was gone again.

☯

Backpack Trekker: A 60's Flashback

> *In the 1969 movie "Once Upon a Time in the West" Ennio Morricone creates the music and Henry Fonda is cold-blooded in Monument Valley.*

When Zen Jazz occupied an orbit around my celestial spirit, the quality of my life improved. When Zen was gone I had only the truncated space of my own mental constellation with no reason to coil up the tension of repartee. After Zen's departure I traveled to Crater Lake National Park, Oregon.

Crater Lake is an extinct volcano. The crater was formed over 6,000 years ago when Mt. Mazama exploded. The hollow mountain caved in on itself and a cauldron was formed. It collected enough water over thousands of years to create a lake. The water is pristine and gorgeous, deep and blue. Wizard Island is a separate volcanic cone that grumbled and poked its head out of the lake.

Often when camping it is difficult to completely get away from noise: parents scolding their garrulous brats; a barking dog tethered to a VW bumper; a generator that breaks the silence to energize a TV; or to elude the traces of humanity such as cans, cigarette butts or pottery shards.

I figured if there was one place in America with no people or telltale signs of nomadic movement, Wizard Island might be the place.

I had to reach the island. While in the campground I saw a man blowing up an air mattress that featured scenes from a "Star Trek" episode. It depicted "The Menagerie" - a two-parter - dealing with illusion.

I staked out the site and when the campers left I lifted the flotation device. I entered the water at night and kicked my way hugging and pointing the raft. I protected my gear with plastic.

The water was cold but I kept warm flapping like Kipling's white seal looking for the place where no people go.

I arrived cold and tired. I removed the plastic and hurriedly crawled into my sleeping bag. My body heat was stable and my breathing returned to normal. I gave thanks to Theodore Roosevelt for making Crater Lake a public reserve.

I thought I heard sounds while falling asleep: trucks, magisterial on the highway, school bells ringing clemency from class, gun shots, random and overhead like the chirping of vultures, all the sounds collected from adventurous wandering. Amidst the clamor of silence I fell asleep, warm and secure.

The next day I awoke to the sound of human voices. A park ranger was giving a guided tour. He explained the geological attributes of the area. It was then I realized that Wizard Island was just another stop on the tourist trail.

TREK 106

In 1969 Ho Chi Minh died. He had fought for Vietnamese independence practically all his life.

On May 19, 1961, Miles Davis blew trumpet with Gil Evans and his 21-piece orchestra at Carnegie Hall in New York. Davis traversed many musical miles in his career.

Tomorrow never found him where yesterday left him. In 1965 he assembled a jazz all star line up: Wayne Shorter on tenor sax; Tony Williams on drums; Ron Carter on bass and Herbie Handcock on piano.

Miles met Hendrix and they talked about music. If Jimi had lived they probably would have made music together. In '69 Miles hit with "Bitches Brew". The album cover reflects the psychedelic revolution.

While listening to jazz music I brooded about military expenditures. A trumpet can create landscapes. A gun only kills. Why not mass-produce musical instruments instead of the M-16? The military never lacks funding.

Why don't we tighten the purse strings on the armed forces? Why don't generals and admirals man bake-sale tables to raise money? Maybe Congress is afraid if they don't feed the beast it will decide to take over.

I mailed off for info on how to join the Navy. But four semesters of ROTC dispelled any thoughts of volunteerism. State supported universities were required to teach military classes. We marched on the parade ground with a band playing and rifles on our shoulders. We learned to dismantle our rifle, shine our brass and spit-and-polish our shoes.

After two years of basic inculcation, a weekly stipend was offered to continue with advanced ROTC. The army had money to lure young men into its ranks while molding and shaping fresh lieutenants. It offered travel to exotic lands to meet strange people and kill them.

Backpack Trekker: A 60's Flashback

There is a story Langston Hughes tells in "I Wonder as I Wander" about a war near the Siberian border. A Soviet barracks has soldiers relaxed, playing cards, when the door opens and a corpse is brought in. One of their comrades has been killed by a "slant-eyed bastard." Another soldier goes to the body and pulls the sheet back so everyone may see and he points out that, "Our comrade's eyes are slant eyes, too."

TREK 107

Published in 1969, "The Very Hungry Caterpillar" by Eric Carle, contains 225 words and has sold 30 million copies.

Querida María,

Out of Boulder I got a ride with a student scurrying to Connecticut. We took turns driving, stopping only to refuel and discharge. We hit NYC at sunrise two days later. I fasted for the duration of the trip. He, Rich House, kept offering food. He couldn't understand anyone turning down a munchable.

On the second day, while driving, I puked my guts into a paper bag. Turning into a rest area I emptied out from both ends, expelling all foodstuff and liquid. Rich construed the action as a sign of the deleterious consequences of fasting. I explained it as my system cleaning itself out. I had several gallons of spring water and I continued to flush.

When he dropped me off in the Bronx, I felt good. I walked a few miles past tall apartment houses with windows metal-barred against intruders, past fleets of smelly trucks rushing to piles of unpicked up garbage. Violators were threatened, "Autos will be towed away at owner's expense." Then I saw a decked-out lady walking a chinchilla. I entered a diner and had a 99-cent Breakfast Special.

Remember the $169 standby flight? I found one cheaper: Freddie Laker's $135 one way, first come first gone.

When I arrived at the ticket office in Queens a line of people extended from the entrance, around the corner and down the block, excluding the possibility of a flight for two days. That afternoon a man invited me to his home.

I experienced the Long Island Expressway on which commuters from the island spend 45-60 minutes to and from work. I want to reach the point where my work place is in the hotel room where I sleep.

During rush hour it becomes the longest parking lot in the world. While we were on it a truck skidded on a slippery road, smashed down a lamppost to hinder incoming traffic, and blocked all three outgoing lanes with its jackknifed body, necessitating the traversal of a muddy shoulder, one slow car at a time.

Warren, my host, had five kids and was also going to Europe. He fed me, gave me a bed and did my laundry. His traveling companion has a pet rabbit with free run of the house. After supper I laid down to rest, planning to rise and see a Randolph Scott western at 10:30 pm on the telly, but when I awoke it was one o'clock. Oh, well, I brushed my teeth and read another page of John Stuart Mill, from a thoughtful essay entitled "On Liberty":

"The worth of a State, in the long run, is the worth of the individuals composing it."

Estoy pensando aplazar mi viaje por Irlanda e ir al sur de España porque está fría en Inglaterra ahora y el cielo llora cada día. Tal vez, en Agosto puedo dormir a gusto sin interrupciones de las lagrimas de Dios cayendo encima de mi cabeza.
Tu hijo

TREK 108

In 1969 the Vietnamese government threatened "Newsweek" magazine with expulsion for publishing unfriendly articles.

I woke up on Wizard Island and washed my face in the huge vat of clean Crater Lake water. I still had the precooked dried pinto beans my mother had provided to keep me alive in remote areas. As I slowly ingested the beans I thought about 1939.

Hollywood had its peak year with studio productions. Also in the late 30's Fascism extended its control over much of the world. The Spanish Civil War changed military history with mass bombing of civilian populations.

Generalíssimo Francisco Franco was outfitted by Hitler and Benito Mussolini. He used Italian conscripts and Moorish mercenaries. The Falange was a brutal group led by a Fascist willing to destroy Spain to secure his power. Standing against him were artists and volunteers from around the world. The Loyalist forces retreated into Madrid where Franco commenced his bombardment of the capital that continued for months. The besieged city would not surrender. *"Madrid, que bien resistes."*

The US did not help the besieged democratic government of Spain. It even set up an embargo so no one else could aid the Spanish. Potential volunteers had to avoid the border crossings and hike through the mountains. In this conflict superior armaments prevailed. In Vietnam in 1969, despite overwhelming firepower and technology, the US fought a winless war.

The American soldier received combat pay, paid no income tax while serving in Vietnam, had free mail service, trips out of the country for R & R and a PX store to buy items cheap.

The VC suffered privation similar to the Loyalists in Madrid, who endured nightly blackouts, no heat, no money, scarcity of food and daily bombing raids.

American soldiers watched B-52's pound infiltrators along the Ho Chi Minh Trail. The soldiers were miles away but the impact of strafing and tons of bombs dropped from high altitudes caused the men to have nosebleeds and severe headaches. They couldn't imagine anything able to survive such destruction. The trail was scarred with craters and scorched earth. Yet next morning, the North Vietnamese army was ready to fight again.

Franco decided to encircle Madrid. When members of the International Brigades realized he was determined to strangle the lifeblood out of the city they retreated to Valencia, Barcelona, and departed the country after their good fight.

There was an audience of *Madrileños* watching "Duck Soup" with the Marx Brothers. From inside the movie theater they heard bombs. They ignored it. When bombs shook the building the projectionist beat it down to the cellar. The audience, fascinated by the magic of tinsel town, continued to watch the movie. A direct hit collapsed the roof and buried the front rows in rubble. When the dust cleared the spectators were still in their seats watching the movie.

TREK 109

On June 15, 1969, some 25,000 people gathered in Tokyo to demonstrate against the Vietnam War.

My day on Wizard Island in Crater Lake was tranquil. I watched a pair of hawks soar in the upper air currents. The wind created patterns on the surface of the lake. A face appeared on the water. It reminded me of a friend Mario Prieta Basura in Berkeley. We met at the Cosmic Carrot Café where he worked as a dishwasher. He had a second job on a crew that cleaned Telegraph Avenue late at night. He wielded a wrench as they plugged into fire hydrants to hose the daily accumulation of garbage. They started at the entrance to the university and worked their way down the avenue. Everybody on the crew was on the lamb.

Mario joined the navy out of high school. He was stationed in Bremerton, Washington, aboard the USS Enterprise. The ship moved down the coast to Alameda Island in the Bay Area. Mario recalled walking on a deck that rose to meet him or fell and made it seem like he was stepping in a hole. When he got down wind of news that the next port of call for the Enterprise was Vietnam, he canceled the idea of further military involvement. He went AWOL.

At a Free Clinic in Haight Ashbury a person in the back room provided him with fake ID. He got a chance to use it late one night when a '59 Chevy wagon pulled up in front of an oriental rug store. Two men threw a concrete block through the window. They loaded three carpets into their car and drove away. Mario's boss called the police. Before the cops arrived, everyone on the crew except Mario had vanished. When asked to show ID he presented his new credentials.

Mario was eventually apprehended and confined to an area near Yerba Buena that was built from garbage and whimsically called Treasure Island. He was restricted to barracks except for one hour a day when he was allowed to walk around like a pet dog. A marine corporal who ran the small slam enjoyed lining the inmates up for shaves in dicks and ass formation, one man's nose in the back of another man's head. From Treasure Island Mario saw boats dock at Alcatraz.

When the Enterprise lifted anchor for Vietnam many seamen jumped ship.

TREK 110

In 1969 Generalíssimo Franco, who had completed 30 years of supreme power in Spain, chose Prince Juan Carlos de Borbón y Borbón as his successor.

I collected enough dead wood for a modest fire and watched the flames as the wind blew a glowing ember onto the air mattress that separated me from volcanic crags. A burn hole deflated the raft. My body temperature rose with anxiety, so I disrobed and swam in the lake. The water was cold. When I felt chilblains attack the efficiency of my heart muscle pumping blood, I removed myself from the water, dressed, and crawled into my sleeping bag. I thought about Lemuel Gulliver and fell asleep.

When Gulliver was captive in the land of the giants, he was transported in a cage with a handle on top. A trusted servant had taken Gulliver to the beach and set him down. He fell asleep in his hammock as the servant wandered off and was awakened by the clapping of wings. An eagle picked up his cage and flew him out to sea.

I woke up dangling in the air. An eagle picked up my sleeping bag with both talons and flew me out of Crater Lake. It must have thought it had a tasty worm.

I was carried for a long distance until I heard the flapping of more wings. Apparently another eagle arrived to contest possession of me, his worm-like meal. The flight pattern became very erratic. Suddenly I felt myself falling. I dropped with such swiftness that I almost lost my breath.

I dropped into a large body of water, salty but not the ocean. I splashed down hard then crawled out of the bag and swam ashore to an island.

There was a man in a boat passing by at a slow pace. I waved to him and he came to fetch me. I asked him where we were and he replied Antelope Island in the Great Salt Lake, Utah.

"How did you get here?" he asked.

I told him I had paddled out to Wizard Island in Oregon to experience a place where men never go, but the idea had proved useless when I learned it was just another fee for a commercial boat trip.

"An eagle snatched me up and dropped me in this salty lake," I told him.

He was an elder in the Church of the Latter Day Saints. He thought my account was pretty far-fetched.

"It is no more fantastic," I said, "than your story of a man finding gold plates under a stone in upstate New York with words delivered to the ancient inhabitants by Jesus."

Despite our philosophic differences he offered to take me home.

☯

TREK 111

In 1969 Elia Kazan directs the movie from his own novel "The Arrangement".

The Mormon elder was named Mr. Byington. He motored around in his boat as diversion from his work with the church. It was his responsibility to rent apartments in all major cities in America to be occupied by Mormon missionaries. Young men were assigned in pairs to various locations and shifted around as needed.

He fed and re-outfitted me then asked if I was interested in a Bible study session. I felt so obliged to him that I would have agreed to mow his lawn.

We bowed our heads as he prayed that Jesus would guide our understanding as we studied his holy word. After our study a young man entered the room.

"This is my son Mosiah," he said. "Visit while I go to the kitchen and fix us some apple juice." He left us alone. His son had curly hair with more locks than the Panama Canal. He stared openly with velvety curiosity.

"Where are you from?" he asked with brown eyes shiny as obsidian.

"To give you a long answer," I said, "my ancestry goes back to a region in Spain where many of the conquistadors were hard-ened - Estremadura.

"I have many cousins named Trujillo, after one of the cities in Spain that benefited from the pillage of the New World. When the Spanish conquered Granada in 1492, the monarchy of Ferdinand and Isabella turned to bankroll Columbus, who sailed in August.

"The end of the war against the Moors meant lack of work for the warrior breed on horseback. The opening of the New World provided new employment for these men of patent-leather skin. But the Americas were not new.

"Civilizations such as Tiahuanaco and Chaco Canyon had flourished and disappeared. It was new to these representatives of adventure whose swordplay prepared the way for the Cross.

"These soldiers fanned out to cover the territory between what is now New Mexico and Buenas Aires, men with names like Ponce de León, Pedro de Mendoza, Francisco Coronado, Her-nando Cortes, Alvor Núñez Carbeza de Vaca and Francisco Pi-zarro.

Backpack Trekker: A 60's Flashback

"One hundred years later another soldier, Miguel de Cervantes, published a satire on these knights errant with his 1605 novel 'Don Quixote'. Cervantes wrote:

En un lugar de La Mancha, de cuyo nombre no quiero acordarme ... se daba a leer libros de caballerías con tanta afición y gusto...que vendió muchas hanegas de tierra de sembradura para comprar libros de caballerías en que leer...

"The men of iron from Estremadura had stamina to endure hardship, and I have a tincture of their blood coursing through my veins. I'm from the Southwest and like Quixote I'd sell portions of my property to buy more books," I summarized.

TREK 112

In the 1969 movie "MacKenna's Gold" desperados travel through Indian land to find a cache of gold.

Elder Byington returned with cold drinks at the end of my harangue of Spanish pollination of the Americas. Mosiah was alert, but looked like a tongue-tied tourist in a foreign country trying to understand why his passport had been confiscated.

"I want to learn Spanish," he said. "Can you teach me?"

"A language cannot be learned in a few days," I said. "Buy some audio tapes. Listen to Spanish every day. Even if you don't understand, the sounds will seep into your collection of symbols like slow rain into topsoil.

"Carry a book and learn vocabulary. Repetition is the key. It's the way the industrial complex promotes its products with their brand names on TV; billboards; outfield walls; racecar helmets; bus benches; everywhere the casual glance might absorb these symbols. Also while you learn, keep in mind that you will visit the country where that language is spoken. The final test is your ability to communicate quickly and fluidly with ticket sellers and native speakers."

"How long did it take you to learn Spanish?" Mosiah asked.

"I'm still learning," I said. "I thought I had a solid chokehold on the language after bantering with taxi drivers and vendors in *El Mercado* in Ciudad Juarez, then I tried to read Cervantes and realized I had a lot to learn."

I told him my mother's first language was Spanish. "She didn't encounter English until she entered public school. The languages did not coexist equally. English had to dominate, driving Spanish out of the classroom and away from the work place. This clash of cultures also occurred between the Spanish explorers and the native people at Hawikuh.

When Coronado was looking for the Seven Cities of Cibola, he only found a little crowded village. He attacked it to steal not gold, but food and blankets."

"You should visit southern Utah," Mosiah suggested. "You will enjoy the petroglyphs and pictographs. Forget about the cultural turmoil, visit places that excite you."

"I think you are right. Thanks for telling me that. I've been wandering around randomly. Your suggestion has inspired me to journey back to where the bones of my ancestors have been ground to dust; where pottery shards and arrowheads can still be found on the surface; where stone and mud were the materials for construction. I want to hike into Grand Gulch Primitive Area or around Navajo Mountain to Rainbow Bridge."

I spoke with a newfound excitement, oblivious to the attentiveness of my audience.

When I paused and regarded my benefactor, I noticed Elder Byington was asleep.

TREK 113

In the 1969 movie "The Italian Job", there is a major traffic jam in Turin with music by Quincy Jones.

While in Salt Lake City I visited the Mormon Tabernacle. The acoustics were so perfect a person was heard whispering on the other side of the room. I got a ride out of Salt Lake with two men from the East Coast, two profligates on the make. They found me walking with a "Book of Mormon". They suggested I trash the book and go with them.

Their names were Jeff and Arnold. Jeff was caramel-colored with nappy hair. Arnold had long, straight brown hair and a muscular frame. Arnold was very talkative while Jeff only interjected occasional comments.

Arnold walked up to a woman at a stoplight and asked if she wanted to get better acquainted. She walked off without responding. He approached another woman walking on the sidewalk.

"Hi gorgeous," he greeted. "How would you like to have my baby?"

"Fuck you," she replied.

"Yes, do fuck me. I'm a love specialist. I can show you such a good time it will be a high-water mark on your social calendar."

"Your high water might drown me," she replied.

"No matter how deep we get, you will float in a sea of ecstasy."

"I'm a landlubber," she said. "Fuck yourself."

Arnold hit on every female within earshot, without convincing any of them to mate with him. We decided to leave town.

"You have a direct approach with women," I said to Arnold. "How often do you score with such a frontal assault?"

"It's like fishing," he said. "Most of the time you reel in an empty hook, but you keep casting out for the moment when the atmospheric conditions are right and they bite solid into your hook. You keep trying because there is the prospect that you will land one."

"I picked up a woman one time in Denver," Arnold recalled. "A one-liner was all it took to lure her into conjugal participation. She even had her own pad nearby. I worked her aperture until it consumed three fingers, then I pinned her to the floor with my purple-headed warrior spike, nailed her down until all she could do was kick her feet in the air like an upturned beetle. I stroked her from an assortment of positions and waited for her to enjoy a series of orgiastic tremors before I shot my mother lode onto her belly. She had such a good time she wanted to introduce me to her friends. I could have stored up a year's supply of 'poon tang'. But I was bound for moving on."

TREK 114

> In 1969 the movie "The Undefeated" features a Confederate and a Yankee who team up to battle for Mexican independence.

We built a fire and wrapped chunks of meat and corn-on-the-cob in foil. Jeff placed the food over the coals and covered them up with dirt. Arnold suggested we stroll and brandish our wit.

When we returned we dug up the food and feasted. Arnold laid down and rested the *"labia majora"* of his thinking process while Jeff and I admired the millions of stars overhead. He had obtained a Bachelor of Arts degree and was half way to a Masters in history but felt inadequate about his education.

"The education system dispenses information which is designed to create certain results," Jeff said. "I could get a job teaching, but all I'd do is reissue the standard material. The history I'm learning does not fully represent who I am. For example, there are plenty of college courses on ancient, medieval and modern Europe, but there are no classes on tribal living in Africa. The university catalogues offer European art courses but there are no extended studies of African art.

"The system always shines the light on its selected icons. I enjoy hearing how Washington led a revolt, but what about Toussaint L'Ouverture? I think Eleanor Roosevelt deserved recognition when she died in 1962, but what about Mary Bethune? The Babe had a powerful bat during the swing era, but Satchel Paige could have struck him out. Greta Garbo was sexy in "Mata Hari" but how about Josephine Baker in "Zou Zou"?

"I agree that the power structure wants to propagate its own symbols," I said. "Take for example the case of Kit Carson. In the Taos area there is a road and a national forest named for him. He is presented to us as frontiersman and scout. The Indians called him the rope thrower. He knew the Indian ways and used this knowledge to destroy them.

"Working as a killer for the army he led soldiers into sacred land like Canyon De Chelly to burn orchards and kill livestock. The army destroyed dwellings and the Indians that escaped bullets found themselves in winter with no food and no shelter. The survivors had little recourse but to move onto reservations. I think they should remove Carson's name from everything and make Kit's house a public restroom.

"Another western icon is Billy the Kid. You can visit his grave in Fort Sumner. His image is still sold on postcards. But why should we remember him? He was a vicious killer."

"Most education only has imitative value," Jeff said. "The main reason I'll return to the university is to keep my student deferment. I prefer the lecture hall to the rice paddies."

TREK 115

On December 1, 1969, the first draft lottery of the decade was held.

Backpack Trekker: A 60's Flashback

Querida María,

It started somewhere. Let's start with the 1930's, climbing out of depression, salvation came not with Jesus riding a lamb and turning swords into pruning hooks and ploughshares, but war. America's major industry became the production of munitions.

War created jobs for everyone, young men became soldiers, older men made plans and shook hands with young men boarding planes for the combat zone. Women moved into jobs in factories and even played baseball until the men returned and sent the women back to the kitchens. Boys sold newspapers of the exciting events. Great minds were tinkering with powerful agents of destruction.

It's best to conduct warfare overseas. In WW II our civilian population did not suffer the indignity of sleeping in subways. We armed nations around the world. We punched east and west with "God on our side" (Dylan's "Masters of War").

The world cheered and danced when the armistice was signed but we were now in the business of making war supplies. What about the production line and the jobs? We had to promote war.

General Eisenhower became a two-term president. Korea provided the next battle ground. What was the reason for three years of fighting a limited war with 33,729 dead and 103,284 wounded? The blanket logic was to stop the spread of communism. In the machinations of world leaders young men are expendable, especially if they come from minority or low-income families.

Ten years later we eased into another war near the previous killing fields. The same pretext was used to help a defenseless people against brutal invaders from the north. Our security was somehow threatened. We continued to beef up the military budget.

The falsehood of our purpose and stupidity of our situation became painfully obvious when even the vets of the Vietnam War protested against it. One man publicly threw his war metals over the fence at the White House.

"History is a nightmare from which I am trying to awake," said James Joyce.

I say claim allegiance to no government that promotes violence. Recognize no border. Believe in the oneness of life: that the life of a gosling or kitten is as important as that of a human child. Believe in the perpetuity of the human spirit. That's my rant for now. Will find the local public library and read for a couple of hours.

Love, your son

TREK 116

In July of 1969, Neil Armstrong became the first human to leave tracks on the moon.

It is healthful to watch the flickering images of a campfire. I sat around the fire pit with Jeff and Arnold. We talked about Vietnam and the Civil Rights Movement. Arnold had two friends die in Vietnam. Jeff had a friend killed by highway patrolmen who fired on protesters in Orangeburg, South Carolina. Jeff thought overseas maneuvers should get less coverage than the victims of our war in America, a war that had more to do with freedom.

"Our soldiers in Vietnam are paid to participate in an unsavory experience," Jeff said.

"The Civil Rights Movement is composed of volunteers, true freedom fighters. I remember the march from Selma to Montgomery in 1965. State troopers beat back the marchers at Edmund Pettus Bridge. Dr. King spoke after that to encourage the people. He said you can't surrender to the forces of intimidation. If they gave up then and lived on to ninety, the extra years would not do them any good because they would have died spiritually when they allowed someone to turn them around.

"They regrouped and before the bruises healed from the first drubbing, they marched successfully across the bridge."

"What did you think about King getting involved in the Memphis strike?" I asked. "It wasn't a scene that he helped organize."

"The sanitation workers strike," Jeff continued, "might have been beaten down if Dr. King had not tipped the scale in their favor by marching in their support. Like at Edmund Pettus Bridge, he was determined to march despite injunctions.

"The beleaguered strikers were hard-pressed to continue. They had no income to pay their bills or buy food, while the Mayor and his people were still on the payroll. The strikers were desperate and needed something extra. Dr. King provided the extra ingredient.

"He was at the beginning of the movement, which came into focus when Rosa Parks was arrested and they all agreed to boycott the public bus system. It took over a year in Montgomery but the situation changed. King was a natural leader and he dressed like a US senator.

"The sanitation workers walkout lasted about six weeks. It came to a conclusion quickly after a march led by Dr. King deteriorated into looting. Tear gas was fired at the marchers. Students became angry for being refused permission to leave school to join the march. Anger is not a good emotion to start a march. After King was killed, Abernathy and Coretta Scott led the strikers to victory.

The struggle for freedom continues, but for me, that phase of the Civil Rights Movement ended at the Lorraine Motel in April of 1968."

TREK 117

In 1969 the book "The Andromeda Strain" by Michael Crichton makes a big hit.

Robert Crumb was the cartoonist of the Haight Ashbury experience. He was not a long-haired, barefoot vagabond, but his "Keep-On-Trucking" man was the logo of the backpacker populace. His Fritz the Cat inspired animated movies. The San Francisco rock group Big Brother and the Holding Company utilized his talent for some cheap thrills on an album cover. His "Zap" comic was an unconscious bubbling up of the psychedelic underground. He was a thin introvert who wore glasses and might easily be ignored if he tried to cash in on some free-love action. He also had two brothers who seldom mingled with women.

R. Crumb's luck changed when his art brought notoriety. He found salvation and expressed his sexuality in the panels of his art. In one episode a little man with a long beard comes to visit riding on the back of a strong, shapely female. We cannot see her head because the beard covers it. When the little man dismounts it is revealed that the woman has no head. The man's intention is to leave the beautiful body with Crumb to enjoy at his leisure. He also leaves a head to put on her if they should go out.

Crumb's little man departs quickly, much like Neal Cassady closing the door on Jack Kerouac at Big Sur post-delivery, of a willing woman to his cabin. Crumb takes advantage of the situation with a stand-up, back-door entrance. In the process her head is damaged. After the sex he feels guilty and wants to dump her. The little man agrees to take her back, but wants Crumb to attach her head to transport her. All Crumb can do is wrap up the nub and put a hat on it. He takes her back and watches as the little man sticks his hand into the hole between her shoulders and pulls out her head by the tongue. Once equipped with a head she becomes contentious.

"How could you leave me with such a creep?" she asks. With a head on her shoulders she becomes more than either of them want to deal with and they exit stage left and right.

The Haight Ashbury provided many opportunities for visual stimulation: head shops with incense burning; bars with boisterous free thinkers and Hell's Angels bending elbows with music blasting; rent-free itinerants carrying bedrolls; young runaways in need of a place to flop; street musicians singing Paul Simon or Buffy Saint Marie songs; friendly talkative people sitting on doorsteps; revelers in the park willing to share their stash for a group high; plenty of escapades and outlandish antics from the subculture to heat up the imagination of a graphic artist like R. Crumb.

TREK 118

In 1969 the movie "Ma Nuit Chez Maud", Eric Rohmer presents one of six moral tales.

The M & M Boys were in a movie called "Safe at Home". It was a film intended to capitalize on the popularity of Mickey Mantle and Roger Maris. Maris did not enjoy breaking the Babe's season home-run record. People tried to qualify his feat, pointing to a livelier ball and the extended playing season, but the stats after the last game were Babe Ruth 60 and Roger Maris 61.

Roger lacked the charisma of the "Bambino". His career soon faded. Mantle, after Sandy Koufax humiliated the Yankees in the 1963 World Series, spent his last years in the majors nursing injuries and saturating his liver with alcohol. If he had known he would live beyond his baseball career maybe he would have taken better care of his body.

Another terror on the mound was Bob Gibson. He could hurl a fastball through a brick wall as he unleashed his speed and fell toward home plate. Henry Aaron was a homerun hitter but not a colorful player. While standing at home plate he looked like he was asleep. He woke up at the last moment to flick his wrists and hit the long ball.

Willie Mays played ball with great gusto. He was so comfortable in center field that he patented a basket catch that made snagging fly balls seem as easy as a yawn. He didn't catch the ball over his head but low around his waist. Yogi Berra of the Yankees and Stan Musial of Saint Louis were solid hitters. But what made them distinctive was their ability to hit in the clutch. If it was a tight game coming down to late innings with two runners on base, the hitters a pitcher least wanted to see were Yogi or "Stan the Man". They were not power hitters like the Mick or "Hammering Hank" but they always got a piece of the ball. They guarded the plate like a chained dog protects its food bowl at feeding time. It was a safe bet they would slam the ball to some unprotected area of the outfield. As catcher Yogi was in a position to provide some dialogue to batters that might distract them from a Whitey Ford curve ball. Stan retired in 1963 and Yogi in 1964.

My favorite manager, Casey Stengel, was dismissed in 1960, but he returned to bring a positive influence on the New York Mets. He broke his hip and had to quit for good in 1965.

When the splendid splinter hit his last home run in Boston another left handed hitter took Ted Williams' place in 1961. They shortened his name to Yaz because Carl Yastrzemski was too long to write even down the leg of his uniform.

TREK 119

> In the 1969 movie "Women in Love", D. H. Lawrence offers the full gamut of possible relationships between men or women.

Encountering a movie set in the wilds of southern Utah was like walking into a Hollywood western. I crossed a creek and wandered into Paria. I felt like the sheriff in "High Noon", staring down a deserted street. I did not tote a gun. A friend once offered to provide me with a revolver for protection, but I shun the company of a destructive device.

The western town of Paria was a facade: hotel, saloon, Wells Fargo office. It was braced and propped up by carpenters to create the illusion of the frontier. It reminded me of the movie "Ride the High Country", where two old geezers join forces to transport money and a bride. The potential bride is repulsed by her lout of a lover who loathes bathing. She opts to return to her curmudgeon father while one of her benefactors falls into moral decrepitude due to the lure of possible wealth.

Then I was reminded of another movie, "How the West Was Won", where river pirates wait to relieve travelers of their wealth. This movie has incredible scenes of a buffalo stampede with shots from underneath the burning hooves and logs rolling off a moving train.

I practiced a fast draw against my shadow on the wooden planks in front of the saloon. With my finger pointed dead ahead I snarled, "You better make yourself scarce. This one-whistle-stop of a town ain't big enough for both of us. If you don't disappear by sunset, bullets will fill the air."

Sure enough, when the sun went down, my imaginary nemesis was gone. I built a fire in the middle of the street using loose lumber from one of the dilapidated buildings. The sky was filled with stars. Electricity and stars are not compatible. In wilderness areas the stars reveal their points of light as if to counterbalance the surrounding darkness of the earth. I saw patterns beyond Orion and the Big Dipper. I saw Philip Whalen on a bear's head practicing Zen Buddhism. I saw Michael McClure as a shaman activist reading slowly at Point Lobos something you may tell to your children. I saw Ed Sanders getting politically vocal with The Fugs. I saw Bob Kaufman eating a golden sardine in silence. I saw Gregory Corso pouring gasoline on the vestal lady. I saw Anne Waldman praying at Saint Mark's Church for a disembodied project. I saw the poet Lew Welch disappear into the mountains. Lew! Don't take that gun.

TREK 120

In 1967 the first issue of "Rolling Stone" was published.

It was perfect timing when "The Improper Bohemians" by Allen Churchill appeared in 1959. A book about Greenwich Village in its heyday manifested at the peak of the Beat movement. The bohemians, beats and hippies all had similar lifestyles. The artists looked for cheap rents near Washington Square. It was hard to beat the reasonable accommodations in North Beach. Birds of a feather flocked together in Haight Ashbury.

If a rainbow was erected in the 20th century like an art installation, one end of it would be planted in the 1920's and the other end in the 1960's. To compare and contrast the two decades, women were very active. Suffragettes gained the vote in 1920, while women like Emma Goldman and Henrietta Rodman practiced free love. If men could flit around in affairs of *amour*, then these women wanted equal rights in the bedroom, as well as at the ballot box.

Prohibition of alcohol began while cannabis was almost unknown in middle-class America. By the 1960's people could drink themselves to death legally, but potheads were arrested.

In 1920 theater experienced a black and white collaboration when Eugene O'Neill created roles for Charles Gilpin and Paul Robeson.

In the 60's blacks and whites worked together to desegregate public transportation. In 1920 Langston Hughes wrote "The Negro Speaks of Rivers" while on a train departing the South. In the early 60's James Baldwin returned to America from Istanbul to visit the South and help in the movement.

In the 1920's jazz recordings became available. By 1960 Berry Gordy had a label in Motown to provide entertainment to the masses. He created miracles and Smoky Robinson helped him sell records. Music lovers could shop around and Motown kept mass-producing hits.

The 1920's roared and the 1960's were psychedelic. Gangsters and a black market were created by Prohibition. Drug dealers and an underground economic network with untaxable incomes was created by the profits of illegal substances. I satisfied my addictions at the public library reading books published during the 1920's.

TREK 121

In "1969 the British sex-film "Nine Ages of Nakedness", topless beauties from the Stone Age to the Space Age strut their stuff.

There was an optimism about the 1920's and 1960's that was contagious. Waldo Frank expressed it in the first issue of "Seven Arts", a literary magazine (1916-1917).

"It is our faith and the faith of many that we are living in the first days of a renascent period, a time which means for America the coming of that national self-consciousness which is the beginning of greatness."

Beatlick Joe Speer

In 1961 President Kennedy spoke of the torch being passed to a new generation. He represented positive change for our culture.

The Immigration Act of 1924 established a quota system which discriminated in favor of countries of northeastern Europe. Under this system Great Britain, Ireland and Germany were allotted more then 70 percent of the quota.

This system was abolished in 1968 in favor of a first-come first-served policy. The era of mass immigration ended soon after WW I.

Black America moved from a rural South of dust and depression to jobs in northern cities. In 1910 in New York the black population was 29,000.

By 1930 the number swelled to 327,000. Harlem became the Mecca of the New Negro. Better to be a dishwasher in Harlem than a school principal in Kansas City.

In 1921 Marcus Garvey was in full swing with the Universal Negro Improvement Association in Harlem.

In 1961 Malcolm X lectured in Harlem. Also in 1961 Peter, Paul and Mary took Greenwich Village to the bitter end.

In 1921 Ku Klux Klan activities ratcheted up the use of fear and terror against people of color and any white sympathizers. In 1961 Reverend King was jailed for anti-segregation demonstrations.

More Freedom Riders followed the example of the original thirteen. Jails became overcrowded with Freedom Riders until Attorney General Robert Kennedy sent U.S. marshals to Montgomery to keep order.

In "The Book of American Negro Poetry" of 1922, James Weldon Johnson wrote, "The status of the Negro in the United States is more a question of national mental attitude toward race than of actual conditions. And nothing will do more to change that mental attitude and raise his status than a demonstration of intellectual parity by the Negro through the production of literature and art."

A host of talent rose to the occasion: Claude McKay, Jean Toomer, Countee Cullen, George Schuyler, Nella Larsen and many others.

I imagined myself disappearing into "Tropic of Cancer". In 1961 it became Miller time as the prohibition against his books was lifted. I wanted to be a book on a shelf sharing pages with you, Henry. I wanted no space between us. Cheek to cheek with your verbal matrix, I wanted a warm hand to open me up so I could leap out with punctilious poetry. I ingested your vision from a distance.

TREK 122

In 1969 the film director Josef von Sternberg dies.

As the dry decade of the 1920's continued, bohemians wet themselves with a dip in Washington Square Fountain. People could still tipple in the Village because speakeasies sprung up like weeds. Thirsty patrons headed to the dark bastions of alcohol to imbibe the forbidden liquid.

In 1922 Eugene O'Neill wrote a play about characters that spent more time in bars than in church. O'Neill was a hard drinker himself and preferred the company of misfits.

In 1962 Ken Kesey presented his bohemian free-thinker Randle Patrick McMurphy, who collides with the power structure and is given a choice between jail, the army or the bughouse.

McMurphy opts to billet with the crazies in "One Flew Over the Cuckoo's Nest". He is like Golden Boy John Reed, full of vim and vigor and instigating revolution at every corner. John goes to Russia to study the 1917 revolution. In America he goes to court for sedition and has his passport revoked. To make McMurphy's behavior more compliant, the institution gives him a lobotomy.

In 1922 Marcel Proust died in his cork-lined room. In 1962 John Steinbeck and his dog went in search of America in "Travels with Charley".

In 1922 Gandhi was sentenced to six years of imprisonment for civil disobedience. In 1962 Alexander Solzhenitsyn wrote a novel about a man confined to a labor camp in "One Day in the Life of Ivan Denisovich".

In 1962 my hair was cut short like the infield lawn on a baseball diamond. My mother converted a room in our house into a beauty shop. Living next door to her place of work meant she could book clients early or late.

Sometimes her first appointment was at 7 a.m. and her last customer was a late night vodka drinker. As long as Mrs. Seabreeze was awake she had a drink in her hand. Mom fixed her drinks as she cut her hair and painted her toenails. Mrs. Seabreeze was a good tipper.

The doorway between the shop and the living room was boarded up except for a small reach-through aperture to answer the phone from either side. The smell of moisturizing shampoo, neutralizing solution and other products for hair color, perms and skin care wafted through constantly.

TREK 123

In the 1969 British drama "A Touch of Love", Sandy Dennis has a job and a nice baby, what more could a single girl want?

Compare the history of the 1920's to the 1960's and the similarities fill the Columbia River Gorge.

In 1923 Edna Saint Vincent Millay burned her candles at both ends. She separated "A Few Figs from Thistles" and rode the Staten Island Ferry back and forth all night.

In 1923 Robert Frost was busy writing poems. In 1963 he turned to frost in the clearing. In 1923 Jean Toomer wrote "Cane". In 1963 W.E.B. DuBois lay down in Ghana in August, almost coinciding with the March on Washington.

On November 22, 1963, John Kennedy was killed. Blood in Dallas. I was in the hallway between class changes. A freshman student with a history book in his hand ran through the hall yelling, "Kennedy was shot!"

The hallway was crowded. I stopped to watch the messenger depart through double doors. Soon I was lost in an enormous vortex of cacophony. I saw crime displayed in bright colors. I became despondent and left the hall for a class on W.B. Yeats. He has warned us: the blood-dimmed tide is loosed upon the land.

I could not believe that Jackie was a widow. It must be a post-Halloween April Fools Day joke, but I won't be fooled again.

Who will be next? When the shooting starts even children are killed. Leave gun play for the movies. Blow up buildings in the movies so extras can be paid to dress up and hang out on the set while snow collects on volcano rim.

But conformation arrived. They turned us out of school early. I watched the news. It was an orchestrated press release. Someone gave the announcer a news release.

The announcer didn't know anymore about it than I did. I felt helpless to turn the tide of blood. I learned to pray. It was the strongest way. Not on my knees but while walking a blue highway.

I prayed incessantly to fill a blank mind. Prayed to defeat the power of destructive forces. Prayed while waiting for a VW to turn over. Prayed for the Chinese to vacate Tibet so I could escort the Dalai Lama back to the sacred heights and help rebuild the walls of the monastery, to plant fruit trees on the way.

I prayed unceasingly and drove into a harem of belly dancers; prayed while soldiers threw their guns into Popocatepetl.

We should pray until we get it right, pray day and night, believe in the power of prayer because it makes more sense than killing people and I can't afford health insurance, so I have to manage myself on a healthy path.

TREK 124

> *In 1969 Dr. Who, a maverick scientist and adventurer, traverses space and time on British TV.*

In 1924 Charles S. Johnson connected Harlem writers with the Greenwich Village community at a Civic Club dinner. "Dixie to Broadway" paraded an all-black revue while O'Neill described infanticide in "Desire Under the Elms".

In 1964 Sidney Poitier won best actor Oscar in "Field of Lilies". The Beatles experienced "A Hard Day's Night". In 1924 Harlem was alive with big jazz bands and high pitched artistic activity. In 1924 in "There is Confusion", Joanna wants to hear a "story 'bout somebody great, Daddy." In 1964 Harlem erupted in riots.

The behavioral patterns of the bohemians, beats and hippies are characteristically freer of social constraints. Couples enjoy each other's favors without sanctimonious marriage. In the 1920's the hemline went up to reveal more leg. In the 1960's women burned their bras. The 1920's Village scene included bohemians who worked hard and carried soirees to heights of sensuality.

Amiee Cortez arrived at Village parties prepared to entertain. She boasted that she had the most beautiful body of any woman present. To prove it she swung into a freestyle, joyous, wild dance that culminated with her removing all her clothes. On occasion, to conclude her show stopping performance, she would throw herself into the arms of a bug-eyed male and they would retire to the nearest bedroom. Guests would pull blankets and pillows off the bed of the host so they could cushion their love-making. The bootleggers kept the revelers supplied with gin.

In the '60s, alternative types were less squeamish about na-kedness. People skinny-dipped together, entered the tight con-fines of a sweat lodge, bodies pressed against bodies, naked together.

We stripped near the pond and plastered mud on each other until it was like a new layer of skin. We laid together on a blanket while the sun dried the mud to a rhinoceros-like hide, totally en-capsulated in earth except our lips that were free to intake elec-tric Kool-Aid through a straw and exchange bird peck kisses.

Couples zipped themselves up in sleeping bags like a split frankfurter in a hotdog bun. Others crawled into the sanctuary of pup tents. Others connected like animals in heat, in plain view of friends, plants and children.

TREK 125

In "Hell's Angels 1969", there is a scheme to rip off Caesar's Palace Casino in Las Vegas.

In 1925 Dr. Alain Locke collected massive material for his book "The New Negro". Malcolm X was born. In 1965 Malcolm left his wife Betty Shabazz in the same straights that his mother had been left in, all alone with many children to raise. When President Kennedy was killed the Honorable Elijah Muhammad advised Malcolm not to comment on it. But he found the occasion too advantageous to pass up the chance to make an historical allusion about the chickens coming home to roost.

Elijah had many steadfast followers. He had been a mentor to Malcolm. Perhaps it was not appropriate for Malcolm to take to task his former leader's sexual indiscretions in a public forum. He could have criticized him in private. If whites were the enemy, he should not have given the white press ammunition to use against the Nation of Islam. Instead of giving a speech in the Audubon Ballroom in Harlem he could have taken his family of young girls to the Catskills for an outing.

Members of the counterculture from the 1920's and 1960's had a flippant attitude toward money. In the '20s Robert Clair-mont was a wealthy, playboy poet who maintained an apartment in the Village. Merrymakers arrived at his residence in droves.

His door was always open and he paid for everything. If the furniture was smashed, he ordered new. If the booze ran low, he called for more. After days of continuous celebration Robert got tired and left town. His doors remained open and the party continued with people ordering more supplies as the need arose and charged it to the absent Robert. Upon his return he picked up the tab. He continued rolling in money until the market crash of 1929. He waited for the market to spring back up, but it never did. When he realized that his wealth was gone, he joined with some of his friends and spent his last $1,000 on a final party. When he woke up next morning he was broke.

TREK 126

"The 1969 British horror movie "The Crucible of Horror" is a chilling story of a terrorized wife who plots to murder her sadistic husband.

In 1926 Wallace Thurman edited a magazine called "Fire". Thurman was not included in "The New Negro". He was a small press editor with a purely artistic focus.

In 1968 the anthology "Black Fire" appeared, edited by Larry Neal and Amiri Baraka. In bulk and scope it was akin to "The New Negro", but in spirit and name it rose from the ashes of "Fire".

In his magazine Thurman wrote a story about Cordelia the Crude, a woman who pays twenty-five cents admission into The Roosevelt Motion Picture Theatre to pick up men. She sits alone until approached by a horny male who plops down next to her and touches her, as if by accident. If she is agreeable they have a petting party and relocate for more extended intercourse.

In 1926 Mae West ran afoul of the Society for the Suppression of Vice for her repartee and suggestive body language. In 1966 "Alfie" scored with as many women as possible.

In 1926 Carl Van Vechten hit with "Nigger Heaven". He used the Harlem material for his best seller. He was privy to inside information, being a trusted member of the Harlem circle of artists. Many voices in the black community responded angrily to the novel. They felt he had betrayed his relationship to Harlem.

The story drew attention to the teeming excitement of the flesh pots and cabarets like the Cotton Club that featured the jazz of Duke Ellington. A tourism developed bringing money into

Harlem from white folks that wanted to hear Cootie Williams pronounce Harlem on his trumpet and watch exuberant dancing.

I think Van Vechten was more memorable as a photographer than as a writer. His main character is a drab loser. Paul Byron wants to be a writer but he is an abysmal failure. The novel has a cheap, violent ending. In 1966 Truman Capote captured the temper of his times with "In Cold Blood". Whereas Van Vechten's characters are superficially treated, Capote explored in great psychological depth the inner life and motivations of two misfits who murder a family.

In 1966 I enjoyed listening to rock-and-roll and dancing at private parties. With the music and spirits flowing, one did not need a partner. Everybody danced together. A room full of flailing arms and smiling faces was not the same as the Savoy Ballroom in Harlem with a thousand jitterbuggers on the floor, but one night I met a fabulous girl from Utah that I wanted to lavish with late-night hospitality. She was most amenable to my raillery until her husband arrived and escorted her away.

TREK 127

In 1969 John and Yoko Ono Lennon lay down in a hotel bed surrounded by journalists and announced their mission for peace.

In 1927 the talkies broke the silence of film. A white man blacked his face and dropped on one knee to sing "Mammy." In 1927 Sacco and Vanzetti were executed. Marcus Garvey was deported.

In 1967 the Swedish film "I Am Curious Yellow" was seized by Customs and banned in the U.S. It was released from the lock-up when the aesthetic-minded supported its artistic merits. It offered nudity and sex, but even more damaging to its distribution was its anti-war sentiment and homage to Dr. King. He had recently called America the great purveyor of violence. A film called "Bonnie and Clyde" confirmed his assessment. It took depiction of cinematic violence to new heights. Bonnie and Clyde were bank robbers, so they deserved to be riddled with bullets from ambush. It disturbed me that violence was acceptable but naked bodies were offensive.

While studying "Troubled Sleep" by Jean Paul Sartre, I fell asleep and experienced the following dream:

Backpack Trekker: A 60's Flashback

I rode a horse-powered buggy with my wife and three children. We were enroute to Boot Hill to place flowers on the grave of the unknown poet. A pack of wolves started to chase us. I tried to out-distance them by whipping the horse with a wet peacock plume. The wolves continued to pursue us until I tried to placate them by throwing my youngest child out as a sacrifice. The wolves devoured the child on the run and continued to gain on us until out of fright I threw my daughter to the wolves. Some of our pursuers slowed to rend my child while others of the pack closed in for a larger meal. Our horse stumbled in a prairie dog hole and the wolves jumped on top of us, teeth first. Suddenly the wolves were killed by random gunfire.

I moved the remainder of my family to the big city. I got a job in a munitions factory and put a down payment on a car. My wife became tired of housework. She filled the washing machine with gifts I had bought for her during our twelve-year marriage. She took all our family photo albums and stored them in the freezer. Then she became a street hooker and contracted a social disease. My remaining son became a dope dealer and was gunned down by federal agents in a low-income neighborhood.

I drove my car and did not come to a complete halt at a stop sign. Suddenly state troopers were chasing me at high speed. I threw my money out the widow. Some cops stopped while others continued the chase. Soon they forced me off the road. They beat me unconscious and I woke up in a pit surrounded by wolves.

TREK 128

> In 1968 The Rolling Stones produced "Rock and Roll Circus".

In 1928 Claude McKay created a best-seller with "Home to Harlem". Charles S. Johnson took a job at Fisk University in Nashville. D. H. Lawrence made a statement for sexuality in "Lady Chatterley's Lover" and William Elmer Harmon bequeathed $500,000 to endow awards for African-American achievement, making possible the first all-Negro exhibition in 1928.

In 1968 the counterculture was presented in a "Hair" raising experience. "The Great White Hope" showed that Jack Johnson still carried a wallop. Motown took a hard hit in 1968 when Dr. Martin Luther King, Jr. was killed. Riots broke out in Detroit. Riotous activity and violence dominated the consciousness of the country as citizens talked about the police action in Vietnam and the war in America. I was on a college campus when I heard the news of our slain spiritual leader.

My friend Ralph, who had protested in Warsaw against governmental interference in cultural affairs, had invited me on a retreat to contemplate devotion to Jesus. The news arrived as we discussed John Lennon's appearance in "Rock and Roll Circus" without the Beatles. The blood of the lamb sullied the Mississippi River.

After Dr. King was killed we were not given to airy songs. I felt we had lost the best. The King was dead and the throne was surrounded by spotted hyena. I went into a depression and had to drop a class on American history to stay at an even keel with my grade-point average.

I told Ralph I would attend the retreat to mourn the loss of Dr. King. After three days of clean mountain air I accepted Jesus as one of the many masters sent by God to guide our misbegotten brood. Three days later we drove to Fort Sill, Oklahoma. At the grave of Geronimo, I touched the stones and closed my eyes to pray. I left my American history text in the Apache cemetery. It had resale value, but I didn't want the blood money.

We drove to Palo Duro Canyon and walked to Lighthouse Rock. I prayed to be as independent as possible because the people I love might not be around when a crisis occurred for me.

Visualize world peace. Visualize a kingdom where spiritual degrees are presented at graduation ceremonies. Wear the cap and gown like a halo and wings. Let sorrow soar. Let joy swing higher than the treetops. Recommit energy flow to a path toward the light. Don't play chess in the dark. Travel without fear. Repeat the names of loved ones like a mantra. Listen for news of the next gathering of kindred spirits.

Join the circus and roll toward freedom.

TREK 129

In 1969 blues record producer Leonard Chess died.

1929 and 1969 closed out two exciting decades. The curtain fell on the sound and fury of artistic expression. In 1929 the economic system took a jolt on Black Friday. The Saint Valentine's Day Massacre left seven dead in a gang-related execution.

Backpack Trekker: A 60's Flashback

Two white men using Negro dialects went on radio as "Amos 'n Andy." Martin Luther King, Jr. was born just as Countee Cullen wrote "The Black Christ".

In 1969 the doors closed on Jim Morrison's concert tour. Diana Ross and the Supremes stopped their hit parade. Tina Turner sang "Proud Mary". At ten years old Michael Jackson was already a professional entertainer.

D.A. Pennebaker filmed a concert of Little Richard at the Toronto Rock and Roll Revival of 1969. Pennebaker also filmed Dylan's tour of England and turned it into a film called, "Don't Look Back".

Why wasn't Dylan involved at the Woodstock Festival? Plenty to point a camera at during the labyrinth of activity: people playing in the mud, exposed and accepting of nature's laconic treatment; people sitting under plastic waiting for something better to happen; the excitement of combining water and electricity; people sleeping on top of their cars; parking lot parties springing up when the stage was too far away and the ice chest too heavy to lug around.

There were some of the best electric rock guitar players ever back then: Alvin Lee; Johnny Winters, Carlos Santana. Carlos was from the Bay Area via Mexico. The East Coast was not familiar with the Latino soaring guitar congas. When Santana was introduced the crowd kept on with whatever they were doing. When Santana left the stage the spell of black magic filled the field.

The Rolling Stones were not on the bill at Woodstock. Leaving no stone unturned, Mick and friends wanted to capitalize on the success of Woodstock and have their own free concert on the West Coast. They announced intentions to join The Grateful Dead and other Bay Area groups for a Golden Gate Park event in December. The city denied them access. The promoters relocated to Altamont Speedway. They wanted to make a movie, too.

At their event violence broke out near the stage. The cameras recorded it. The Dead opted not to play even without viewing the footage. The Stones rolled on like the muddy waters of music. Maybe the movie would give them shelter. They had recorded with Chess Records. They knew how to strategize the game. Both the '20s and '60s ended with violent imagery.

Beatlick Joe Speer

In 1969 sax player Coleman Hawkins died.

Anton Chekhov wrote a story called "The Bet" with a character who changes his attitude in regards to the control money will have on his life. Some men are arguing about the death penalty versus life imprisonment. One man feels a quick execution is preferable to a slow death by confinement. Another man disagrees, saying the continuance of life under incarceration is better than having the life force snuffed out prematurely. They make a bet. A millionaire banker bets two million rubles that one of the men cannot endure a five-year voluntary lock up. The man responds with the bravado of a "Cool Hand Luke" when he asserted he could eat fifty eggs instead of thirty-five. The man avows he will endure fifteen years of isolation to earn the money.

He is locked up and the banker retains the key. Early in his confinement the man is heard to weep and utter disconsolate sounds, but after a time he settles into his separate existence. He requisitions books and wine. He studies languages and comparative religion. Five years pass. Ten years elapse. Finally he has twenty-four hours left to complete his term.

The banker is very agitated about having to pay up because during the intervening years his financial status has changed. He is no longer an economic mogul. To lose the bet will be his financial ruin. The banker determines the only way out is for the prisoner to die. No stay of execution is possible while he stands to lose two million rubles. He decides to smother him to make it look like he died in his sleep.

With the key he lets himself into the room. The prisoner is at his table. The banker sneaks up from behind to execute the dastardly deed, but finds the man asleep. He hesitates long enough to notice a letter on the table. The prisoner has undergone a change of attitude. He no longer values money and to prove it he has decided to leave his confinement five minutes before his time is complete. The banker shutters at the audacity of his potential homicidal act. He retreats without waking the inmate.

The next day news arrives that the prisoner has disappeared. The banker goes to confirm the fact that he wins the bet. He sees the note on the table and removes it. He locks it up in his safe.

Russian writers have a history of being jailed or exiled for their literary contributions. Dostoevsky was arrested and sent to

Backpack Trekker: A 60's Flashback

Siberia. Vladimir Korolenko spent a great part of his life in exile. Maxim Gorky was exiled at the height of his career. Boris Pasternak was expelled by the Soviet Writers Union. Alexander Solzhenitsyn spent years in labor camps and in exile, accused of slandering his country.

TREK 131

In 1969 The Grinnell Natural Area was established at the University of California at Berkeley.

I camped for three days at Paria, an old movie set in southern Utah. It was an enjoyable location because it had the appearance of a town, but no inhabitants.

On my second day there a man arrived in a station wagon with lodge pole pines sticking out the back. His name was Raymond Manning. He was a part-time prospector from the eastern slopes of the Sierra Nevadas.

He also earned money as a handyman laying flagstone patios or doing plaster and stucco work. His faded blue bandanna was mostly hidden by a black beard. A dusty black hat shaded his squinted eyes.

He carried his accommodations with him in the form of a tepee. The canvas he used was made from sturdy hemp. I helped him set up his shelter and was amazed to discover hand-painted designs of the devil's cornfield. The floor of his tepee was composed of sheep skins. The covering flap for the entrance was the hide of a white buffalo. We made a campfire in the middle of the street. As it turned out we both had an affinity for desolate areas.

"I haven't lived in a city for seven years," he remarked. "The closest I've come to city life is holding up on the outskirts of Mexican Hat while waiting for a piece of mail to arrive general delivery."

"I like the population of this community," I said. "I'm sure it has a low crime rate. And where else can we camp in the middle of the street? In most cities the long arm of the law knocks on your window after midnight to inform you it's illegal to sleep in your vehicle."

"Did you ever read 'The Brave Cowboy' by Edward Abbey?" he asked.

"No," I replied, "but I saw the movie based on the novel called 'Lonely are the Brave' with Kirk Douglas and Walter Matthau.

Kirk leaves his girlfriend and flees into the wilderness, but the gum chewing cop is in hot pursuit."

"And civilization eliminates him like a canker," Raymond continued. "On a rainy night a semi-truck kills him and his horse. The mechanized world wipes him off the visage of the earth, like a windshield wiper slapping a bug to one side."

"That's right," I said. "And what appropriate symbolism. The horse was the main means of transportation of the old west. The conquistadors explored on horseback. The Plains Indians traveled by horse, following the buffalo and transporting their belongings by travois. The Apaches used horses to flee into Mexico to hide from federal troops. When the train appeared they called it the iron horse. When the car arrived the horse became a toy for the rich. Horse trails were replaced with concrete highways."

We talked for most of the night without disagreement on any topic.

TREK 132

In 1969 Arna Bontemps released
his book "Great Slave Narratives".

Raymond Manning had worked as editor of his school newspaper. He caught heat from the administration for espousing unpopular causes. Several of his editorials were inspired when local law enforcement agents began a crackdown on street prostitutes. A female cop in a leather mini-dress arrested his sports editor when he approached her for service. Raymond became indignant and wrote a scathing article about prostitution. He insisted that if it was illegal to solicit skin trade on the street then the female cop pretending to be in business was also breaking the law. Raymond said there was one law for the poor and a separate scenario for the rich. Why is it, he asked, that a well heeled business man from out of state can arrive in town, settle into his hotel room, call an escort service, and have the merchandise delivered to his room? Why are only the lower-echelon prostitutes subjected to constant crackdowns? The top-dollar call girls are not busted. Why are the independent operators run out of business while the women who make their pimps rich are permitted to continue?

People can be promiscuous and share their bodies for free without legal recriminations, but offer sex for sale and the law gets involved. This indicates that the legal concern is over economics and not morality. Raymond felt the demonizing of streetwalkers was conducted for economic control. The state wants to shut down people making undisclosed amounts of money. The independent women are put out of business so the big-time sex vendors can control the market. They want us to have one choice instead of freedom of choice.

Manning believed through legalization of prostitution the health problems involved could be better dealt with. Since the government is mainly concerned about the exchange of money, they could better control the process legally and augment their revenues by selling more business licenses. The administration took him to task for his views. He was soon reduced to typesetting ads.

"I quit the paper," he said, "and submitted to underground publications. I had articles published but it didn't change anything. I gave up writing and learned to play guitar. I used music to deliver my message. People were more willing to listen when I incorporated rhythm. With music I entered through the back door of their consciousness. My guitar was my M-16. With music I took aim at the smallmindedness around me."

TREK 133

> In 1970 the movie "Hell's Belles" features a biker
> who has his ride stolen and chases the offenders
> across the Arizona desert.

Life in Paria was calm and uneventful until Raymond Manning arrived. He played guitar and sang original tunes at night as we burned boards off the sidewalk for a fire. His motive for playing music was to capture an audience. He had strong ideas to convey and felt expression through music was stronger than the written or spoken word.

The determination of his grandmother had a lasting influence on his will to succeed. He told me a story about how she stopped driving even though she still had her driver's license. Raymond took over driving her to the store and waited in the car as she pushed her shopping cart up and down the aisles, matching coupons with products. The waiting gave him time to practice chord changes in the car. She insisted that he serenade her after he unloaded her groceries. She did not want to hear his protest songs. She enjoyed songs like "The Old Rugged Cross" and "Rocky Top". He tried to introduce her to recent music, especially the late Yardbirds lineup with lead guitarists Jeff Beck and Jimmy Page. But she rejected that as a devil's brew.

One day after not driving for a year she felt very spunky. She wanted to cruise the strip and find out what the young people were doing. Raymond did not consider this a good idea. Before she stopped driving she had knocked down two mailboxes and almost ran over a lady pushing a perambulator. He felt she was lucky to call it quits before having to file insurance claims or incur extensive medical bills. The idea of her behind the wheel again was frightening. But he knew if he negated her freedom of choice she would be on the road again in no time. So he encouraged her by changing the oil and filling the tank up with high-octane gas. This startled her because she expected resistance. He even suggested she drive at night to avoid traffic. Raymond had secretly set her car up on blocks.

One dark night he rousted her up and offered to accompany her as she drove the car. She was reluctant, but he hustled her out to the driveway and helped her into the driver's seat. She was nervous and didn't realize the car was propped up. She started the car and shifted it into drive. Raymond directed her.

"Step on it Granny. Stop here. Turn left. Turn right. Look out. You almost hit that kid on a bike." After ten minutes of "driving", she wanted to park it. He directed her back home and helped her out of the car. She was shaky after the experience, but she never talked about driving again. Raymond continued to rib her with comments like: "Hey Granny, let's make a cross country trip. We can take turns driving. You can take the easy parts like coming down Tioga Pass."

TREK 134

Louis Malle takes a six-month voyage to India and makes a feature-length documentary entitled "Calcutta", released in 1969.

My friendships that summer did not have much carry-over value. When I was with someone we spoke in cozy conversation to share details and representative anecdotes, but when we separated I lost the connection. I should add people to an expandable address book and include them on a postcard list.

Backpack Trekker: A 60's Flashback

Traveling and meeting different people every day found me afloat in the wash of events. Relationships turned into wind patterns. I became separated from people.

I was like flowing water, not connected to the shore, no money in the bank and refusing to drive a tank. I felt like a person squeezed in the crowd trying to get a better view of the stage. I was a solitary stick figure on a kaleidoscopic landscape.

Any stranger may spill words from an unknown source that might yield bountiful poetic treasure. I wrote them down before they blew away like clouds over Monument Valley. I felt the aloneness of time like a stone butte on Navajo land. I enjoyed the frenzied activity of urban areas, but I felt most complete in a forgotten ghost town. My heart pumped blood like any other living organism, but it exemplified as much sentiment as a hard tree trunk from the petrified forest.

My two lifelines to humanity were Zen Jazz and my mother María. As I traveled in the summer the relationship with María was conducted through the mail.

I relished my student deferment and enjoyed a regiment of required reading at the university. Sometimes in my off-campus housing I thought how smooth to pass through the world unnoticed, leaving no trace and moving silently like the wind or water. But the winds can increase in velocity and fell trees or tear a roof off a housetop. Water can swell to torrential proportions and displace solid land mass or gradually wear away stone.

I dreamed of performing random acts of kindness. I considered Jude the obscure my brother. I saw myself passing through life like a shadow moving across the rim of the Grand Canyon. Only in my dreams did I experience any ongoing semblance of connectedness. I dreamed of achievement through hard work; of creation through original manipulation of DNA cells; of standing on Pike's Peak to wave a ten-foot red banner; of shouting across the gorge of despondency and hearing my voice echo; of seeing my image refracted by a pendant prism dangling from the claw of an eagle in flight.

In dreams I expanded beyond the narrow limits of my road map. In the world I accepted my aloneness like a prison term of indefinite duration.

Beatlick Joe Speer

*In "Phantom India" of 1969, Louis Malle makes a
seven-part TV series on poverty, overcrowding,
and other aspects of life in India.*

When Raymond Manning told me the story of his grandmother driving him around in a car that was propped up on cinder
blocks, it reminded me of my *abuela*. My grandma never drove a
car. She used a horse and buggy until the encroachment of
paved roads made it impossible or illegal to use a horse. When
the grid pattern of fences and roads was established it precluded
even going for a walk unless it was along the side of the road.

The practice of pedestrianism was past. She sold her horse
and used her wagon as a flower bed. Her children drove her to
church on Sunday and to the farmer's market. She always maintained a large garden so she sold and bartered vegetables. She
irrigated and aerated her rows of green chile, then she weeded
and kneaded flour tortillas. Her main job was providing nourishment for eleven children and three grandchildren born to a
daughter who died of pneumonia at a young age. She never
bought a television so she had no need for English. Her children
did not speak English until they enrolled in public school, where
Spanish was not allowed.

In good weather my *abuelita* spent the day out of doors.
When she rested from hoeing her rows she sat in the shade. She
exchanged baby-sitting services for cords of pine and oak for her
wood stove. A hatchet was her tool to prepare kindling from dead
branches collected on her property. With her crusted right hand
she split wood to fit into the fire trough of the stove. With a hot
stove she prepared seven tortillas at a time, flipping them over
with her fingers. As she was reluctant to hook up electricity, she
stayed outdoors most nights until it was time to go to bed. Her
last act of the day was to say her rosary. She said the prayers
aloud, lying on her back with her head on a pillow. It was her desire to die peacefully in her sleep. The end finally came after her
children were married, in the military, or moved out. It came one
fall when the harvest was in and the fruit trees had delivered their
bounty. It came at the close of a day full of hard work. It was a
perfect day with colors changing and the nights turning cool.

They found her in the morning lying on her back, a smile on
her face and a rosary in her hand.

Backpack Trekker: A 60's Flashback

In 1969 three top-rated TV shows were "Bonanza", "Gunsmoke" and "The Beverly Hillbillies".

Robert Rosy dropped out of high school in 1969 because after his class visited Ann Arbor, Michigan, he realized certain areas had a buzz on and his hometown was not happening. He rode the bus to LA where he earned some money selling copies of the "LA Free Press".

Single copies sold for twenty-five cents and that left eleven cents for him. He waved the papers in a driver's face, as cars stopped at a red light on Hollywood Boulevard. As long as he kept one foot on the curb he could reach out and shake the paper at motorists.

At the end of his selling period he returned the unsold papers and received his payment in cash. He sold the papers for three weeks, but never bothered to read one. At the Twin Pools in Topanga Canyon he first discovered group nudity. The experience was so enjoyable he went several days without wearing clothes. One day in Palm Springs he found a cozy spot in the city park to stretch out for a nap. He dreamed it was raining, but when he opened his eyes the sky was azure and the sun was shining. He realized the lawn sprinklers were on so he ran out of reach of the watering system. Two city employees stood together laughing.

Robert tried his hand at hitchhiking and his longest ride was with a furniture moving van. The driver's name was Walter McClung from Imperial Beach, San Diego. Walter was a sturdy sixty-year old and liked to tell jokes. Robert's laughing at the jokes led to a job offer and two months of work. The driver paid him cash and bought his meals. Robert saved most of his money and got to see California from the elevated trucker position. They loaded and unloaded. Robert learned to strap a refrigerator to his back and heft it up stairs. He finally parted company with Walter in Salinas.

After the adventure wore off the road grew tiresome. Robert felt the days turn cold and he was suddenly anxious to finish his education. His madcap dash filled him with the desire to take a raft down the Colorado River, hike the Appalachian Trail, visit Horseshoe Falls with a red mackintosh, but he wanted to elevate his income so he could visit places with a greater deal of comfort.

He dedicated himself to academic life and studied with recrudescent vigor. His freshman year he became my fencing opponent for the fall semester.

TREK 137

> *In 1969 Jan Palach, a 21-year-old student, committed suicide by fire to protest the rollback of reform in Czechoslovakia.*

Querida María,

Being useful means having a positive influence on the lives of others. Fiction is interesting, but not always utilitarian. A 450-page novel by Sinclair Lewis like "Main Street" doesn't make it to the end of the street, whereas one verse from the New Testament gives a day's worth of meditation. A verse that recently plunged me into a whirligig of thought:

> *"Where is the wise? Where is the scholar? Hath not God made foolish the wisdom of this world?...the foolishness of God is wiser than men; and the weakness of God is stronger than men."*
> I Corinthians, 1:20

History tells us how the Greeks defeated Troy, Rome conquered Greece, the Vandals sacked Rome. Civilization tells us how the Mayans built pyramids in the jungle, how the Phoenicians sailed the seas, how the Incas constructed stone highways to traverse the Andes ... but there is a vast difference between man's knowledge and god's wisdom.

Man's ken can be catalogued or studied for amusement or gain, such as auto mechanics, atomic power, filmdom, cosmetology ... or it can be left at the grave side with tools, money, cosmetics ... Man's knowledge is useful for movement in this world, language to ask for a job, fossil fuels as energy ... Man's knowledge will advance the human mind, the science of life, the economic index ... It can be gained from newspaper articles, magazines, business college, experience ... God's knowledge promotes the human spirit ... It helps us move from this world to the next and can be obtained only by asking.

Colombia tiene un ocasión que se llama el día de los Inocentes; un dia para echar agua en cubetas o globos llenos de fluido, y tirar agua a cualquiera persona. Estuve sentado en el fondo del bus con la ventanilla abrierta cuando un arrastrado fulano de afuera me tiró con agua. Un chiste malecho, pero todos los pasajeros saltaron en risas. Después del incidente, cerré el vidrio, pero era como trancando el corral despues que se escapó el caballo. También los niños bloquearon la carretera en varios puestos para detener tráfico y pedir moneda. En Ipiales habián gente en los balcones echando agua encima de los caminantes abajo. En las cordilleras de los Andes los cultivadores sembran en las cuestas, taludes, de las montañas, dependiente en la lluvia por regar. Los nativos cortaron todos los árboles, por eso, las lomas son muy despobladas de madera.

Tu hijo

TREK 138

In 1969 Communist journalists met in North Korea to deal with the task of fighting "aggression of U.S. Imperialism."

"The Movie Goer" by Walker Percy peeked my interest because the main character is a film buff and the story opens in New Orleans during Mardi Gras. I thought he would trip off into cult or classic films like *"La Ronde"* by Max Ophuls, with dimly-lit interiors and the merry-go-round symbolizing human relationships, or "The Seventh Seal" with the knight playing chess with death. Visions of a scene like the travelers in "Easy Rider" tripping on acid in a cemetery filled my mind.

I thought the author would be in the thick of the February festival with thousands of bodies pressed together, helpless to scratch their noses while compressed like bundles of recycled cardboard; wildly costumed revelers cavorting; strangers giving in to passion; people lined up on Canal Street to vie for doubloons thrown from floats. But I was disappointed with the novel.

The main character, Binx, even leaves New Orleans during the festival for a trip to Chicago. He returns to the Big Easy on Mardi Gras Day, but his arrival is conducted like a traveler in a bus station of a strange city. He is oblivious to the festivities. "The Movie Goer" is probably a satisfactory novel to most readers, but since my expectations were dashed I cannot recommend it to anyone.

I spent several wonderful days in Paria then decided to relocate to Bryce Canyon National Park. Highway 89 west then north into the park was the easy route, but I decided to follow the Paria

Beatlick Joe Speer

River north to Cannonville and pick up Highway 12 which cuts across the northern top of the park. I boiled five pounds of pinto beans and dried them out to have plenty of nourishment for a wilderness experience. After walking twelve miles the first day I pitched my tent in a dry arroyo bed.

An arroyo is a smooth place to set up a tent. It is usually sandy, flat and free of unwanted protrusions of roots or rocks. The only problem with an arroyo was that if it rained upstream the water ran down smack into your camp site.

That night I enjoyed a lightening show off in the distance. The thunder sounded like an occasional timpani drum. I fell asleep and soon had a dream of floating on the river with Huck Finn. The rainfall in the north took about an hour to run down and inundate my camp. The next day I drug my belongings out of the arroyo and waited for the sun to dry me off.

TREK 139

In 1969 the United States and Mexico completed construction of Amistad Dam on the Rio Grande near Del Rio, Texas.

One day while sitting quietly in the shade, a roadrunner slammed on its breaks in front of me. A person can tramp through nature and never see local wildlife. Human chatter and movement caused animals to hide or hightail it. But when one is blended into the environment, when their heart rate is a balanced rhythm and not a distress signal, then animals appeared unafraid. The roadrunner and I made visual contact. Something in me changed. I felt a shiver down my spine and spoke Spanish to the bird. It understood my lingo and responded by scratching on the ground. When I examined the marks I discovered its easy familiarity with Castilian. The accents and tildes were all appropriately placed. The runner wrote that Spanish was learned many summers ago from bearded men on horseback searching for riches. The fleet-footed birds knew the indigenous dialects and were able to serve as translators for the Spaniards.

As letter writers in India transcribed dictation for illiterate persons, the runners served as liaisons between the European and Native American cultures. The difference between the service was that the Indian secretaries requested a stipend whereas the runners had no use for money. They mediated for the two groups to stave off the hacking broadsword, the thrust of the rapier, the pull of a halberd and the litany of warm blood exposed to the air.

The runner was appalled by my paltry diet of dried pinto beans. It offered to provide a meal of meat.

It killed a rattlesnake and dragged it over to me. I skinned it with my knife and cut *hors d'oeuvre*-sized strips to feed the runner. I cooked my bits on juniper skewers. We pulverized the rattle and made a tea. We discoursed until sunset. I could not decipher the markings in the dirt after dark. The runner was headed for the Kanab Plateau to participate in a feather swap.

The runner was excited about the event because a large macaw contingent from Guatemala was expected to attend. It flicked its tail and disappeared in the dark.

The wind blew hard that night. In the morning the words in the earth were erased.

There was no trace of our relationship.

TREK 140

In 1969 a revolt against the Pentagon was started because of its huge budget and its close link between the armed services and defense contractors – the "military-industrial complex."

While walking north along the Paria River in Utah, I met a coyote with one leg caught in a steel trap. It had been thus detained for many hours.

All its resistance had been squeezed out. I petted it tentatively because I didn't want a bite to infuse me with rabies.

The coyote was as passive as a flower child placing the stem of a white rose down the barrel of an M-16. I grabbed the jaws of the trap like Samson manhandling the lion's mouth and released the frightened animal.

Blessings to the canon of pantheistic deities. The leg was not broken. I gave him water and four ounces of roasted rattlesnake meat. I carried him to a spot of shade and applied shiatsu therapeutics.

He responded so quickly that I was encouraged to use a discarded porcupine quill one-twentieth the size of a hypodermic needle. This technique created no bleeding and minimal side effects. I completed the cure with a session in reflexology.

The last time I was stricken by a pesky virus I had a room rented with an octogenarian artist who used crutches to move around. Her name was Mrs. Smith and she served as den mother to three under-graduate students.

I retired to my room one day, emaciated and silent. She entered my room with a presentiment that an undertow of sibilant infirmity had weakened my limbs.

She sat by my bedside and told me a story about a nightingale that sang for a monarch and made him feel good. Some jealous underlings introduced a mechanical nightingale that sang as beautifully as the real bird. The king paid more attention to the fake bird. The real bird felt neglected and flew away. The fake broke and the king was left without the beautiful singing of the nightingale.

Mrs. Smith told me stories until I forgot about being sick. I decided to apply the same cure to the coyote, so I invented a random narrative about traveling on foot through Big Bend National Park and encountering a hungry *javelina* that chased me to the hot springs. The hot water was contained in an old foundation along the Rio Grande near the mouth of Boquillas Canyon.

I climbed into the water and the wild pig followed me with teeth foremost. The soothing effects of warm water calmed the pig. We became amicable and splashed around like two kids in a backyard pool. My stories were avidly absorbed by the wounded coyote. He forgot about his hurt limb, stood up on his own legs and was ready to start trucking.

TREK 141

> In 1969 the Bay Area Rapid Transit sank the last
> section of its prefabricated Transbay Tube under
> San Francisco Bay.

The coyote was on its way to a consortium of carnivores when the trap unexpectedly detained his progress. Once released from the trap he rested and rebounded to a state of vigorous health. We joined forces and walked north together.

The coyote had a tuft of red hair above his forehead and an amatory expression on his face. He reminded me of my Zen jazz-poet friend so much that I called him Coyote Zen.

"Are you ready to go Coyote Zen?" I asked. The coyote walked ahead of me, stopping sporadically to look back and see if I was maintaining the pace. I enjoyed traveling with Coyote Zen. We communicated with our eyes and body movements. Conversation was unnecessary. We traveled smoothly without discourse or conflict. It reminded me of when my friend Zen Jazz and I traveled to California. Zen conducted all the verbal exchanges as I took a vow of silence. Since the words between us had no special meaning I decided to practice my French on the coyote.

"Je suis un petit peu fatiguée."

From the intonation the coyote inferred my meaning and stopped to rest before I did. When I called it *"le gardien de la campagne,"* he smiled in agreement.

When I shouted *"Allez!"* he was up and trotting.

After I enunciated *"J'ai beaucoup de faim,"* the coyote ran off. I thought he had become exasperated with my mundane comments and decided to abandon me without a farewell, but after ten minutes he reappeared with a small rabbit in his mouth.

"Je suis très heureux a manger viande," I said. He dropped the hare at me feet. I skinned and cooked it. After the meal and the twenty miles we had walked that day I felt exhausted.

"Je voudrais reposer." The coyote curled up at the foot of my sleeping bag. We howled at the night. Our voices blended together. We slept soundly.

During the night our thoughts and dreams meshed and overlapped. *C'est vrai*!

In my dreams I shouted poetry at the moon. I dug a burrow in the side of a hill and waited for my dinner to pass by. I was nonplussed as I covered fifty miles a day while avoiding roads and dodging bullets from ranchers.

J'essaye d'ouvirir la porte mais je ne peux pas. Tu vois?

I was weary of every extraneous sound as I wandered incessantly in search of food and a safe place to sleep.

TREK 142

In 1969 the United States and the Soviet Union held Strategic Arms Limitation Talks (SALT) in Helsinki, Finland.

Coyote Zen and I awoke simultaneously three minutes before the sun appeared on the horizon. We usually drank water and broke camp to a quick march for two consecutive hours. The sun can be unrelenting and unforgiving if one is exposed to its radiant force all day. Human skin is too delicate to absorb this energy that continuously presses downward and inward. From waterfall to meandering river, from the stiletto stabs of straight up noon to filtered light of pine tree forest, contact with nature is infallible choreography.

After putting some miles under our feet the coyote and I stopped in the shade for a leisurely breakfast. I always have green tea in the morning with honey. I boil a pot of water and pour off enough for two cups. The remaining water is for oatmeal with a smidgen of trail mix dropped in; afterwards the pot is removed from the heat to set five minutes on a flat stone.

I gave Coyote Zen some plain oatmeal with dried crushed sage sprinkled in and he swallowed it down without even masticating. The coyote spent most of his waking hours with at least one eye cocked for any auspicious tidbit. We shared a smooth togetherness until we discovered several recent cat prints in the dirt. It looked like a large mountain lion was just ahead of us. Coyote Zen processed a sample of air and his eyes validated the danger.

We walked more deliberately, like soldiers on patrol in the Cam Lo Valley in Vietnam. I stepped lightly as if doing a cakewalk around land mines. The big cat tracks continued to follow the Paria River. That was our direction and we did not want to veer off course and get lost.

We hiked one time from Caballo Lake to Isleta Pueblo in New Mexico. It was a 200-mile journey, but we followed the Rio Grande and arrived without any wasted effort. We could have stopped and waited until the lion changed direction or outdistanced us, but we looked at each other and decided to keep walking. The coyote and I were tight and more than willing to engage any feline hostility. After we sealed our determination with a howling duet, we spread out and continued to move in a unified direction, like two of the Magnificent Seven transporting a corpse to Boot Hill.

When the lion appeared we were as ready as the New York Jets offensive squad. The big cat growled at us and I let fly with a rock that clipped it on the right leg. I had a stone the size of a grapefruit in reserve. We kept walking and the lion did not pursue. We stayed on red alert for the next hour, but no confrontation ensued.

Backpack Trekker: A 60's Flashback

In 1969 a group of officers led by Captain Mohammad al-Qadafi toppled the ailing King of Libya in a coup d'etat and established a republic headed by a Revolutionary Command Council.

Querida María,

I was delayed two days at the Canadian border because the official who conducted the interview classified me as an undesirable. Fortunately his front desk did not carry the final clout. I protested, which kicked me up to another official with a private office. Unable to decide (he was a wishy-washy namby-pamby), he arranged a meeting for the following day with the judge. The reasons for my negative classification were:

1. no permanent address
2. no permanent employment
3. no means of transportation
4. not sufficiently funded.

I was offered counsel, but decided to plead my own case. The trial began and I swore on a book to tell the truth.

There was me, the adjudicator, and a man playing devil's advocate. He grilled me. In turn I replied to the accusations. I mentioned the initial official who discovered my shortcomings, resulting in my tramp, "burden to society" status. He was elderly, conservative, fixed in his ways. His logic amounted to the sum total of his value system, a system I had consciously rejected. His judgment of me was predicated on elements I had factored out of my life.

The opposition again attacked me. In my summation I was requested to present evidence to gainsay the four objections.

"I have no reservation at the Holiday Inn, no airplane ticket from Montreal to Quebec, no dignitaries waiting with bubbly to drink to my health. I learned my lifestyle from a master whose words are contained in the book I swore on at the commencement of the proceedings. He said take no care of what you shall eat, or wear, or where you shall sleep. He said if you have abundant faith you can perform wonders. What I offer as evidence is my faith that God will provide for me wherever I go, with whatever I need. I have traveled all over North America. While on extended nomadism I had no reason to maintain a domicile or a job. At times I had moolah galore but my funds were dwindling.

But whether I was well-heeled or down on my uppers I felt capable of a short visit to French Canada without being an imposition to Prime Minister Pierre Trudeau. My visit would fortify the channels of communications so necessary to the effective conduct of our two countries."

The trial adjourned for twenty minutes for the adjudicator to review the case and arrive at a decision. Thirty minutes later I was walking the open road toward Montreal.

TREK 144

In 1969 Richard Benjamin played a librarian from the Bronx who falls for college girl Ali MacGraw in the film "Goodbye Columbus".

As Coyote Zen and I slept under a cliff overhang one stormy night, our dreams and memories meshed together. We roamed the southwest like the Spaniards, outside all day, keeping an eye on the sarcophagus sky ready to intermeddle on our progress. We had two hours to make some arrangements before the storm hit. We ducked under the overhang as the first drops stirred up the dust and built a small fire for visual comfort. Then we slept to the sound of rain. An engorged Chama River blocked our route near Abiquiu. Coyote Zen was a good digger so he suggested we burrow a tunnel beneath the flowing water. That sounded like facetious crap spooned up by an avid waster of precious moments.

I suggested instead to construct a raft out of cottonwood logs tied together with barbed wire. We unraveled strands of wire from a nearby fence to secure a selection of downed logs. When our project was complete Coyote Zen stood on the deck of our craft like the captain. In lieu of a rudder, I hung onto the back, submerged in the water and kicking like a beaver en route to its underwater home. We navigated the river safely. Upon reaching the other side, Coyote Zen stood up and walked on two legs. I found myself unable to stand erect. I crawled like a quadruped. We traveled thus until sunset and made camp on the riverbank.

Coyote Zen built a fire. During the night I rolled over onto the hot coals and caught fire. I was so deep in sleep I could not move. I burnt slowly all night and in the morning only my teeth remained. Coyote Zen licked up the ashes and swallowed me. I mixed with his gastric juices. My essence secreted through his skin and hair. When I touched the earth my cells regrouped and I returned to my original human upright form.

Coyote Zen was so glad to see me he began to howl. We howled together until the moon appeared in the sky at midday. We heard explosions like batteries of cannons firing at each other. We woke to the sound of thunder. The rain fell forcefully in front of our sanctuary.

I put more wood on the coals and read to Coyote Zen from "The Brothers Karamazov". I explained how the three brothers represent the three parts of a person: Alyosha the spiritual, Ivan the intellectual, and Dmitri the emotional. But then we have the half-brother Smerdyakoz, the product of a scurrilous relationship. The illegitimate used murder to legitimatize itself.

Hypnotize me away from the lascivious use of dark force.

TREK 145

In 1969 Arlo Guthrie revealed he was not military material as he was briefly inducted into the U.S. Army in the film "Alice's Restaurant".

Coyote Zen and I hit the highway after days of hiking. I polished up my thumb and figured we could hook a ride on Highway 54 into the Pink Cliffs and check out the eroded rocks of Bryce Canyon. I've seen travelers hitchhike with a dog, so I figured there would be no problem with a small animal that could move with suavity. It took us ten minutes to snag a ride in a station wagon. It had extension ladders protruding out the back window. The driver was dressed in overalls with various buttons attached to his suspenders. He even had a "Free Huey" button. I liked the Black Panthers. Huey P. Newton was very photogenic with his sun glasses and black clothes. The Panthers were on the side of the North Vietnamese against U.S. aggression. They wanted to patrol their own neighborhoods and not be harassed by police who acted as occupational forces. They wanted to stand on the steps of the courthouse and shout, "Power to the People." They wanted someone from their party to be elected mayor. I say let's have a party, a Black Panther Party.

"Thanks for stopping sir," I said. "I have my friend Coyote Zen with me."

"Climb in," he said. Coyote Zen sat between us. "My name is Elmore Culiver. Where are you going?"

"Bryce Canyon."

"Just a few miles up the road," he said. "Your friend seems right comfortable traveling."

Sometimes while traveling I image myself as a character in a story, somebody like Alibi Ike, who Ring Lardner described as a ball player that never comes clean about why he does things. I explained to our host that we were on our way to a consortium of environmental warriors.

We planned to meet at Thor's Hammer in the Park, wear green armbands and talk about chaining ourselves to the last tree on Shakespeare Peak.

"You can stop at our place if you take a notion. My mother loves visitors and she can do justice to a banquet table. It looks like you need to elbow your way to some home-cooked vittles and stay until your clothes fit."

I looked at Coyote Zen and smiled. Coyote Zen blinked and cleaned his teeth several times with his tongue. "We thank you kindly sir," I said. "Our diet has suffered a dearth of protein lately. We'd be glad to help out with any work."

"Since you mention it, I have some hay that needs to be unloaded."

"We'd be more than willing to chuck a few bales around."

"Will your friend Coyote Zen help too?"

"Yo-heave-ho. We pull together. Coyote Zen will make sure there are no shirkers."

TREK 146

The 1969 film "Last Summer" set four teenagers on Fire Island to explore their sexual stirrings.

Mr. Culiver drove us in his station wagon to a ranch for the hot, home-cooked meal. He lived at the end of a narrow dirt road. As we pulled into the yard a group of mares were clustered near a fence where a stallion tried to dispose of a hard-on.

One of the mares had her rear end against the fence. The stud tried to mount her with the fence in between and got tangled up in the strands of barbed wire.

Coyote Zen jumped out of the car and went to work immediately, snapping at the horses heels and driving them away from taunting the stud. Mr. Culiver disengaged the stallion from its embarrassing position.

His mother emerged from the ranch house and stood in the yard with her hands on her hips. Mr. Culiver introduced her as Alice. She had layers of turquoise jewelry around her neck. Her wrists displayed enough silver and stone to give a weight lifter a serious hernia. She had straight gray hair and a friendly smile. We shook hands and she had a grip like a stone mason. She was fascinated with Coyote Zen as a domesticated wild animal. She loved animals and provided a home for a slew of cats, a pack of dogs, a small herd of horses and goats and a bevy of fowl. She probably spent more money feeding her menagerie than paying her taxes.

Coyote Zen and Alice got on swimmingly and he ended up in her kitchen with a bowl of goat's milk while *"Die Meistersinger von Nurnberg"* played on her turntable.

Mr. Culiver and I worked unloading bales of hay from his truck. He used two hooks to dig into the hay for maneuverability. He loaned me a pair of gloves and I picked the bales up by the wire and stacked them in the barn. We finished and washed off at the pump in cold water from a spring on their property. Once we were squeaky clean Alice called us inside.

Coyote Zen was already seated at the table with a plate in front of him and a napkin around his neck. She treated us to a meal of tuna-noodle casserole; spiced beef with dumplings; dandelion greens; zucchini; corn; asparagus covered with Hollandaise; cheese-frosted cauliflower and finished off with a fresh strawberry chiffon pie. It was the most delicious food I had eaten since my mother's enchiladas and posole.

TREK 147

In 1969 Richard Burton played Henry VIII in a compelling account of a famous love affair that involved adultery in the film "Anne of the Thousand Days".

The gray-haired Alice invited us to partake in an after-dinner cup of instant coffee. Her son referred to her as a buck Mormon. Despite this she still knew about Christ's appearance in the New World.

She was related to Ebenezer and Mary Bryce who were the first settlers to run cattle in the spectacular canyon lands of southern Utah. The history of the Latter Day Saints was familiar to her, but she liked to smoke and drink wine, and was adept at slinging colloquialisms with a rodeo rowdy or itinerant handyman.

For many years she operated a summer camp for girls. Nobody in her area was interested in a resort for youngsters. She traveled vast distances to drum up business for her ranch. No place was too far as she traveled to Chicago to distribute fliers in neighborhoods like Oak Park, Berwyn and Evanston. She offered special rates for church groups and YWCA members. When her business became solvent after several years, 80 percent of her clients came from the Chicago area. Camp girls were motivated by a free summer session if they could sell the idea to five other girls. Some girls enjoyed the experience so much that they returned year after year.

"This young man is a hardy worker," Mr. Culiver said to his mother. Alice's eyes dilated as if she had handled the plates which the Prophet had translated. She lit a cigarette and cleared her throat.

"We could use someone of your ilk to help out with the chores," she said. "Would you consider working here in exchange for room and board and $100 a month?" I looked at Coyote Zen. He smiled and showed his teeth. That was his way of acknowledging consent.

"I'm only available until the end of summer, then I have to return to the university. But as long as you do the cooking, I'd be happy to work for you. Coyote Zen is ready to sign a contract now."

"You don't have to sign anything," she said, "except to endorse your paycheck." We shook hands. Mr. Culiver showed me to my quarters and I settled in for a new experience.

TREK 148

> As a business executive Jack Lemmon runs off to Paris with Catherine Deneuve in the 1969 film "The April Fools".

Coyote Zen moved into the big house with the proprietress of the ranch. Mr. Culiver's mother Alice owned 600 acres, the source of the fire wood she collected for a stove she kept glowing from mid-October to mid-March. She had given birth to five children and gained many creative grandchildren who took turns staying with her, helping her out with tending the land. During

Backpack Trekker: A 60's Flashback

girl's camp she often took groups into Bryce Canyon. The girls experienced the towering hoodoos and the lonely slender shape of the Sentinel, a rock that resembles a fist, with all the fingers eroded away except the middle finger that is still fully extended.

Her own children had separate residences in Provo and Salt Lake City. They attended to their own affairs so she often took on a hired hand, preferably an opera *aficionado,* who loved animals. My score on opera was zip, but because I was tight with Coyote Zen she hired me.

My relationship with Alice was fun and educational. She loved to read even more than I did. As she passed the piano she read the sheet music looming over the ivory keys. She read whole sections of old newspapers before tearing them up to ignite the kindling in her wood stove. She read cookbooks like some people read romance novels. Stacks of magazines were consumed like flapjacks.

I was surprised to find issues of "The Little Review" and "Dial", two magazines that folded in 1929. She read the "Encyclopedia Britannica" from Aardvark to Zion with complete retention. I asked her questions like "what was the population of Ankara in 1960?"

"Six-hundred-fifty-thousand and sixty-seven," she responded without squinting her face in thought. I thumbed randomly through the volumes looking for obscure facts to trip her up.

"What is Makalu?" I asked.

"It is a mountain in the Himalayas between Nepal and Tibet," she replied. And if that wasn't enough she added, "Its elevation is 27,790 feet."

Every room and hallway contained bookshelves filled with text books and National Geographic Magazines. A bibliophile could make a routine visit to the water closet and get lost for hours in piles of picture books and short-story anthologies.

Alice was an immense repository of knowledge living near many natural wonders in southern Utah. When she spoke even Alfred Stieglitz would have hushed up. She was a great soul and once she gave utterance, all surrounding conversation stopped. She was a believer in the world as a living entity. She believed that we served as stewards to creation for what was provided to us in trust. Her father was the sun and her mother was the earth.

Beatlick Joe Speer

In 1969 Mario Puzo hits with his novel "The Godfather".

"The world was destroyed three times that we know of," Alice said one morning while straining goat's milk from a plastic bucket through a white cloth. "The first time was destruction by fire. Volcanoes exploded and ringed the earth with a dense collar of impenetrable ash. Boulders crumbled from the heat and were carried miles away from their origin by flowing lava.

"A certain group of people were saved. They lived with the ants underground. After the earth cooled the remnants reappeared to occupy and repopulate the land. But this situation could not last. Members of the race turned to wickedness and corruption. The world had to be destroyed again. This time everything froze. It was so cold that blind fish at the bottom of the ocean were encapsulated in ice. But once again a select percentage was saved."

"Was it the talented tenth that was saved?" I asked.

"The people who survived had a high spiritual content," she answered, "talent had naught to do with it. They lived underground until it was safe to reemerge. Life continued only to be destroyed a third time. This was where Genesis picked up the story with flooding as the mode of purification."

"When the waters subsided," she continued, "they found themselves on a crag of jagged rocks. They had to crush rocks to make soil to grow food. The water retreated until the people found themselves in a barren and stark landscape where they had to depend on rainfall for water. This worked for them because they had a strong connection with the Great Spirit. When they needed rain they prayed together as a community. Their prayers were very powerful and the Great Spirit granted their needs.

"They migrated and used magic to obtain water. One person of the clan was entrusted with the water jar. When water was needed the keeper of the sacred jar fasted for three days. The jar was buried in the ground and the person chanted over it while moving in a circular pattern around the jar. If there was no blemish in their purity or sincerity, the jar began to overflow with water, and flowed continuously until they broke camp to travel onward." We suddenly heard a loud knock at the door. This startled both of us because we were not expecting company.

Backpack Trekker: A 60's Flashback

In 1968 "Petulia", starring Julie Christie and George C. Scott, tells the tale about a San Francisco kook in the Summer of Love with flash forwards and The Grateful Dead sound track.

In 1964 Francois Truffaut directed a black-and white-film called *"Le Peau Douce"*. I loved watching Francois Dorleac as the airline hostess who distracts a married man. I enjoyed the musical score by Georges Delerue. The camera work was reminiscent of Hitchcock, the editing smooth.

But it took two hours to unfold a story that could be summarized verbally in one minute: Married man sparks new passion with young mistress. His wife finds out. She confronts him. He denies any wrong doing. She throws his suitcase out the door. Relationship with mistress cools. The wife discovers incriminating photos and shoots him in a restaurant.

The violent death provided an emotional and visual conclusion to the movie, but I don't think it was a realistic ending. The wife had already reconciled herself to their separation.

Instead of resorting to gunfire, a French victim of infidelity is more apt to activate their own *affair d'amour*. The wife of a fickle husband is more likely to emerge clandestinely from her own hotel tryst than to bump off her hubby. I give this movie two stars.

In 1960 Harper Lee took us to Alabama in the 1930's with her novel "To Kill a Mockingbird". It is a joyful story from the point of view of a young girl in a small town.

The girl Scout has a wonderful relationship with her lawyer father Atticus Finch. He hates guns and never went to war, but he is a dead shot with a rifle. If he shoots fifteen times and misses once he figures he wasted ammunition. Scout never knew about his remarkable marksmanship.

"People in their right minds never take pride in their talents," Mr. Finch's housekeeper Miss Mandy explains to Scout. The book also presents a fascinating courtroom battle between the forces of good and evil.

The combatants are easily identifiable. Atticus represents moral rectitude while the opposing faction, the Yules, could easily be related to the Snopes in Faulkner's saga of Yoknapatawpha County. The Yules accuse a crippled black man of raping their daughter. Atticus methodically breaks down their facade of false-hood to reveal their lies as an attempt to cover up family abuse.

The novel was wonderfully translated to film in 1962 with Gregory Peck showing great aplomb as the Southern attorney. I give this film four stars.

TREK 151

> In the 1969 movie "Sabata," a gunslinger por-trayed by Lee Van Cleef shoots it up in a spaghetti western filmed in Spain and Italy.

In 1960 the book "Black Like Me" appeared, based on a true story of a white man who turned himself black to experience the indignities of second-class citizenship. The film version came out in 1964 with James Whitmore in the lead role. The idea for this book may have been inspired by George Schuyler's 1931 novel "Black No More", where a young black man becomes white due to the scientific discovery of a brilliant physician. Another book I enjoyed was "Summer Job Directory", a compilation of listings of fun jobs in resorts all over America.

I used it to secure a job one summer near a Pike's Peak Colorado dude ranch. I wrote the director of the ranch extolling my virtues and emphasizing my suavity in personal relationships. They hired me through the mail. I was elated to receive a salary plus room and board. They started me out as a scullion, washing dishes and waiting tables in the employee's dining room. Within three days my stellar characteristic of amiability was recognized and I was bumped up to desk clerk.

In this position I discovered the concept of tipping. I unreserv-edly helped guests with luggage, or any special needs such as advice on what to see and do in the area, or to make arrange-ments with housekeeping for an extra bed in their room. I tried to ameliorate everyone's visit as a matter of course. My first tip left me flabbergasted. One woman who stayed a week visited me every day with questions about recreational opportunities. I told her about the Garden of the Gods, Seven Falls, and the Will Rogers Shrine of the Sun. I procured ice and other off-hours de-lectables from the kitchen. When she departed she left me a sealed envelope. It contained a crisp twenty-dollar bill. Despite this increased awareness of my earning potential, I did not alter my behavior. I continued to serve everyone, regardless of what

Backpack Trekker: A 60's Flashback

might cross my palm due to special efforts. It got to where I made enough in tips for fun money and deposited my checks.

While in the area I visited Pike's Peak. At over 14,000 feet elevation it was the closest to divinity I had been on the physical plane. But proximity to the most high had its consequences. I returned to the ranch sun burned. The ranch closed for the season in early September and I returned to the university. I enjoyed this adventure due to a book that arrived in the mail. It substantiated even more my inseparability from books and the postal service.

TREK 152

In 1969 Bruce Lee served as stunt supervisor in the films "Marlowe" and "The Wrecking Crew".

One summer my brother Paul and I hitchhiked to Alaska. We traveled up the coast from Cabo San Lucas in Mexico to Seattle where we boarded a ferry as walk-on passengers. Our main objective was to visit Denali, the highest point in North America. We marveled at the vast fields of tundra, a mama grizzly with two cubs grubbing for roots, and at the majestic mountain range that pops up from a flat plain.

The only trouble we encountered on the journey was with Canadian Customs while leaving Alaska. Gadding about Alaska was easy until we arrived in Tok Junction headed east.

Alas, after Tok we had no ride offers so we started walking. We trekked for seven days while thumbing the occasional vehicle that passed by too loaded down with supplies to even consider us as passengers. We arrived at James Store, not even big enough for a whistle stop, and bought tickets on a bus for Whitehorse in the Yukon. The agents at the border crossing detained us. I'd been through this scenario before. They asked intrusive questions like how much money we had.

"Forty dollars," I replied.

"Each?"

"No, together." We had to step down from the bus. They refused us entrance into Canada because we did not have sufficient ways and means. I explained we were not planning to immigrate, we were just passing through back to the USA.

We had no worries about sustaining ourselves on a pittance of cash, but they had grave concerns about us being a burden on their economy. They put us on a bus and within hours we were back in Tok Junction.

Converging on Tok simultaneously was a circus from North Hollywood touring Alaska and Canada. We started a conversation with a muscular man sporting round brass earrings. He invited us for coffee and introduced us to other members of the troupe. The cook of the outfit was a homosexual who wore his pants so low that his crack was exposed. He asked us if we needed a job. We nodded affirmatively. He connected us to the owner. They needed two roustabouts to swing sledge hammers and help set up and take down the big top. They paid $35 a week plus room and board. The room was a bunk bed in the bull truck where the elephant was kept. We accepted the offer and when the circus broke camp, we went with them as employees of the Dwayne Brothers Circus. We arrived again at the border. The same guards were on duty. They had no choice but to let us pass as members of the circus. We smiled and waved as we crossed the border into Canada.

TREK 153

In 1969 the Santa Fe Opera in New Mexico presents "Help! Help! The Globolinks!".

In 1963 Frank Waters wrote about the Native Americans with his "Book of the Hopi". It details the myths, legends and history of the Hopi - a tribe that made their migrations and settled in northern Arizona. He compares their religious ceremonies and symbols with the European Christians.

The kiva is the Hopi underground ceremonial chamber. It penetrates Mother Earth and is entered from the roof by a ladder. The altar level is sunken. The priests occupy the lowest level. They are barefoot to show humility. The Spanish mission is above ground in an ostentatious display of bulk with its steeple thrusting into the sky. The Christian priests perform on an elevated platform, above the congregation. They are adorned in colorful vestments. The Native American and the Spanish Christian symbols were completely incompatible. The Spanish built missions at what today are the Salinas and Gran Quivira National Monuments in New Mexico. The Spanish arrived there in 1598 and immediately renamed the village. They conscripted locals to help build their church and drew from the native population as the base for their congregation. The Christians and their mission latched onto the pueblo culture like a cancer. In 1670 the inhabitants of the Salinas Valley found a cure for this intrusion. They decamped suddenly to take refuge along the Rio Grande. Historians explain this exodus was due to drought and raids from hostile Plains tribes. I don't subscribe to this theory. The population at Gran Quivira at the time of their evacuation was 1,500 people. They were situated on elevated land where they could see all around for miles. Marauders could not easily sneak up on them. They were dug in behind stone walls. I demur the drought theory. It is an easy explanation, but they lived about 30 miles from the river. They were dependant on rainfall for their crops but they had an ability to petition the Great Spirit for what they needed. They realized the power of prayer and if they lived righteously they were provided with their needs. I think they abandoned their long established village to eliminate the Spanish. They chose to cut off the Christian canker by removing themselves *en masse*. After they departed, the Spanish also gave up their presence in the area. The mission became a ruin. The cure was effective.

In 1680 there was a general revolt of all the tribes in what is now New Mexico. They chased the Spanish south as far as El Paso because they could no longer tolerate the oppression. The northern tribes employed violent means to remove the Spanish. My theory is that the people at Gran Quivira followed a more passive approach.

TREK 154

> *In 1969 Marlon Brando played a British agent in the film "Burn" who is sent to investigate a slave revolt on a Portuguese controlled island.*

I responded to the knock on Alice's kitchen door. Three helmeted men with clean blue shirts stood silently.

"Can we help you?" I asked.

"We are looking for José Cuervo," one of them said. I knew I should stall them long enough to run out the side door and disappear into the protection of the forest. Even with a short head-start I could lose them in the trees. I knew I should tell them that José had moved to Findhorn in northeast Scotland, that he had gone back in time to become a citizen of Flanders, he had joined a jazzology vodka club and was lost in the delirium of taking in the confusion which surrounded him, or that he was working as a librarian in Buenos Aires, or anything but.

"That's me." José Cuervo was not my real name but it was a moniker I fixed upon while traveling. These men represented a special squad sent out to track down offenders of minor traffic violations. I had two parking meter tickets on my record from several years back. But since I did not drive a vehicle, the chance of the cops finding me was like a Hindu from Himachal Pradesh reading Denise Levertov backwards. Of all the places in America where I might have been, such as watching *"Belle de Jour"* in a small art theater in Albuquerque, scouring the shelves in Cody's Bookstore in Berkeley for a copy of "Infants of the Spring" by Wallace Thurman, or listening to a record of the Reverend Gary Davis sing "I Won't Be Back No More" in a second story Denver walk-up, they randomly roused me out and arrested me.

I said goodbye to Alice. They handcuffed me and walked me out to a squad car. I howled when Coyote Zen appeared. We stared at each other and knew it was time to ring down the curtain on our relationship. As we drove away he ran after the patrol car. He ran as fast as he could but gradually the distance between us increased. When we reached the paved road Coyote Zen disappeared into a tiny speck.

We drove for several hours until we arrived in a town. They fingerprinted me then locked me in a jail with three other men. The men were asleep as I climbed into an upper bunk. When they discovered me one of the men wanted to pound me just for the exercise. I discouraged this by describing myself as a serial killer who consumed broken glass. I asked what offenses had brought them to such an impasse.

One man had been arrested for growing marijuana. He traveled around the country planting hemp seeds on public lands and in federal building flower beds. Another man was arrested for painting "Bring Home the Troops" on the walls of abandoned buildings. The aggressive dude had been locked up for driving off at a gas station without paying for his fuel. We bonded quickly. We all felt unduly punished for innocuous actions while the government paid men to kill people and destroy vegetation with Agent Orange. I started a petition requesting immediate reevaluation of our situation. We all signed it. We felt it was a valuable document but when we showed it to the guard, he laughed and tore it into pieces.

❦

Backpack Trekker: A 60's Flashback

In 1969 the film "Bob & Carol & Ted & Alice" featured wife-swapping, psychotherapy, pot smoking and other trendy modern couple situations.

Querida María,

Some of the sunflowers in Alice's garden are over six feet high. The squash leafage unfolds a luxuriant green. The wood piles grow like a wealthy miser's savings. Alice has 72 apple trees. A wooden press is near-by to separate the juice from the pulp. She has apricot trees big enough to climb into and build a tree house. We talk *apriori,* drink apricot puree, eat apple leather, tarts, *empañadas* and dried apricots.

When my brother hits the big time with his music I'll sell tickets or help with the sound check. There are backyard musicians as talented as the ones who cut records and travel on concert tours. Hope we can use the technology to disseminate our work. The goal, whether on the porch or in the studio, is creation. Some artists need the stimulus of a contract or a percentage of the take in order to do serious work. To make a commitment they need $100 bills tightly packed into a portmanteau. The unknown itinerant artist playing for love is as hard to find as altruistic barbed wire. Getting your work out-and-away stimulates growth. Imagine playing the same songs on every record or if I retold the same story every time I signed up for an open-mic. Stagnation. To feed the machine, meet the quota, fulfill the demand, uphold the contract, can be reasons to work but the transitory favors of the media can be nebulous on an overcast day. The goal is creativity onto which everything else is added, like a paycheck or a sack of apricots. Do you want to be a workaholic like Betty Davis? Bring lovers in the front door and have them leave by the back door as contracts scurry in search of signatures.

Work comes in many forms. Reading all of Shakespeare's plays is work; learning another language; watching all the films produced in 1969; visiting all the National Parks in North America; tending a garden of giant sunflowers; or building a home with stones collected from the beach.

I saw *"La Muerte de un Burocrata"*, a 1966 film from Cuba. You will probably never see it due to our government's belligerent attitude toward Cuba and any products from Havana. It is a funny story about a working man who dies. The film opens with his funeral. His widow goes to an office to secure her pension. The agent needs to see her husband's worker's card. But she buried it with her husband and she cannot secure her pension until they have the card. The nephew goes to the cemetery to see about opening the coffin. He must have an exhumation permit to move the body. But he does not want to move the body, he just wants to open the lid and remove the card. He must wait two years or have a special signature from some bigwig in some office. So he goes from office to office. Franz Kafka would love it. Finally he hires some thugs to help dig it up.

Late one night they raise the coffin, but a security guard hears them and the nephew rolls the coffin out of the cemetery. Off with the lid and then he pries the card from the corpse's fingers. When he tries to return the coffin the gate is locked. He takes the coffin home and tries to complete the paper work to rebury the dead man. That turns out to be more of a problem because you cannot bury the same person twice. He returns home one day after a futile paper chase and sees vultures circling his residence. It's in Spanish with English subtitles.

I think the most dolorous battle of the Civil Rights Movement was in Memphis against Mayor Loeb. To find an equal to his obdurate mentality one need go to a slave ship captain or plantation master. "Yes sir, massah."

What pressed the sanitation workers into walking off the job was the death of two men on a garbage packer. A hydraulic ram crushed Echol Cole and Robert Walker. Faulty equipment, no workmen's compensation and no life insurance made the starvation wages unable to commiserate with reality. All the mayor could say was that it was against the law not to work. Neither side would give in. The strike continued for 65 days. It went from a local racist situation to a national labor dispute. The workers needed a second wind to blow away the fetid resistance. They asked Dr. King to come and take a stand by the river. Dr. King came to Memphis and suggested that all workers leave their jobs and students leave the class and march. Marching in March. Marching with Martin. As he prepared to go out, near sunset, leaving his room at the motel, a single bullet killed him. The workers won the strike and most of their demands, including an immediate pay raise. Deep in the forest, comfortable in my sleeping bag, I heard the report of a rifle and woke up crying.

Your son

Backpack Trekker: A 60's Flashback

In October of 1969 the Weather Underground (a splinter group from the Students for a Democratic Society) organized their first demonstration and marched through an upscale Chicago shopping district, pummeling parked cars and smashing shop windows.

My most extroverted cell mate was Humphrey Boorman. He loved The Beatles. He saw them on the "Ed Sullivan Show" and was the first in line to see the films "A Hard Day's Night" (1964) and "Help" (1965).

The two promo films blend together in the light zaniness of their antics. In one of the movies Ringo acquires a ring and is constantly on the go. He becomes the target for a series of assassination attempts. The group sings and runs around like youngsters in a home movie. A tapster pulls a tap to draw a beer and Ringo falls through a trap door. A tiger appears with an appreciation for Beethoven. They do a number in a concert hall where young screaming girls are brought into position like artillery to make lots of noise. Neither film has any dramatic tension.

"Yellow Submarine" (1968) however, is classic animation directed by Canadian George Dunning. It has a good story and a "Strawberry Fields" sound track. The Beatles benefited from collaborations with people like Dunning and George Martin. They learned a few licks from Indian sitar players which enhanced their sound.

But they were smart to quit touring and performing live. Late 60's groups like Cream, or Jethrow Tull, or Led Zeppelin could overpower them with energetic jams and electrifying leads. When The Beatles were cashing in their chips, The Who were reaching artistic high latitudes with "Tommy" (1969), a story about a blind boy who "sure plays a mean pinball".

Boorman was not a boring man. He moved to Canada in 1966 to avoid the draft and then flew from Montreal to London. In Soho he met a Turk who sold hash. The Turk had established routes for vendors with steady customers. Boorman took over one of these sales jobs in Colchester. He lived in London and took the train under the guise of a student, reading Jane Austen novels while all along his bag was loaded with contraband.

Once a month he traveled from Harwich to Hook of Holland on another job he pursued in distributing bootleg tapes. He sold many copies of "Blond on Blond". As he made the rounds selling hash he introduced his customers to Bob Dylan. "Rainy Day Women #12 and #35" was popular with everybody hooting and hollering. Another song his clients enjoyed was "Like A Rolling Stone". He always smoked the first bowl or bong hit with his clients to demonstrate the effectiveness of his product.

After Dylan's motorcycle accident in 1966 Boorman was glad to leave America. He only returned briefly, retracing his path through Canada, to be with his mother as she died of cancer. She left him a small inheritance which he used back in England to buy a van. He hosted a smoke-in and directed the communal painting of his van. They even painted the rims, exhaust pipes and underneath the frame.

TREK 157

In 1969 Robert Redford gave an appealing performance in "Downhill Racer".

My most introverted cell mate was an artist named Patrick O'Brian. He had been arrested several times for creating large chalk drawings on downtown sidewalks. This was an art form he learned as an artist in Dublin, Ireland. Patrick attended art school for two semesters before the instructor O'Casey, told him to consider work as a carpet cleaner.

After such advise, Patrick quit school and used his money to travel Europe, where he visited many museums like El Prado in Madrid and The Louvre in Paris. While walking on Stephen's Green he met a sidewalk artist who reproduced exact replicas of paintings by European masters. He used colored chalks and always set his cap in a prominent place for people to toss coins.

When Patrick returned to America he tried to earn a living depicting paintings like "Rape of the Daughters of Leucippus" by Rubens, but very little money fell into his cap. He fared slightly better portraying American works like "Nighthawks" and "American Gothic", but still his earnings were meager.

He changed his subject matter to culture shakers like Angela Davis with a huge 'fro and short skirt. This generated more revenue, so he was encouraged to expand his representations to include Jane Fonda strip-teasing out of a space suit. He earned money as he practiced his art near universities in Ann Arbor, Boulder and Berkeley. But when he plied his art in Utah his efforts were not appreciated. He was jailed for despoiling public property.

"What was the most fun you ever had with your art Patrick?" I asked.

"The most fun was returning to the sidewalk in front of the art school where my erstwhile teacher told me to forget about art. O'Casey's favorite painter was Claude Monet. For his benefit I drew a picture using the impressionistic style of Monet. It was not an actual reproduction of Monet's work, but an invented subject. It caught the attention of the art instructors and they gathered around my picture to analyze in detail. One man said it was from Monet's period at Argenteuil, where he constructed a studio on a small boat and painted on the river. Another man described it as a late Monet after his blindness changed how he applied paint. O'Casey expounded how the work was probably a Monet from a private collection and seldom seen. It started to rain as they stood around discussing my work. They pulled out an umbrella to try and protect the drawing but the colors began to run as the drops fell.

"Do you have any chalk on you now?" I asked. He took a pack of cigarettes from his sock. He brought out three slender stems of chalk.

"Can you give us a sample of your work here on the floor?"

"I can depict a detail from 'Garden of Delights' by Hieronymus Bosch." He proceeded to cover the floor of our cell with grisly images. When our jailer discovered Patrick's handiwork, he was not amused. He confiscated the chalk and forced Patrick to scrub the floor after he splashed a bucket of water over the drawing. The colors merged and ran down the drain.

TREK 158

> In 1969 Italian film director Luchino Visconti made "The Damned", depicting the decadence of Nazi munitions makers from 1933.

I saw the movie "The Brothers Karamazov" (1957). Some strong acting, but I was disappointed with the Hollywood treatment. A far cry from "Dr. Zhivago". David Lean made "The Bridge on the River Kwai" (also 1957) on location. But "Brothers" was filmed on a MGM back lot. All of the outdoor shots were done in the same restricted confines of a drab half-acre. The worst offense is how Hollywood changed the ending. In the film Dmitri walks off smiling with a beautiful woman by his side. In the novel Dmitri is found guilty of killing his father, a crime he did not commit. There isn't the slightest extenuating comment made in his defense. Dmitri is simply taken away as a few exclamations are heard on the steps of the courthouse.

"He'll have a twenty-years trip to the mines." The peasants stand firm and condemn Dmitri. What makes this verdict grim is Dmitri's yell: "I am not guilty of my father's blood."

He knows he is innocent but the evidence is against him. The real culprit, the bastard brother Smerdyakov, hangs himself. The novel ends with the funeral of a boy. The innocent victim, Dmitri, dreams of escape, as his brother Alyosha follows the little flower-decked coffin to the church. The boy Ilusha dies two days after Dmitri is sentenced.

I spent part of every day in the summer of 1969 reading about the "Brothers". It disturbed me that a film version would give it a truncated treatment and a less than authentic interpretation. One of Smerdyakov's motivations for killing his father is Ivan's dictum: "everything is lawful". The film doesn't even delve into one of my favorite parts of the book, Ivan's hallucination, his attack of brain fever that produces a conversation with the devil. Ivan loses consciousness, but he goes on talking incoherently. Alyosha puts him to bed.

In 1964 George Burns put Gracie Allen to bed. He was at her side as she died. Some of Gracie's dialogue during their routines seemed incoherent, like when she described cooking two turkeys at once, a little one and a big one. She said when the little one burned you know that the big one was ready. George visited Gracie's tomb once a month. He talked to her and told her jokes. Someone asked George what his doctor thought of him drinking cocktails and smoking cigars. George said his doctor was dead.

TREK 159

In 1969 the film "Tell Them Willie Boy Is Here" explodes the cruel treatment of the American Indian by white men.

The third member of our billeted cell block was Jonathan Highlow. His crime was cutting a huge peace sign in the lawn in front of the court house. He was the only one of us who enjoyed his restricted confines. The accommodations were actually better than what he was accustomed to as a free man. He normally slept on the outside stairwell of an office building. The office personnel departed after 5 p.m. and returned at 7 a.m. He usually lay down at ten and cleared out by 6 a.m. He did not outfit himself like Kerouac at his job in the fire tower. The most comfort he enjoyed was a doormat or cardboard. The advantage of the location was that he was out of the rain and there was no traffic on the stairs after dark.

There was a McDonald's that opened at six where he went to use the facilities and buy coffee. He loved McDonald's. They gave him a free refill and he sat as long as he liked and talked to people. He usually read the newspaper, starting with the front page and finishing off with a close perusal of the classifieds. A dream job might be there, such as: Live in companion wanted, no experience necessary, all expenses paid, plus generous salary and benefits.

But no want ad ever tempted him enough to even call from the pay phone. A real meal deal did not appear until noon when he lined up for free food at a church-sponsored "Feed the Hungry" program. A message was forced on the guests and a reading from the Bible, but he didn't mind as long as he ate and stayed out of the weather. Most afternoons he hung out in the public library. He sat in a chair and looked through picture books, especially of faraway places.

Sometimes he dozed off with the book open in front of him. He left the library at five to connect with another free meal. The early evening hours he panhandled in front of different restaurants. This minimal expenditure of energy provided enough to cover his daily expenses. His lifestyle seemed so uneventful I wondered where he got the inspiration and the equipment to perform the yard work that landed him in the calaboose.

"So what motivated you to engage in freelance landscaping, Jonathan?" I asked.

"I was asleep one night when the boisterous voices from the landing below woke me up. It was two men sharing a bottle and talking about sports. I decided to join them. I had seen them before in the park.

"They were liquored-up and lookin' for some kicks. One of them knew where to lay hands on a lawn mower. So we borrowed it and rolled it to the court house. They pulled the rope to fire it up and cut this huge peace sign in the grass. When the mower ran out of gas they told me to wait with the machine while they went for more fuel. While they were gone the police came by. They arrested me.

"I tried to explain that I had only been an observer, but hey, you try telling the cops anything without money or ID. Forget it! I'm innocent, but I don't really mind. I enjoy talking to you fellows," he said.

TREK 160

In 1969 the movie "The Royal Hunt of the Sun" depicts Spanish conquistadors pillaging South America for gold.

The turnkey who brought us cheeseburgers in our Utah jail cell was not amused with our continued frivolous attitude. At night, after lights out, he had to shush us. During the day he yelled at us because we carried on like attendees to a biregional convention of circus clowns. We accepted our incarceration with aplomb and ease. I just wanted to lie in the bunk and read. We had been detained for minor offenses and didn't anticipate any serious punishment. We badgered the guard to send us a priest. Cleric counsel before sentence is passed should be a right. Much to our surprise, a religious representative did arrive at our cell. I was delighted to see him. I immediately asked if he would hear my confession. He admitted that he was not an official priest but he could listen to my confession and administer communion.

"Bless me father," I began. "It has been three years since my last confession. These are my sins. I married three women at the same time. I've committed nineteen armed robberies. I used God's name in vain many times. I've deserted my children and raped a retarded bar maid in Saint Augustine. Father, can you forgive me?"

The ecclesiastical personage suggested I say five Our Fathers and five Hail Mary's.

"But reverend sir," I protested. "You don't understand. I've been exceedingly bad. I stole money from my child's piggy bank to buy drugs. I poisoned the city drinking water. I planted bombs on random perambulators. I put Ex-Lax in the brownie mix at the old folks home. I played with myself while reading the Bible. Can you forgive me father?"

The man sensed I was pulling his leg. He rose angrily and called the turnkey to let him out. After his departure I continued to mock the system.

Backpack Trekker: A 60's Flashback

"No matter how severe the list of sins, they always assign five and five as penance. One time my friend Zen Jazz got so peeved at the five and five routine that he threatened to molest the priest. The reverend father got excited. He offered Zen fifty dollars.

"He hadn't been buggered since his seminary days. Zen gave him a list of sins that took Satan and his cohorts a week to classify. Zen yelled at the priest. Father, what do I have to do to get the punishment I deserve?

"Just live, my son," the priest replied. "Just live."

TREK 161

In the 1967 book "Spain, the Vital Years" author Luis Brolin argues that the Nationalists denied bombing Guernica and attempted to blame the Republicans.

Late one night, while the four of us were asleep in our jail cell, I was visited by the spirit of Zen Jazz. He reprimanded me for my willingness to accept the loss of my freedom. I was reminded of our affinity with the anarchists of Barcelona before Franco's bombs in 1939 squashed the concept.

"We maintain our freedom by exercising our freedom," Zen said. "Remember how we studied the catalogue of classes and located where the biology students examined different strains of bacteria. The students looked through microscopes as we arrived to stand outside the classroom with binoculars around our necks. We discussed the problem of a lethal virus in a small Arizona town that could spread by a gentle wind. The professor told us to move along but we informed him that we were practicing our freedom of expression."

I recalled another example of our freewheeling freedom. We attended a school assembly with invited speakers who sat behind the podium. In between speakers, Zen rushed the stage and commandeered the mic. He did not have time to deliver his harangue before representatives of the university escorted him away. There was a definite predictability and edgy inevitability about people's response to our moving freedom of speech into taboo territory.

For example, if we milled around near the entrance to the Berkeley campus where Telegraph Avenue starts, and argued about whether Christ was black, no one would shut us down. But if we talked about C.S. Lewis loudly in the nave of a church during the service, we were encouraged to depart before they passed the tithing baskets.

I knew how a situation would resolve itself when Zen attended the drama department's production of a Chekhov play and started reciting Shakespearean soliloquies up and down the aisles. Zen also knew it was a matter of time before his freedom of speech would be curtailed.

Only one time was his intrusive style welcomed. He entered from the back of the room of an American history class and interrupted the professor with an explanation of why Mary Todd Lincoln should not have been consigned to a state insane asylum.

"If she spent money extravagantly, it was her money." The professor challenged Zen to a debate then and there.

I don't know how Zen entered our jail cell, but he resembled the gentile man who visited Ivan Karamazov in his room. Suddenly I was delirious for my freedom.

Zen smiled and disappeared. My desire for freedom manifested in freedom. The cell door was ajar. I walked out and departed from my captivity, sauntering past the townspeople as if they were dead.

TREK 162

In 1967 the British folk rock group Fairport Convention was formed by bassist Ashley Hutchings and the following year vocalist Sandy Denny joined the band.

In 1962 the Ambrose Bierce short story, "An Occurrence at Owl Creek Bridge", was made into a short film. During the Civil War a man is about to be hanged. The rope breaks and he falls into the river below and escapes.

He returns to his home where his wife awaits him. They run toward each other. Cut to her. Cut to him. Cut to her. Cut to him running. An emotional scene elongated by editing. When they meet in a loving embrace the scene switches back to the bridge. The rope goes taut. His feet swing freely over the river.

Most of the 29-minute film takes place in the few seconds it takes the man to step off the bridge and hit the end of the rope. During those few seconds the man fantasizes his escape and reunion with his wife. Not even Sergei Eisenstein with the angry sailor in "Battleship Potemkin" breaking a plate, was so successful in extending real time.

Backpack Trekker: A 60's Flashback

I walked all night thinking mostly about films. One of my favorite directors is Jacques Tati. He is also an actor. He's a combination of Harpo Marx and Noel Coward. He doesn't speak, but he generates a suave meticulous comic style. Tati is a precursor of Woody Allen in that he will write, direct and act in his comic movies. His scripts are plotless holidays told mostly in visuals and pantomime. Tati is a throw-back to Charlie Chaplin.

Just after sunrise I got a ride with an unemployed actor from Los Angeles. His name was Jeff Star and he was fed up with Tinsel Town. He felt the money and the most desirous roles were in LA but he decided to relocate to New York City, share an apartment on the Lower East Side, and pursue a career in theater. Samuel Beckett's work was important to him. Jeff had memorized the novel "How It Is". Realizing that being a cab driver or waiting tables would be his livelihood, he was ready for a change; he would study Stanislavski at night. He asked if I would help him drive to the east coast. I declined and asked if he liked movies.

"Cactus Flower" was his favorite film. Goldie Hawn held her own with Ingrid Bergman and Walter Matthau.

"I love Goldie," Jeff said. "Saw her dance in "Can-Can" at the Texas Pavilion at the New York World's Fair."

"Did you see "Mondo Cane"? I asked.

"No, what is that?"

"An Italian film from 1962 documenting unusual rituals and strange human habits. I think the director Jacopetti even fabricated situations to add punch."

Jeff dropped me near Hovenweep National Monument in southeastern Utah.

TREK 163

In 1967 the novel "The Confessions of Nate Turner" by William Styron, retold the story of a black man resorting to violence against white oppression.

Hovenweep is an Anasazi site with mysterious stone towers. There is no definitive explanation of why the towers were built or what purpose the structures served the community. Some of the towers are located near natural springs. Greenery flourishes where the water runs off. Water leaks through the soil at the back of a cave. The water is cool and clean. I cupped my hands and drank. This was the same spot where people drank 1,000 years ago. I have a great affinity for the Anasazi, the ancient ones. They traveled on foot. I decided to fast for three days, drink water and meditate. When initiating a fast, the first two days are the most difficult. The hunger pangs dig into your belly like cat claws ripping through skin. The transition from regular intake of food to nothing solid going down the gullet is a shock to the system. But after the body adjusts to no food, it then becomes easy not to eat. The body gives up any resistance. It gets weaker as the fast continues. It would be easier to starve than to die of cancer. As the days pass you just want to rest. No energy to talk. Just go to sleep.

On the third day of my fast I hallucinated in color. I saw myself as a member of a tribe. We traveled from east to west, from Atlantic to Pacific, and from north to south, from North Pole to Tierra del Fuego. When we settled down we selected a spot near water. We realized the significance of our location, that others might try to occupy the same area. We collected smooth flat stones and built a tower on the edge of a ravine to protect our territory. After completion of the tower we were set upon by a roving clan of nefarious stone carvers.

They wanted to disassemble our tower and draw their symbols on our stones. We resisted their encroachment, but allowed them access to the spring for one hour a day. They built their own tower on the opposite side of the arroyo and created a pink dye to imbue the stones with an artificial tint. During the day the ostentatious glare was absorbed by the sun. The pinkish element retained light and continued to glow for half the night. We could not sleep until early in the morning. Without sufficient sleep we could not function well.

While their tower was neglected we dismantled it. But the stones spread all over the ground continued to glow at night. The only other solution was to bury the stones. That seemed like too much work, so we decided to relocate to another spring. We moved completely out of the area to what is today southwest Colorado.

I stopped fasting after five days. I hitchhiked to Cortez and ordered a meal in a restaurant. When they presented the check I explained there was no money in my pockets. The manager let me work off my debt by washing dishes. He even gave me a sack of fruit and half a key-lime pie to take away.

☯

Backpack Trekker: A 60's Flashback

In 1969 "The Sterile Cuckoo" stars Liza Minnelli
as a neurotic college student in her first affair.

I visited Mesa Verde National Monument in Colorado, where I met a Navajo man at Spruce Tree House. He invited me to his hogan. We sat on a hand-woven blanket that could have come down from a museum wall. His name was Four Corners, after the area where he lived on roasted mutton and piñon. He said he remembered seeing me on Alcatraz Island.

"I was ripped off on The Rock," I said.

"An apology is in order," he said. I had no foreboding of what he was about to repent.

"I went into your tent after watching your comings and goings. I knew you were not an Indian so I felt justified in stealing from you. I thought maybe you were a reporter with a top-of-the-line camera, but I never saw you take pictures. You were not there for political reasons so I figured nobody would raise a ruckus for your sake," he confessed.

"After my tour in Vietnam I couldn't maintain a regular job. I had no access to money except to steal and take the goods to a pawnshop where they knew I wasn't coming back to reclaim. I went to prison for robbing the pawnbroker where I sold my stuff. I learned most of what I know about thievery behind bars. I developed patience to stake out a building or campsite until I knew the time was right to strike.

"In Nam I used to watch for Charlie and set an ambush. I'd hit fast, then disappear like a crack of lightning in the sky. Your tent provided cash. I didn't have to carry off anything like an urban looter. When I saw you headed for the ocean I knew I'd have a clear shot. But I've changed since then. I fasted and prayed. I moved back to our traditional homeland. Now I must make atonement. I'm sorry for any pain I caused you. I want to repay you now." He handed me a wad of hundred-dollar bills. I accepted his gift with great joy. Will you forgive me?"

"Sure," I said, shaking his hand.

"I was very distraught at the time by the sudden change in my financial status. I felt antsy like an inmate with a life sentence. The Rock is a hard place. You Native Americans lived there for a cause. I was there to lend support and absorb the vibes. The Rock is too damp to enjoy any extended stay. Let it become an open aviary. Hire a boatman to motor out once a day to throw food in the exercise yard. Invite Mary Poppins to sing 'Feed the Birds.'"

I was depressed at the time but I accepted the pain in silence. I couldn't exactly complain to the Coast Guard. I felt elated now. If I had to experience that pain to feel this good now, it was worth it. I left Four Corners and headed north toward Telluride.

TREK 165

The first implantation of an artificial heart in a human being occurred in April of 1969.

Telluride is a small town 9,000 feet in the mountains. I found a health food restaurant where I ordered a tofu burger with fried bananas. Then I hit a mountaineering store and bought all new tent, back pack, sleeping bag, canteen, flashlight, rain slicker and dried foods. The bar, doors wide-open, provided draft beer while blasting out "The Thrill is Gone" by B.B. King. There was a man at the bar reading "As I Lay Dying" by William Faulkner.

"Excuse me," I said. "How do you like the book?"

"The complexities of his narrative technique leave me in the dark at times about who does what. And I don't know if I can tolerate his sordid naturalism. I don't know what to make of a family dragging death around with them."

"It's a comic novel," I said. "When it was published in 1930, America had little to laugh about. The title is symbolic because of the stock market crash and the economy dying.

"It's hilarious that Addie Bundren watches her oldest son construct her coffin. And after her death they position her upside down in the box to accommodate the dress they want to bury her in. Then they have to transport her to Jefferson to be buried. The journey is fraught with trouble.

The wagon breaks down. They have to cross a flooded river and the coffin spills out and floats away. After retrieving the coffin, they spend so much time with their mother's corpse that they become inured to the stench.

They are surprised when they stop in a town to buy something and the sheriff compares the contents of the coffin to rotten cheese. People cross to the opposite side of the street with handkerchiefs to their noses. The ghastly caravan can only attract buzzards and deprecating remarks."

"So when they arrive in Jefferson do they park Mom some-where and forget about her? Where is the ceremony of her in-ternment?"

"There is no pomp and circumstance. They borrow shovels and the final deed takes place like an afterthought."

"So Anse buries his wife and shortly thereafter buys a new set of teeth and takes up with a new Mrs. Bundren?"

I nodded and polished off my beer.

"Can I buy you a beer?" he asked.

"Put your money away," I said. "Meet your new benefactor."

TREK 166

In 1969 "The Mousetrap" celebrates its 7,000th performance in a London theater.

Querida María,

Que tal? I had an unanticipated windfall blow into my lap, again. While in the Shiprock area, my ship came in. A Navajo man bank rolled me. I am in the chips, flush with C-notes. I asked where he got the money. You have instilled good principles in me and I don't want to benefit from *lucre* that was stolen from funds allocated to buy Little League equipment. He had stolen it from me in San Francisco and returned it in Colorado. He bestowed a boon on me and made himself feel good about it.

I will call you every Sunday at ten a.m. We can catch up be-fore you go to mass at eleven. You are an exemplary mother and a reliable friend. Your faith is strong as a connecting cable on a suspension bridge, a golden gate between this world and the next. If I fell off a ship in the Indian Ocean, your faith would pull me back to your front door. I feel blessed and invincible, like the Indians who believed the sacred dance would make them im-mune to the devastation of bullets.

I'm in Telluride. I traveled here to find an altitude comparable to my state of mind. I had a delightful conversation with a man working here for the summer. We discussed the intricacies of Faulkner's style. He was addled by Faulkner's multiple points of view. I told him it took the critics twenty years to realize there was more than sound and fury coming out of his barn. He told me about an abandoned hydroelectric plant above the waterfall. I plan to hike there and set up camp. The sound of running water is the symphonic movement I want to hear. I love places where the inhabitants have long since departed. Why is that? I like houses where the windows are jagged, broken glass and torn screens, where the doors have fallen off the hinges or are immobile due to the dirt collected against the threshold. I prefer ruins to lived in cities. I prefer Bodie to Los Angeles.

Anyway, I'm having a great time traveling. I know people die every day in Vietnam. I wish the war would end before the next decade begins, but the munitions factories have orders to fill and the testimony of blood has plenty of momentum to spill over.

Peace and Love, Joe

TREK 167

N. Scott Momaday, the nation's best-known Native American writer, received the 1969 Pulitzer Prize.

I set up my tent near enough to hear the water falling over the edge of the cliff. I felt like Hans Castorp without the immeasurable and monstrous snow fall. The constant sound of moving water invigorated my psyche and provided me with nights of glorious slumber. It was like falling asleep in a snow bank while listening to Beethoven.

Dreams seldom come in my dormant phase, but the swift rush of liquid churned up my subconscious and provided a plethora of imagery. Flashes of the Buddhist monk in the Grand Tetons nourishing himself with inhalations of clean air. He created poems in his sleep. Yearning to write a love poem while not in love, but to write about it, might allow amour to develop. I start with one line.

When I think of you ... I visualize world peace billboards ... replay French movies on the back curtain of my eyelids ... forget the subtitles ... read the body language ... communica-linguist waiting for a scene of enthusiastic assimilation ... When I think of you ... we trek to the stars with lazar guns set on the stun mode ... we motorcycle on the Isle of Skye ... we do masonry work at Stonehenge ... we stroll under an El Greco sky in Toledo ... on a train in Spain drinking beer and discussing "The Sun Also Rises" ... in a four-star hotel calling down for room service to send up the drug of the day ... barefoot in a warm climate ... encased in mud on the savanna ... we let it dry on our skin like epidermal husk ... then wash it off under Victoria Falls ...

When I think of you, my mind expands beyond the limits of possibility, and it rains poetry on a clear day.

I woke up in the night and lit a candle, but the moisture in the air finally extinguished the flame. During the interim I wrote this love poem while under the influence of rushing water and continued to write in the dark on the bedrock of timelessness for a pallet. Then I gave up writing and prayed to find a permanent friend to travel with and collect memories and work with on projects and study a map of Mexico and pick a city to visit on the Pacific Ocean and to warm the bed up first on cold nights and share meals and teach and preach about what excites and with concern for each other we learn to love the world.

TREK 168

John Kerry returned from Vietnam in April of 1969
with war decorations - and a troubled conscience.

A Japanese backpacker hiked into the upper falls area from the opposite direction. I waved at him and yelled positive greetings. He waved back but didn't respond verbally. Soon a cozy fire reflected off his dome tent. A voice that sounded like Toshiro Mifuni called to me with an invitation for tea.

"Hello," I said. "Welcome to the Telluride Heights low-rent district."

He responded with a series of grunts that sounded like an airplane with engine malfunction. This reminded me of the 1968 film "Hell in the Pacific" where a Japanese and American soldier are trapped on a small island together and do not speak each others' language.

We sat down and he served tea. I nodded and bowed my head. He took a dried mushroom and broke off a piece. After soaking it until the piece was bloated with heated moisture, he swallowed it. This nourishment caused him to speak like Lee Marvin.

"Hello," he said suddenly. "I don't normally speak English, but this species of mushroom empowers me to speak any language for five minutes at a time. My father gave it to me to help fulfill my quest. I'm walking across America to spread the ashes of my grandfather near places that would honor his spirit."

"His last wish was the cremation of his remains. He wanted his ashes carried to America and sprinkled in different places. I left a smidgen near the base of the Statue of Liberty. Left a pinch in Los Alamos where they invented the A-bomb. I'm going to the north side of the Grand Canyon and my last place will be Disneyland. The small box that contains Grandpa, I'll throw into the Pacific Ocean.

"Grandpa was a hermit until he suffered a stroke. Then we had to place him in a rest home. They wanted to medicate him, but he refused any pills. At home as it got cold, he put on more clothes to keep warm. He always slept in his shoes. The staff at the facility undressed him for bed. He was miserable and troublesome.

"At his request the family took him back home. He promised not to be a burden and quit eating. After five days he was dead. We found him in his rocking chair. He died in his sleep, peacefully and with his shoes on. It is my honor now to carry out his last request. At sunrise I'll drop a few ashes over the waterfall. I wanted to tell you this so you won't think I'm just an awkward tourist, blithely blundering along. The effect of the mushroom is wearing off. I will slip back into my native tongue."

Once again he sounded like an irate Japanese soldier left to die on a small island.

TREK 169

> *Released in 1968, the massive Russian production of Leo Tolstoy's novel, "War and Peace", took more than five years to finish and offers great battle scenes and aristocratic life.*

Querida María,

The summer is winding down. My experiment of traveling without money was successful, plus, not having to grind the hours away on the commercial treadmill gave me lots of time to read. I just finished two novels by Nella Larsen that were published late in the Harlem Renaissance.

The novels of Nella Larsen: The opening of "Quicksand" (1928) finds the heroine, Helga Crane, in pleasant circumstances, teaching at a school in the South. She soon becomes dissatisfied and quits in midterm. Some nameless discontent drives her to seek fulfillment in South Chicago. After a short stint in the Windy City, her spirits drop and she departs for NYC. Harlem in the 1920's sucked in most of the Negro artists in the Western Hemisphere. For a while Helga is fascinated by the music, social gatherings with high class entertainment and lavish food, dance halls, the mass of people on the street. She did not live in a dank cellar or an overcrowded YWCA. Through a connection she had a plush apartment. Nevertheless, her ennui set in again and she takes a liner to Copenhagen. In Denmark she lives comfortably with relatives, rejects an offer of marriage from a prominent portrait painter, and eventually beats it back to Harlem with a nagging emptiness.

One evening while walking, she gets caught in a downpour. She stumbles into a church revival. Several of the attendees experience religious orgasm. This spiritual assemblage activates Helga's libido. She immediately sets her heart on the Reverend Mr. Pleasant Green, "who had so kindly, so unctuously, proffered his escort to her hotel on the memorable night of her conversion." The rural yokel cannot resist her charms and they are united before her clothes can dry from the rainstorm. She takes up housekeeping in a backwater town in Alabama. At first the novelty of it excites her; then, the boredom and poverty set in and she wants to flee her retched environs. But now she has children that trap and drag her down into quicksand.

If Larsen's objective is to show that faith in Christianity is a dead end, if she wants to say that putting your life in the hands of the Lord, like her ignorant neighbors, is a hoax then it comes too late in the story to have an impact. Does Larsen suggest that marriage and the ensuing offspring are the pitfall? Without the responsibility of children Helga could take it on the lam again.

Her message is so slim she could have fleshed it out in a short story rather than dragging it out in a novel. Helga Crane is a namby-pamby. Her behavior is shilly-shally. The pattern of her relocations to escape the boredom of her life becomes excessively repetitious. Helga is educated, attractive and likeable, but she squanders her potential. She never approaches the level of tragic character. Her final decision to live in a converted horse barn surrounded by illiterates is stupid.

The characters of Larsen's second novel "Passing" (1929) are equally as vapid as the ones mired in "Quicksand". Irene Redfield and Clare Kendry deal with the issue of Negro women passing themselves off as white. But the covert theme is that of the lesbian relationship between Irene and Clare. Both women are married but their marriages are hollow arrangements. Irene has two sons but she and her husband sleep in separate bedrooms and bicker constantly. Clare is married to a white man who does not know that she has been "painted by the tar brush."

She is glad when he leaves town so she can visit Irene. The two women compliment and caress each other in a romantic manner never displayed to their husbands. Irene is so sexually repressed that from insecurity and fear she kills her friend Clare.

Larsen has her main character describe the slow passage of time: "The day dragged on to its end." To describe "Passing" I only need to alter one word: The novel dragged on to its end. I think the reason she got published was the paucity of African-American female novelists of the time. By the late 20's Harlem writers were in vogue and selling books. Claude McKay had a bestseller in 1929. Larsen had a manuscript and her friend Van Vechten gave the nod to his cohorts at Knopf. In 1930 Larsen quit writing and returned to nursing at a hospital in Brooklyn. After the stock market crash of 1929 the Harlem Renaissance began gearing down. It came to a complete halt with the riot in 1935.

Hope to see you soon, then register for another year at the university.

Hasta la Vista

TREK 170

In 1969 Walt Disney Productions created a VW with a mind of its own in the film "The Love Bug".

I walked to the outskirts before hitching a ride out of Telluride. When I finally raised my thumb, a dark-haired lady in a VW bug stopped to pick me up. She lived in the area and worked selling original jewelry.

She had at least one ring on every finger. Her ears had multiple piercings from which dangled feathers and twisted silver. Her name was Doris Norris and she asked if I could drive her bug so she could paint her fingernails.

The Volkswagen was a major tool for reliable low-budget travel. A ten-gallon tank could easily cover 300 miles of freeway or back-country dirt roads.

Backpack Trekker: A 60's Flashback

When I got behind the wheel and prepared to enter traffic, the car took off by itself. It moved so fast and unexpectedly that it tossed us upside down until our feet stuck out the window. Doris accused me of reckless driving, but I protested. The bug navigated us on its own volition. When the car stopped, she insisted that we switch places.

She took over the controls and demonstrated her mastery over the machine. When she was most confident, the car reared up on its back wheels and shot forward like a race car heading for the finish line. The car took us onto a dirt road. Doris spun the wheel and slammed on the brakes, even turned off the ignition key, but nothing stopped the bug from careening around corners at breakneck speed and climbing a steep grade up into the mountains.

The road dead-ended into a ghost town. The bug stopped near an abandoned two story hotel. The VW shut itself off and wouldn't start again. Doris tried to open the door. The mechanism did not respond. She accused me of some legerdemain trickery, but I explained to her that the car itself was making the decisions.

She became inflamed when she was not in control of her life. She banged on the dashboard and railed against this tortuous turn of events.

I'm sure her protestations carried for miles, like the vociferant voice of a lioness growling across the savanna. I opened the door and decided to look around while Doris could relax. We were at Altus Lakes. The air was pungent with adventure.

TREK 171

In 1967 Arlo Guthrie created a sensation at the Newport Folk Festival with "Alice's Restaurant Massacree," an 18-minute talking saga about littering and avoiding the draft.

I climbed into the dilapidated two-story hotel. All the windows were broken out. The inside walls had been covered with graffiti. There was a newspaper on the floor with an article about Georges Pompidou being elected President of France.

There was a long hallway with rooms on either side. What kind of people stayed in these rooms? Perhaps they were hard-nosed miners or weather-beaten foresters. Perhaps raucous revelers and merrymakers crossed the hall to egg on celebrants with rum-enriched eggnog.

Maybe there was a sluice box where men looked for the mother lode and used gold dust to pay for their goods and services. Many high-elevation Western ghost towns were founded because of valuable ore. When they extracted all the gold teeth from Mother Earth, there was nothing left to sustain an economy and the environment was usually harsh.

The inside stairs to the second floor were shaky but traversable. The sound of a flute filled the upper level. The player's genealogy must run in a straight line from Orpheus. At the source of the music there was a man on a flute and a young woman weaving on a loom. She noticed me first and stopped her work. He sensed her anxiety and withdrew the reed from his mouth.

"Hello," I said. "I didn't realize anybody resided here." They had a large piece of plastic over the window. Their belongings were strewn across the floor. They had bedding in one corner of the room and had obviously been ensconced there for several days. He reached under a blanket and brought out a revolver. "Don't shoot. I'm just a harmless victim of circumstantial juxtaposition."

"What are you doing sneaking around?" he demanded.

"I'm sorry to disturb your serenity. I'm not the absentee landlord making a surprise visit. Squatters have rights too."

"Squatters? The ones with rights have the greatest firepower. I'll show you what right is." He squeezed the trigger and fired off a round near my head.

TREK 172

> In 1969 the doctors suggested Louis Armstrong
> not play the trumpet again.

"I got your attention," said the man after shooting a bullet that whizzed past my cranium. I collapsed on the floor and writhed like Bonnie and Clyde after the birds took sudden flight and the ambush riddled them in slow motion. For several moments I felt bitten by the jaws of death.

"Let that be a lesson to you," he said. "Don't skulk around. Now we can be friends. My name is Daniel and this is my girlfriend Penny."

"I apologize profusely for barging in on your mountain resort," I said taking a subterranean breath. "I had no inkling this dilapidated structure was inhabited by anything except spirits unable to connect completely with the next world."

"We moved in here three days ago. We were in Telluride, but ran short of moolah and needed a place where Penny could work. She is a weaver of colorful carpets that we can sell for hundreds of dollars. After we have restored our inventory, we can stop by the side of the road and stretch out a rope. We hang the rugs up so any passerby can go goggle-eyed and pull over to negotiate.

"I usually start with a plucky price then drop down so people think they are dickering a major discount from two destitute travelers. We can always sell or barter the rugs to subsidize our next venture. Once we traded a rug for some automotive work on our van. Another time we swapped for two months free rent in a beach house in Florida. So what brings you to this neck of the woods?"

"I got a ride with Doris Norris. She is in her VW bug right now."

"You seem like a square shooter," Penny said. "Why don't you invite your sweetie inside so we can chew the fat? We haven't hobnobbed with anyone for several days."

"Doris was kind to pick me up and then her bug hightailed it up here. She thinks I cast a spell on her car. She had an emotional crisis earlier, but she's probably calm by now and will be glad to meet you."

"After the trauma she will need an attitude adjustment. See if you can coax her up for a visit and I'll show her something that will change her state of mind on the dead level."

I went down the rickety stairs to fetch Doris Norris.

TREK 173

In 1969 George Cukor directs "Justine", the story of a Middle Eastern prostitute who rises to a position of power in her country.

I left the old hotel and walked back to the VW bug where Doris Norris sat behind the wheel. Her face was smooth and blissful.

"How do you feel?" I asked. Doris opened her eyes wide and smiled. Her former furor had passed like a mountain storm. "I feel better. The air is so delicious at this elevation. There are two lakes nearby. I've heard about this place and wanted to check it out. I guess my love bug wanted to bring us here."

Her eyebrows fluttered calmness. She rested her hands on the steering wheel as I leaned against the door and looked in. She had beautiful soft hands. In T'ai Chi the soft will overcome the hard, like water deteriorating rock. An energy emerged from her diaphragm. I had an urge to hold her hand.

Clashing with this was my mental process that pointed to our unacquainted condition and she might take umbrage. The desire to dive into the deep waters of intimacy was stronger than my fears of rejection to my heartfelt extended probe. I broke through the web of timidity and reached for her hand. She accepted my touch and we connected like two slices of bread on a peanut butter and jelly sandwich. The simple gesture broke the hypothetical barrier that separates people. We were ingenuous innocents opening our eyes to carnal blessedness.

"You have elegant hands," I said. Her smile massaged my internal organs. All the enjoyment of my hours spent traveling alone melted into a previous incarnation. A surgeon or doctor was not needed to check my temperature and explain I was healthier than on the previous day. I felt more invigorated from the inexplicable combination of compatible energies. I felt protracted excitement as she opened the car door.

"I encountered a couple squatting in the upper level of this abandoned hotel," I said. "They invited us to tarry and be merry. What do you say we sashay up?" She stepped out of the car.

"Was there a gun shot? she asked.

"Probably just a marmot backfiring," I replied.

TREK 174

> In 1969 George C. Scott is in a re-edited feature
> from two episodes of the TV series "The Road
> West". It is entitled "This Savage Land."

Querida María,

I have a concrete revelation to announce in this letter. Met a girl in the high country of Colorado. Can't say I will stand next to her while a priest dispenses permission for us to kiss, but she is as emotive as Marlene Dietrich in "Destry Rides Again".

You are anxious for me to connect with someone. When I opted not to attend the prom, you were disappointed. Then there was the occasion when you asked me to help one of our pretty neighbors carry her books home. I returned from that assignment and you were crestfallen when nothing developed. The library was more interesting than dates or frittering away time with my peers. It's my fault for being contrary-wise to normal behavior.

Earl Hines on piano is more exciting than The Beach Boys. I'll take Willie "The Lion" Smith playing at a rent party over any Elvis movie.

This girl is named Doris Norris. She stands out because of her alternative style of appearance. Plus she has a strong mind of her own. I'll keep you posted on future developments. I'm working my way into the Southwest. Not to imply I have a job. I'm simply moving in a southwestwardly direction.

Since my financial windfall I hike around well-heeled. Feeling wealthy doesn't alter my summer experiment. I guess it is like having a gun in my backpack. I can use the money anytime for a trip to Chaco Canyon to stand on La Fajada Butte and watch the sun set; to sit in the great kiva at Pueblo Bonito and listen to the bats fly up from the sipapuni; to emerge refreshed into a new world or return undaunted into a vanished civilization; to listen to the sound of memory gushing down a dry arroyo; to watch shadows collect on sandstone and cut them out like cookie patterns.

I seldom watch TV but I miss "Gunsmoke". Saw the evening news one day during happy-hour in a bar. The body bag count is odious. The amount of energy and money expended on warfare is misplaced. They could rebuild ghettos in America. Imagine instead of defoliating Vietnam and dropping bombs on civilians we put billions of new dollars into education and public art. We have nothing to win in Vietnam. Why not invade Mexico instead? We wouldn't have to travel so far and maybe we could extend our borders. We need a pretext so let's attack because they sell dope to our kids. We cry for our own dead, but also remember many more wounded Vietnamese shattered mentally or crippled and in wheelchairs with no legs because they stepped on a land mine made in America.

Anyway, love you, your son ...

☯

Beatlick Joe Speer

In 1968 Louis Armstrong recorded
"What a Wonderful World".

I escorted Doris Norris to the second floor of the abandoned hotel where the squatters were ensconced.

"Meet Doris Norris," I said, introducing her to the couple.

"Greetings," Daniel replied. "Sorry we have no divan. The room comes unfurnished. Pull up the floor and have a seat. Would you like a cup of tea?"

"I'd rather a mixed drink," Doris replied.

"Our liquor cabinet is empty."

"A cup of tea is fine," I said. "If it's no trouble."

"No trouble. We boil water and plop in a tea bag." He pumped up the fuel tank on his Coleman stove and lit the flame under a pot.

"While the water heats up I want to show you a strange phenomenon. I don't know if you believe in ghosts, but we have experienced a visitation. It's the spirit of some western character. It paces and moans disconsolately. We have since learned to summon it up from its vaporous existence by chanting in unison. We have not spoken with it but you are welcome to ask it a question."

Daniel led us to an empty room where we bunched up and chanted. After a few minutes we heard the lamentations. Then a vague transparent image appeared.

"Who are you?" I asked.

"I'm a ball of disturbed mist, an unquiet soul that cannot make the transition into the next world. In life I was known as Kit Carson."

"Why do you prowl this desolate place a hundred years after your death?" I asked.

"In history I'm known as a frontiersman and scout. In New Mexico they named a national forest after me. In Taos they have a museum dedicated to me. This false adulation keeps me in a state of painful abeyance. I am worse than Judas because I betrayed not just one man but an entire race of people. I helped U.S. soldiers kill Indians and led them into Canyon de Chelly. We burned their orchards and destroyed their food supply. We decimated their villages so when winter arrived they had no choice but to surrender. I was a mercenary who killed people that did nothing to deserve such treatment. As long as I am celebrated by the world, I am doomed to spiritual unrest. Tell the world not to honor me. Tell the world the truth and set me free."

The spirit of Kit Carson dissolved like smoke in a twisted wind.

TREK 176

In 1969 Rod McKuen was very busy with two books: "In Someone's Shadow" and "The Songs of Rod McKuen".

Doris Norris and I departed the dilapidated buildings. As we walked toward her self-willed '69 VW bug, I felt it was an auspicious moment to perform a bold action. I liked Doris and wanted to solidify our relationship. The bug started up and we drove down the dirt road back to the highway. I carefully crafted my proposal.

"I think you are a superior specimen of free-form femininity. I don't know how adamant your schedule is, but I'd like to spend more time with you. How would you like to visit Rainbow Bridge in Utah?"

"I don't have time to dilly-dally," she replied. "I have to sell some jewelry and pay off some bills.

"How much do you owe?"

"I need a thousand bucks to make me feel relaxed."

I reached into my pouch and took out my roll of green energy. I peeled off twelve C notes and handed it to her.

"Here is $1200. Will that placate your financial worries?"

"Is this for real?"

"As real as a churchyard with a gaping vacancy."

"I'm not a hooker. You can't buy your way into my pants."

"It is a gift. I share resources with my friends. I don't expect you to do anything you don't want to do."

"This is incredible. Nobody has ever been so generous to me, especially on such a short term acquaintance. What's your whimsy?"

"I've traveled all summer around North America. Mostly alone except for my friend Zen Jazz, who comes at random times. I thought you might add more alliteration to my life. Maybe we can create alleviating memories. If it doesn't pan out you can drop me off at Chaco Canyon. Keep the money. Keep everything in your name."

She touched my arm and shushed me with her eyes. "When I saw you walking along the highway, I thought what a hunk of traveling man. I don't pick up hitchhikers. You are the first, but before we embark on any new adventures, I want to pick up some personal items from my apartment."

"Forget about the past," I said. "Let's go forward. We can stop in Cortez and I'll buy you anything you need. What do you say?"

She tapped on the steering wheel and looked out the window with an avid gleam in her eyes.

"Let's go," she said.

TREK 177

In 1969 Captain Beefheart and the Magic Band caused mouth-frothing enthusiasm with "Trout Mask Replica".

Doris Norris was born in San Antonio, Texas. She borrowed money from her brother for a bus ticket to San Francisco where she joined a religious cult that demanded no friendships beyond the group. It required all financial holdings or portable wealth be turned over to the spiritual leaders. She had to cut her hair and sell incense on the street to earn money for the group. At meal time the members ate off wax paper that was rolled out onto the floor like an extended table cloth. A ladleful of gruel was dropped in front of each of them and they ate with their fingers.

Everyone rose at four a.m. to chant and pray. She stayed until a man on the outside invited her to a concert at the Fillmore West in June of '67. She changed her opinion after listening to The Who and never returned to the cult again.

The idea of communal living was fascinating but not under such stifling circumstances. Some people in Golden Gate Park told her about a commune in New Mexico that excited her. It was located in the mountains with big trees. People still had to work, but in a less subservient system. The rigidity of the urban pattern created an impasse for Doris. Arrangements were made to leave San Francisco for Questa, New Mexico. Just before she left a mailman approached her and said, "Be here now."

Near Questa she saw a llama standing next to the foundation of a geodesic dome. For the first three days at the new commune she had to observe a vow of silence. After that she rotated work duties, serving as kitchen scullion and tending the garden. Sufi dancing and the drum circle became a vital part of her routine. In her off-time she learned to make feather earrings and acquired tools to work with soft metals like silver. With her new skills and equipment she felt confident about making a living anywhere.

Her father coaxed her back to San Antonio with an offer to buy her a new VW bug. She stayed in Texas for several weeks, then cut the tethers and started a new life in Telluride, Colorado. She supplemented her jewelry earnings by stringing hishi stones in the back room of a head shop. Her work was on commission in several prominent locations. Doris was a highly motivated person with urgent aspirations.

TREK 178

In 1968 Baba Ram Dass, spiritual mendicant and wandering Sadu, returned to North America from India.

Doris Norris and I parked the VW on a Durango side street. What better way to enhance a relationship that was developed in a ghost town than to go on a shopping spree. We entered many a boutique and haberdashery. I encouraged her not to buy the first outfit that emitted symptoms of wanting to quit the shop. We were serious shoppers with money to exchange for the rush of owning something new.

A friendly attendant who played Herman's Hermits "I'm Into Something Good", finally got our money. Doris wore stylishly wrinkled clothes. She bought broomstick skirts and crepe blouses of corresponding colors that she could tie in knots and pack into a haversack. We both bought broad-rimmed hats to protect us from the unrelenting sun in the canyon we planned to visit.

The light of August in Chaco Canyon is like a studio set swept by a barrage of ellipsoidal spotlights.

After we had Doris clothed, she helped me pick an outback outfit and a seersucker suit at the Saint Vincent de Paul thrift store.

Doris was hungry after shopping and picked us out a restaurant so we could tackle some viands. She chose one called the Chinese Dragon with a six-foot Buddha near the entrance. Inside were six prayer wheels we turned as we were greeted by a hostess from Hong Kong.

She had relatives living on boats. She did not divulge this information but it came to me in a flash. I don't know what elicited this power, but I accepted it and said nothing to Doris. Maybe because we were approaching sacred topography. Maybe because August was the culmination of the summer march of events.

The music will expand and carry us home. The pages and letters will collect like Native-American medicine cards and be placed in a blue box by an ingenious young student who recently won a spelling bee. The decade approached a peak experience. I drank hot tea and she consumed a cold beer. I scissor-locked her legs under the table.

"I am lucky to have you share these nicks of time," I said.

"You rouse the spirit of the earth and move the rolling sky," she replied.

"We are kindred spirits. I want to take you to a special place."

"When?"

"Now. So indulge the urban urge before we descend into the valley of death?"

"Whatever you have in mind," she said. "I have the wheels to get us there."

"I love to hear that. I think you and my mother would hit it off," I said. "Her name is María and she has a debonair spirituality. She converted a room in our house into a beauty shop. She can book appointments early or pamper eccentrics late at night while serving them mixed drinks. She makes good money working on hair and listening to her customers unload.

"Actually, while women chew the fat in front of the mirror or have their hair shampooed, my mother prays or thinks about a land investment. She even gets us involved taking the rolling papers off the curlers and straightening them out so she can use them again.

"She believes God is people and their needs. She serves the needs of others every day. In her spare time cleans up dearth gurgles when other family members are asleep."

"Your mother sounds like a saint."

"If sainthood comes from hard work, she fits the bill." We talked until the restaurant closed.

"Let's pick up a bottle of champagne and find a hotel," Doris said.

☯

Backpack Trekker: A 60's Flashback

> *In 1969 the Spanish government gave Pablo Pi-*
> *casso permission to return to his native Spain.*

I shared my enthusiasm for ancient sites with Doris and convinced her it would behoove us to visit Mesa Verde and the stone
structures that glint in the protected cliffs. Her VW greeted the
steep climb up to the National Park with grinding downshifting
vigor.

We arrived mid-morning and were lucky to find a group of
campers leaving so that we immediately claimed their spot. The
first day we joined a ranger-guided hike of Cliff Palace. Doris was
amazed at the well-preserved ruins. That night around the campfire we talked about the Anasazi way of life.

"These people had a network of routes connecting them to
other communities. They traded with people as far away as central Mexico," I said.

"How do they know that?" Doris asked.

"Excavations at certain digs have revealed macaw feathers.
The macaw is a tropical bird with extraordinary plumage. It was
not indigenous to the southwest. There has been material found
around Chaco Canyon that is not of this earth. This confirms to
me the idea that human life is not the supreme form. I feel nature
has been penurious in its gifts to man. I think there are life forms
that far exceed our imagination. Just as we care for pets and domestic animals that are indifferent or ignorant of our accomplishments, I think there are other levels of consciousness that make
us look like hangers on to the lower rungs on the life chain," I answered.

"Are you a teacher at a free school?" Doris asked.

"No. I study literature at the university," I said. "You know, I
think I saw you in Golden Gate Park this summer. You were
dancing by yourself at a free concert."

"That's incredible," she replied. "Another reason I picked you
up is that you remind me of a head shop with black-light posters
and beads for sale. To go from Texas to San Fran involved some
shape changing, but I believe the kids are all right. I feel like people under thirty could start a new political party or have a certain
extended territory where we would have control of our affairs.
Can you dig it? We would own the property and abolish taxes if
we saw fit."

"That's like a protracted case of amnesia. If we forgot everything then we'd have to start over and one of the changes could be the eradication of the cumbersome concept of private property. Most wars are conducted to obtain or hold on to property. Selling deeds to land was concocted by a cursory cynic," I said.

A three-quarter-ton pick-up truck with a camper parked in the site next to us. I stirred the coals around with a designated fire stick. I cross-stacked some little logs over the fire and blew on the red-and-orange glow, which pulsated with my warm breath onto its even warmer surface.

Our camping neighbor was an old man with a poodle he called "Charley". They were traveling in search of America. His vehicle was capable of rigorous conditions. The name Rocinante was painted on the side of his truck. He was very friendly and shared numerous stories with us. He recapped the plot of a novel he wrote about people traveling to California with all their belongings, knowing they would never return to till their native soil or give birth to any new life on their farms.

He claimed Hollywood made a movie based on his book, but they couldn't quite agree on his ending, so they attached a more Emersonian conclusion.

When we woke in the morning, the old man and his dog were gone. I pumped up the Coleman stove to boil coffee water. "That was a wonderful visitation we had last night."

"Yes," Doris said. "I bet that man has a granite backbone."

"Despite his stature as a writer, I bet few people recognize him. That was John Steinbeck that sat by our fire last night. He died in 1968."

TREK 180

In 1969 Boston Red Sox star Ted Williams returned to baseball to manage the Washington Senators.

Doris referred to her VW as "our little bug." We shared resources from the outset. The VW took us to the Shiprock area. The Navajo call it *"tae-bidahi."* The rock resembles a ship at full sail on a tranquil ocean. The Navajo tell a story about fighting the Utes. The conflict took a downward turn for the Navajo and they were hard pressed to depart the area alive. The medicine men chanted and prayed. All the Navajo chanted and prayed. The ground beneath their feet rose up and floated away. They left the enemy far behind. At sundown the next day the floating earth settled on a vast plain. It is now a sacred mountain.

We talked about how books change when made into movies. The Boris Karloff 1931 version of "Frankenstein" is monstrously altered from the Mary Shelley novel. Boris burns up. I guess fires are more exciting than blocks of ice. In her ending, Shelley has Frankenstein jump out the cabin window and onto an ice raft.

"He was soon borne away by the waves, and lost in darkness and distance," she writes. Shelly has a concentrated style and unrelenting gift to spin the dynamo of text, but she skirts over realistic details. How does the monster remain unnoticed while traveling around Europe or live next door to a family for months despite his size and horrid demeanor?

If I ask too many questions, it might distract me from enjoying the story. I decided to leave off the questions. The rock came into view. It was there before the Four Corners or before the petroglyphs in Chama Canyon. The magic rock is on the Navajo Reservation. The Navajo adapted better than the Apache to the commercial way of life. The Apache had generations of plundering to redirect before they could blend into American culture. The Apache had to forget Chief Victorio who left the Mescalero Reservation. The Apache had to forget about Geronimo who departed the San Carlos confinement in Arizona. The Navajo learned to sell sand paintings, silversmithing and weaving. Many Navajo ceremonial songs have been recorded. They cultivated the horse and sheep and learned to sell fuel for the automobile.

As we drove along, Doris and I created a friendship poem:

Our friendship transports memories in its hull
Its rigging is taut with connecting tissue
Our friendship is a kayak in icy waters
It is a canoe for upstream tributaries
It is a speed boat to navigate meandering rivers
It is a luxury liner for the long haul
Across the vastness of liquid space
As we walk the deck of our friendship
The prow is set to prowl
Sounding new depths
Cutting through the waters of time
Headed for the safe harbor of continued friendship.

The VW pulled off onto the side of the road. We wondered why we stopped so we looked around. Our little bug had provided us with an advantageous view of the frozen magic vessel.

Shiprock loomed up and sent us a telepathic transmission from another place.

TREK 181

In 1969 Norman Mailer received a National Book Award for "The Armies of the Night".

Shiprock sent us images of a festival on private property. On the first day the grass was a lush landscape of waving green guitars . Stepping on the plush verdure was free and fresh. A fence was going up as people arrived. The area was overrun with thousands so it was like pulling out an umbrella after walking a city block in a downpour. The heels of anticipation and the oncoming horde were the *coup de grace* on the fencing.

Traffic backed up so all who wanted to cut a caper at the fete had to park and walk in with their festive accouterments. The Shiprock pointed straight up. The transmissions of the rock had not found spots on the AM band, but a device appeared at our window that resembled a loud speaker at a drive-in. We heard the bamboo didgeridoo from Vermont. We heard a drummers' circle rotating jabs and rhythm. We smelled the scent of heated oils filling a tent as they combined and entered through a causeway of delight. Doris listened intently and took notes. The rock began to vibrate like a circus calliope.

We heard screaming napalm flash out to burn villagers in a rice field. We saw children running down a dirt road with their skin on fire. We saw heat rays sending spires of fires to swiftly dispatch curious citizenry. We saw the blood from a wounded soldier trail across the ground to the coast and shoot like a torpedo across the ocean and under the Golden Gate Bridge.

The blood hit the beach at Alameda Island and flowed up the steps of an office building where a woman worked. The blood came to an abrupt stop at her feet. In an instant she knew her son was dead.

We saw the highway open up like in the 1969 novel *"Conversación en la Catedral"* by Mario Vargas Llosa. We saw arrows moving toward the stone like spermatozoa advancing for a head-on collision with the egg. We saw the Apache eating the pulp of the mescal plant. We saw them living off the land as they traveled deep into Mexico. We saw them distill their artistry into warfare, an art which they cultivated with businesslike punctiliousness.

"Let's mount the deck of that Shiprock," I said. "I want to touch it."

We drove as close as we could, then parked and walked. Doris wanted to scratch our names onto the base of the rock. I suggested we write them in the sand. I saw the face of Zen Jazz appear in the rock. He was dressed as a priest. He blessed us and I kissed his ring. He touched our heads with a palm branch from Rome. It had been blessed by Pope Paul VI. We stood next to each other while Zen made the sign of the cross several times.

Zen surrounded us with his glow and began our ceremony without relatives and the catered food. The three of us melded together into a familial whole to celebrate the joy of conjugal commitment and to cheer the prospect of our sexual unison.

"I do" was written in our eyes. It felt like the rock was prepared to lift off. The face of Zen disappeared and I knew we would see him soon in the flesh.

TREK 182

In 1969 W.S. Merwin secured by copyright an English translation of poems by Pablo Neruda from "20 Poemas de Amor y Una Canción Desesperada".

The VW drove us to Aztec Ruins National Monument. In reality, the Aztec did not build outreaches in northern New Mexico. The Aztec built Tenochtitlan in what is now Mexico City. It was 7,000 feet above sea level and walled on three sides by mountains. Their big mistake was inviting Cortes as a house guest.

But their influence was enduring enough for people hundreds of years later to name this place in remembrance of that valley. At the Aztec Ruins monument Doris and I sat in a reconstructed kiva to enjoy the ancient ambiance. Doris recounted a traumatic experience from her past.

"There was a drummer in a TexMex band in San Antonio. I fantasized about meeting him along the River Walk and making out on a bench as people walked past. My girlfriend at the time had a crush on the bass player. We arrived early at one of their gigs and secured a place up front. An invitation was forthcoming to meet the band afterwards. We were especially emotive with our appreciation. Brian Epstein could have hired us as part of the frenzied groupies greeting the Beatles when they arrived in America. They offered us shots of tequila and Mexican beer with lime. We paired off and I departed with the drummer. His name was Antonio Ramon. He was very sweet. We stayed together all night and finished off with breakfast at a sunrise truck stop.

"Several weeks later I got a taste of morning sickness. I knew what was wrong with me. An examination confirmed that I was pregnant. The same day I heard Antonio was flown to Vietnam. For some reason I didn't tell him and decided an abortion was the way out. I discovered a place in Mexico that performs the procedure. I traveled to Nuevo Laredo and took a cab to a certain address and was waiting to remove the intruder from my womb.

"It was a matter of moments before they called me into the next room. It wasn't the child's fault that we called it into life. Maybe the stirring in my body was the movement of a future world leader. I decided to have the baby and walked straight out of there. I had to support the life force.

"On the day my daughter was born we received news that Antonio was dead in Vietnam. My parents shipped me off to an unwed mothers' home in Nashville, Tennessee. I finally gave her up for adoption to the Florence Crittendon Home where I was staying. They were capable and caring people. I felt like she would have a better opportunity with parents who wanted a child and were prepared to love it.

"Never did I realize the one night of enjoyment had such resounding concussions. It forced a situation on me that I detested. It allowed me to consider the destruction of another life. It alienated me from my parents.

"It forced me to part from a child that otherwise would bring joy into my life. I carry a sadness with me that I plan to rectify when we meet years later.

"She won't know me, but I'll recognize her intuitively and perform some great act of kindness."

A group of tourists entered the big kiva and we decided to move along.

☯

Backpack Trekker: A 60's Flashback

In the 1969 movie "The File of the Golden Goose", police-men go undercover to infiltrate a gang of counterfeiters, with cross and double-cross and plenty of London location work.

Querida María,

What do we know concerning the creator of the universe? Not enough to formulate a complete sentence and yet so much that people attack infidels for not sharing the same sentiments.

What do we know of the creator of "King Lear" and "The Tempest"? The straight dope on the Shake is sketchy. As creators on a conscious level we are aware of ourselves and the products of our freedom. But when we reach into the unconscious, we enter the unknown, an area that expresses no personality because it includes everything. The more an artist taps the unconscious, the more universal the work will be, and the more apt it is to live into succeeding generations. The more a work depends on personality, the less chance it has of surviving after its particular creator is gone.

The more I travel in time and space, the more vast distance becomes, the smaller I become, and however much I add to my experience and knowledge, the more difficult it is to satisfy the persistent desire for more and more that strives toward complete knowledge.

The eventual frustration of this desire, the futility of it when confronted with eternity, makes me want to stop and select a single object and study it until I know every aspect of it.

If I can isolate a moment of time, I can encompass all of it. This reaction will be futile, however, because for even if I did dominate a single subject, space, or moment, it would become a bore and such a paltry accomplishment that it will not placate the desire for more.

We have an inborn drive for more that has moved us from the Stone to the Nuclear Age. Is there a shut-off valve for experience or a time when we lock ourselves in a room and not desire more?

"Don Quijote de la Mancha" is on my top-ten list for best novels. Maybe because Don takes to the road alone then returns home to regroup his wanderlust with friend Sancho Panza.

"La Segunda Parte del Ingenioso Hidalgo" is richer because they kick it around at night or while traveling to the next adven-

ture. Maybe I respond to that motif currently because Doris and I enjoy that situation.

Another book on my top-ten list is "The Odyssey" by Homer. It is not a novel but presents one exciting adventure after another. Odysseus is dependent on boats to reach his destinations.

Although "The Air-Conditioned Nightmare" and "The Big Sea" are contenders for the list, a travel theme is not a prerequisite for making my list. "The Magic Mountain" by Thomas Mann is on my list. The hero Hans Castorp is "an unassuming young man traveling in midsummer" and stays in one place after he arrives at a sanatorium.

It is mid-August and I feel events are coming to a head. Most people I meet are helpful and friendly. The worst I had to deal with was human chicanery. Some travelers become irate about being cheated or becoming a victim of a pickpocket. The possibility of being hoodwinked or taken advantage of makes them suspicious of everyone and on guard like a gazelle at a water hole where a lion might lurk.

I can't live with mistrust in my heart. Yes, someone did rip me off and they might think dishonesty is the way to get ahead. They know not what they do. If someone is resolute in their desire for money, I'd rather give it to them than fight over it. And after they take what they feel is valuable, I'll ask if there is anything else they want. If nothing else, then leave because the next thing I will give them is a hard time. Money is given to me and I give it to someone else. As the song says, "There is one thing for certain, when it comes my time I'll leave this old world, with a satisfied mind."

Mucho amor, your son ...

TREK 184

"In the Year of the Pig" a film from 1969, presents a hard-hitting anti-war documentary on the Vietnam War.

Doris Norris and I both loved August. I liked the August month because no holidays are listed on my calendar. This leaves room for augury. While driving we saw the outline of a hitchhiker flicker like a midtown jaywalker. I started to motion for Doris to slow down but the VW slowed down on its own.

"What's up?" Doris inquired.

Backpack Trekker: A 60's Flashback

"If I know this traveler walking on the side of the road, let's pick him up."

"I don't think we have room for a passenger," Doris protested.

"Only if I know him, otherwise all bets are off."

The pedestrian did not turn his hand to procure a ride. We pulled up behind him and saw a disheveled face like the flute player for Jethro Tull. As he turned to stand on one leg, I recognized Zen Jazz. I jumped out for an embrace and to introduce him to Doris. It was our tradition upon meeting that we retire into the nearest coffeehouse to imbibe java and exchange information. We stopped in Bloomfield at a restaurant that also had a liquor license. We ordered coffee and I asked Zen what had transpired since we last met.

"I'm working on a story about a man who watched his son dwindle away, emaciated by a debilitating disease. The illness was untreatable and nothing could curb the disease. All they could do was provide relief from pain. A morphine drip. The father spent every day in the hospital, holding his son's hand and speaking soothingly as his son's grasp grew weaker and he lost his ability to communicate except through his eyes. The son asked his father to hold him, he wanted his dad to hold him again, the way he had held him as a child. On their last night together the father undressed and climbed into bed. He gradually felt the heat leave his son's body. When the nurse arrived early in the morning, she found the father in the son's death bed."

"Gruesome and cathartic," Doris commented. "That story reminds me of my cat. Some kids gave kittens away in front of the grocery store. I was not in the market for a pet, but when I came out of the store there was one cat left, and I fell in love with it and took it back to my apartment.

"We lived happily together until I lost my job and could no longer pay the rent. The landlord suddenly changed from a jovial character to a pit bull with language skills. At the same time my car broke down. I was desperate and luckily a friend invited me to move in with her. She was allergic to cats. I had to vacate but could not take Feliz with me. I named her Feliz because she was always so happy. I felt terrible but I had no choice, so I left her bowls of water and food underneath the stairwell on the outside of the complex. I came back to check on her every day.

"On our last day together I found the bowls turned over. I heard her weak voice from under a hedge. A dog must have taken a chomp on her hind quarters. She could not walk. I sang the 'Black Mountain Blues' to her. I used my tears to moisten her lips as she died in my arms."

Tears appeared on Doris's cheeks as she recreated the painful scene. I moved next to her and gave her a hug. Then Zen moved in and hugged us both.

TREK 185

In 1969 "Putney Swope" offers a comedy about a black ad man with spoofs on commercials.

It was half a tick past noon and my companions and I had a blatant caffeine buzz. We decided to switch over to beer. Zen Jazz and Doris had told stories about death. I resolved to contribute a true tale about an artist with a billowing eccentricity.

"I want to tell you about the potter George E. Ohr. He was an unmanageable eccentric who was not fully appreciated during his lifetime. Not knowing how to direct his vast energy until a friend introduced the wheel to him in New Orleans. From then on he devoted his life to what he called Pot-Ohr-E.

"He learned every aspect of his art from digging his own clay, to firing the huge kiln, to glazing the pieces, to setting them on prodigious display. He created one-of-a-kind pottery. At home in Biloxi, Mississippi, with his beautiful wife, he fabricated legions of pots that he called his 'mud babies.'

"George did not agree with the mass-production techniques of the Industrial Revolution but he utilized photography to capture his image while assuming various wild and outrageous expressions.

"His eyes were intense and bespoke a dashingly robust and muscular man. Using unshackled hucksterism to draw attention to himself, like a mustache long enough to tie at the back of his head, he created a wild man persona that put people off and distracted them from his art.

"Many were the setbacks in his career but he composed himself and rose to new heights. While attending an exposition to expose his art, many of his pieces were stolen. Even more devastating was a fire that destroyed much of Biloxi, including his workshop and pottery. After each disaster he rebuilt and his work assumed even greater proportions.

"At his workshop he erected huge signs to advertise his work. Not everyone could afford big one-of-a-kind pots, so George created pieces for the tourist trade like coffee cups, chamber pots and novelty items such as a pile of fake feces and a glazed phallus.

"Despite his attempts to garner attention, he did not receive job offers to work in Paris or sell enough to keep his inventory from becoming overstocked. By 1910 he realized his fame would blast out in another era. He crated up many of his pots and buried them in the ground. He stopped making pots. His sons converted his workshop into an auto-repair garage. He helped his sons in the garage and was the first to own a motorcycle in his hometown. Many of his pots were stored in the attic above the garage. George knew he would become famous and stipulated in his will that his work not be sold until fifty years after his death, which caught up with him in 1918. In 1968 a dealer from the east coast began negotiations to buy Ohr's work for $50,000. The time was right to mine the ore. The work of George Ohr is well."

After my story an alcohol buzz began to overlap the effects of the coffee. We informed Zen that we were en route to Chaco Canyon and invited him to accompany us. By way of accepting the offer Zen created a riff about the National Park that requires driving over miles of dirt road:

Drivin' to Chaco where they cannot find the bones
Drivin' to Chaco where spirits drop the ashes of loved ones into the great kiva
Drivin' to Chaco where the canyon echoes with the voice of the diva.

Let's go," said Zen.

TREK 186

In 1969 Great Britain presented a portrait stamp of Mohandas K. Gandhi, making the former leader of India the first foreigner to appear on a British stamp.

My colleagues and I pulled off the road to visit Angel Peak. At almost 7,000 feet it commands respect. We found a comfortable spot to have a picnic of oysters and crackers. Doris said oysters would cause a flashlight to turn on by itself or make a flag go stiff on a breezeless day. I told her that after eating oysters before a date I had a constant throbbing in my scrotum. At a movie I cut a hole in the bottom of the popcorn box and inserted my wanger. When she dug down, she found an unexpected protein source. After the meal Zen and I went for a walk. He offered me some dried mushroom. I popped a stem into my mouth and let my saliva gradually break it down. Then he offered me a cigarette.

"You know I don't ingest tobacco, Zen. You handing me a cig reminds me of a situation I experienced in downtown Houston, Texas. The tobacco industry hired women dressed in orange negligees to attract attention. They occupied street corners and passed out free samples. The companies calculated that if they could get people smoking, they would become addicted and steady customers until death.

"I predict a future time when cigarettes will be out of favor. The time is coming when images of glamorous film stars sucking on fags will be banned. Huge signs promoting this nefarious product will not be permitted. By the 22nd century the status of cigarettes will be diminished. Smokers will be vilified. Smoking will be banned from all buildings except designated smoke cells. These units will resemble an execution chamber at the end of death row. The special smoking rooms where cigarette addicts can go to puff will be monitored by trained staff. The rooms will be airtight so none of the odorous smoke can escape. Clothing designed to keep the smoke off the body will be required: caps to protect the hair, gloves to keep the fingertips from glowing yellow and a cape to stop the stench from infecting the garments."

While I spoke to Zen, he took an antique hare's foot on a long silver chain out of his pocket to wipe his upper lip and groom his beard. He ran the grisly claws through his hair like a rake.

"There will be equipment installed in the workplace to detect the presence of cigarettes. Any cigarettes discovered in restricted areas will be confiscated," I continued.

"Smoking will not be permitted in the home. Smoke detectors will be installed in every private residence. If someone lights up illegally, an alarm will sound at police headquarters, and a squad will be dispatched to break in the door of the culprit and arrest everyone in the house.

"Their assets will be seized. Smoking will be allowed but only under controlled circumstances. This will put many tobacco growers out of business. To salvage their generations of farming skills, the farmers will be allowed to grow a species of nonsmokeable hemp for use in the fabric industry, producing products like clothing, rope, tents and non-chemically treated pulp for paper.

Backpack Trekker: A 60's Flashback

"The importance of tobacco goes back to the Native Americans who grew and used it for religious ceremonies. The ravaged tobacco industry will survive by promoting snuff. Their advertising staff will devise new slogans like 'snuff is the real stuff' or 'snuff is enough.' They will enlist athletes to snort during time-outs at games. They will introduce a new line of paraphernalia, such as silver snuff spoons, silk snuff sacks and a snuffkerchief for wiping the nostrils. A snuff lite will be marketed for children. Also to attract juvenile dollars, there will be special musical snuff boxes."

That night we made a small fire and burned the cigarettes. Zen asked about Doris Norris. I told him I found a delightful companion to share my travels. Zen said he wanted to put the make on her.

As Aleister Crowley said, "Do what thou wilt shall be the whole of the Law."

To give Zen optimal opportunity, I walked around for an hour before returning to the VW. When I did return, Doris was asleep on a blanket and Zen was nowhere in sight.

TREK 187

> In the 1969 film "The Secret of Santa Vittoria" a
> drunk mayor of an Italian village hides bottles of
> wine from the Nazis.

Doris Norris did all the driving as we traveled toward Chaco Canyon. To keep her entertained I recounted anecdotes from travel books. One of my favorites is "The Big Sea" by Langston Hughes. He spoke of rivers in 1919, and in the 30's he traveled the world. Langston tells of working at a low-paying, boring job in New York City. He decided he had nothing to lose so he applied for a position on a ship. An acceptance came and so much excitement that he did not ask for the destination. At the harbor he walked across planks to assume his new duties. When he inquired where they were bound, they informed him that the ship was permanently docked.

He became part of a skeleton crew to maintain a dead fleet of ships left in mothballs since World War I.

Langston finally did go to sea on a merchant ship. On a voyage to Africa he bought a monkey. He returned home with his simian friend, Jacko, and caused an imbroglio with his mother. His stepfather was amused by Jacko and they bathed and spiffed him up for a trip to the local pool hall. They set him on a pool table where boisterous men gathered around smoking cigarettes.

Jacko was so unsettled by such scrutiny that he took a dump on the table. The stepfather found that comical until the proprietor presented him with a bill to replace the table cover.

On another trip Langston found himself in Genoa, Italy, low on money but wanting to eat some meat. He entered a restaurant and could not read the menu so he pointed to what looked like a meat item. It was indeed meat, a gamey piece of old liver. A reluctance to even poke it with the fork set in but he couldn't afford another meal and he was famished. That night in a flophouse while he slept, there was an earthquake. Sickness of the stomach awoke him before the tremors as the taste of liver was on his breath like maggots. Everyone else ran out into the street in case the building collapsed. Langston was too sick to move. If he was going to die anyway, why make a fuss?

Langston was a precursor to Henry Miller. Miller's books were autobiographical and he writes about his hand-to-mouth existence in Paris during the 1930's. Langston was in Paris in the 1920's. Some of his menial jobs proved to be influential to his style. As a dishwasher in a cabaret, he had the good fortune to hear live jazz every night. The music was reflected in his poetry. He also had a job as a doorman at a club. To make some extra money he trotted down to the corner store to buy cigarettes for the customers. As part of his duties he was supposed to stop any fights that broke out. As a writer he decided to amble to the tabac and buy some smokes when fisticuffs broke out. By the time he returned the altercations were settled and he didn't have to jump into the fray.

Doris Norris loved to laugh. I enjoyed this quality and worked overtime to feed her funny bone. From "The Big Sea" I jumped into "Tropic of Cancer" and described how Henry Miller was being evicted from a Paris apartment and was still typing on a story as the movers carried his desk out into the street.

TREK 188

In 1969 "The Learning Tree" presented an auto-biographical film, based on photographer Gordon Parks's 1963 novel, about the coming of age of a black teenager in rural Kansas during the 1920's.

Backpack Trekker: A 60's Flashback

As we drove south on Highway 44, we saw a speck gradually grow into a human form on the side of the road. It was a man dressed like a Tibetan monk. His head was shaved and it gave him the embodiment of the Buddha. I asked him through the open window if he wanted a ride.

He did not ride in cars and was walking to the site where the first atom bomb was developed. I told him we were not going to Los Alamos, but we could move him down the road a few miles in our magic VW.

He refused to ride with us until I compared him to the monk I met in the Grand Tetons. This piqued his attention as he knew a fellow monk who camped in the mountains and wrote poems based on his dreams.

"Excuse my reluctance to join you," he said. "Too many people die in car crashes. It is an extremely unnatural death."

"I know what you mean," I said. "James Dean. Jane Mansfield gone in a car mishap. James Weldon Johnson died when his car was hit by a train. Bessie Smith died after an auto accident."

"I do not relish such a statistic."

"Relax. You are safer with us than on a Greyhound Bus pass. Would you like a beer?"

"Alcohol and driving do not mix," said the monk.

"You are right. In our country alone 20,000 people die every year when the driver fills his gullet with alcohol. But Doris does the driving and she is sober as a saint. So if you want a cold import, the bar is open."

"Since you define your concept in such fluid terms, I feel the occasion merits a liquid libation," he said.

I gave him a beer and asked about our monk friend.

"As he dwelt in sublime heights he meditated on death, on the pain of the children strapped with explosives and told to pull the plug on a grenade when surrounded by American soldiers, on the pain of an Air Force officer who sent bodies back to America that he knew were not complete. Sometimes he sent a foot and said, 'This is your son.' Our friend felt something get hold of him and he went to Vietnam.

"My name is Rinpoche. I give lectures around the world. Now I'm walking to where the minds engaged on the secret project in the mountains. At the time the bomb destroyed Hiroshima, I was a child. I still have scars as a connection with Oppenheimer. He died in 1967 and I was glad. He failed to kill me and now I am alive and he is dead. I want to work out every negative inclination. I was angry for many years. It was a painful time. The survivors were all scarred. I had to get away from that mirror of pain. We need to invoke Jesus and Buddha at the same time. We need each other."

TREK 189

> *In the 1969 film "Castle Keep", eight battle-weary soldiers defend a medieval castle against a German assault in WWII.*

The sky was clear and the road was straight. As we drove down the dirt road toward Chaco Canyon, Doris Norris commented on how our last passenger reminded her of a story called "The Black Monk" by Anton Chekhov.

"That is one of my all time favorites," I exclaimed with joy. "You are nonpareil and a paragon of brilliance."

"There is a character," Doris continued, "who has visitations from a black monk. But whereas we saw and spoke to the monk we picked up on the highway, the protagonist of this story is the only person to see the monk. This leaves you with the possibility that he is touched. He is obsessed and has hallucinations. In short, an unreliable narrator."

"I think Chekhov was influenced by Dostoevsky. There is a scene in 'The Brothers Karamazov' where Ivan has an extended meeting with a distinguished gentleman. Ivan suffers from brain fever and ends up breaking down.

"I think his visitation is a creation of his diseased mind. In Chekhov's story, however, I think the black monk does exist. One proof is that Kovrin is emotionally altered and invigorated from his meetings with the monk."

"I beg to differ with you," Doris said.

"No one else sees or hears the monk. Kovrin doesn't share his experience with his family. His relationship with the monk isolates him from others," she argued.

"After they cure him of his mania he turns on his wife and becomes cruel. His dependence on the monk is like a drug addiction that destroys him."

"It's the treatment that destroys him," I protested. "Before his cure he is fun and original. Afterward he is a mediocrity and life is irksome."

"The treatment strips him of his delusion," Doris retorted. "It is his own weakness that causes him to spiral down after his rehab. He collapsed after his separation from his addiction."

"We need an arbitrator to resolve this dispute," I suggested. "Turn down this road and we'll ask one of the local residents."

Doris drove along a single-lane road to a closed gate. We passed through and arrived at a dead end where an old Indian woman sat in the shade. We pulled up and greeted her. She sat inscrutably silent. I explained our disagreement about the monk. Her only response was to flick flies away from her face with an eagle feather. After abortive attempts to communicate we decided to offer her a beverage. "Would you like a can of juice or a Coke?"

"Coke," she suddenly replied perking up. "Coke." I gave her a bottle from the ice chest and she smiled. She handed us a leather bag and kept repeating Coke as we drove away. In the bag was a talisman.

"The message of the monk is silence."

TREK 190

The 1969 film "True Grit" has Rooster Cogburn hired by a young girl to find her father's killer.

The area around Chaco Canyon is as inhospitable in August as "A Season in Hell". It seldom rains but when lightning tracks the sky, the thunder iterates its rumble a thousand times. The downpour makes the dirt road difficult. Even a "Drunken Boat" would become bogged down in the mud.

The campground was full so we were directed to an overflow site off park property. It was a bulldozed acre with no facilities. We set up a canopy to create some shade. There was a smattering of other campers.

"This place is the other side of Telluride," Doris commented. "No trees. No water. How can people live here?"

"The inhabitants abandoned this location around 1300," I explained. "Drought is one of the reasons given for its abandonment. I had a friend named Cecil, who worked driving supplies into the park. He could drive in and out regardless of the road conditions. He lived with his girlfriend Kathy in Thoreau. He gave away copies of Walden Pond to people he picked up hitchhiking. They had a garden and kept chickens and bees. They lived in a shotgun-style house. When the end room eroded, they moved one room closer to the front. Cecil never answered the front door. I was there once when someone knocked on their door and Kathy responded totally nude. Cecil yelled at her that it was impolite to be naked while someone else was fully dressed. She vanished into the bedroom and reappeared wearing a hat."

"That reminds me," Doris said, "of some folks who lived in a walk-up on Carleton in Berkeley. There was a lot of traffic at their house, but everyone walked up the driveway and into the back apartment. Anyone who knocked on the front door apartment was a target for prankster attacks. One morning two men in suits knocked on the front door. My friend Stanley answered with a Bible in his hand. The men wanted to discuss his religious preference.

"Stanley assured them that he was a true believer. He asked them if they had heard about the recent discovery that implicated Jesus in a sex orgy. The men shook their heads in disbelief. Stanley went on about how it had been published with enough detail to qualify as verbal foreplay. The men were grossed out and departed in a huff. Stanley followed them down the block with erotic details of a naked Jesus bumping into warm moist flesh. They never knocked on that door again."

TREK 191

In 1969 President Richard Nixon and South Vietnam President Nguyen Van Thieu jointly announced the withdrawal of 25,000 GI's by August. It was the first break in an escalation program started in 1965 that reached over 500,000 by the time Nixon took office in January.

Late one afternoon as Doris and I scanned the campground, we noticed a VW bus with an eye-catching paint job. It looked familiar so I walked over to reconnoiter, and sure enough I saw friends Zachary and Scooter, whom I met in Yellowstone National Park.

They prepared for a trip to New York where a music festival was set for August 15-17. I suggested they meet Doris and we all drove to the big kiva to experience the changing of the light. When we arrived at the kiva and sat with our backs against the ancient stone wall, Zachary sang "Clouds" by Joni Mitchell. He was oblivious to us as we watched a bat circle the kiva.

Backpack Trekker: A 60's Flashback

"He loves Joni," Scooter explained. "He would collect maple leaves across Canada for her, or volunteer to be an immediate organ donor for her, or live in a Siberian work camp to share a glass of wine with Joni."

"How did you get the idea to paint your bus?" Doris asked.

"We got the idea from Ken Kesey. In 1964 he painted up his bus and left Oregon to make a national statement for freedom of expression. We love his 'Cuckoo's Nest', but feel the bus trip was his greatest accomplishment. We hope to take it further."

Just at sunset a large bat appeared and flew around the kiva. Zachary sang "The Big Yellow Taxi" and we all joined in. The bat picked up on our harmonies and landed near the sipapu.

As we sang, I saw ghostly figures emerge from the hole that leads into the underworld. Barefoot men with long hair marched out into the kiva. I saw Chacoans combine architectural designs with astronomical alignments and geometry to create urban centers where some 5,000 people lived.

We drove back to the campsite in the dark. Zachary was full of hullabaloo so he chopped up two wooden chairs and started a fire. He distributed percussion instruments and Doris, and I accompanied Zachary and Scooter as they sang songs from Joe McDonald and Arlo Gurthrie.

The next day we said goodbye as they headed out for the Catskill Mountains.

TREK 192

In 1969 air headlines went to cut-rate flights across the Atlantic.

Querida María,

The light of August melts us down. I've had many mirthful moments this travel season but one of the best is Doris Norris. Wait until you meet her. Not every event is so agreeable. Here is a story I wrote about theft called "The Guitar".

I walked with my newly acquired guitar out to the highway to thumb a ride. The instrument was a gift from a friend for help on a building project. We made adobes used on a home he designed for the extended family. His in-laws lived with them and two grandchildren. As I walked, a car pulled over.

"You want a ride '*ese*'?" asked a youth with a red bandanna over his eyes.

"Where are you going?" I asked.

"'Burque."

After the exchange of preliminary travel banter, I agreed to ride with him and put the guitar in the backseat. He asked if I would spring for a six pack in trade for the ride.

"Sure." What kind of beer do you drink?"

"Coorrrs," he said, rolling his r's. We stopped at a convenience store and I got out to buy the beer. When I walked out of the store, he had the car running and facing the highway. As I approached the car from the back, he suddenly peeled out and drove off. I stood flabbergasted but had the presence of mind to note the license number. I walked to the police station in Española and reported the fresh crime. We filled out some paperwork and they obtained the driver's name and address from the license number. I asked if a policeman would accompany me to the residence so I could confront the thief. They agreed and as we approached the house, I recognized the car parked in the driveway. I asked the policeman to stop just down from the house. I didn't want to startle the thief. I walked to the front door with the six pack. There was loud music that sounded like a Santana riff. I knocked and waited. No one answered so I knocked louder. The door opened. It was the man who drove off with my guitar.

"We meet again," I said. He made a motion to close the door but I blocked the move with my foot as I saw the guitar. "Don't get nervous," I reassured him. "When you drove off with my guitar, you forgot the beer." I handed him the six-pack and snagged my guitar while he stood pie-eyed. "Adios amigo." I skedaddled out of his yard.

"Wait," he yelled. "I'm sorry I stole your *guitara*. Come back and let's party, *vato*." I ended up staying there all weekend.

Doris asked why I'm not protesting the war, why I didn't march with Martin. I told her I want to use my stamina to know the beautiful places in North America. Hiking into Rainbow Bridge has no politics. When they find this war an embarrassment, the military industrial complex will shut it down and start a new one somewhere else. Why are we still in Korea? Anyway, will see you soon as the summer winds down and another semester ahead.

Your son

☯

Backpack Trekker: A 60's Flashback

In 1969 "Topaz" looks at Russian espionage in Cuba.

As Doris Norris and I sat in the big kiva at sunset, she admitted doing something once she felt was futile.

"I know exactly what you mean," I said. "It reminds me of a situation in Dublin, Ireland, in 1916. I call it 'The Rising.'"

"At twelve noon on Easter Monday, a group of Irish volunteers marched to the General Post Office. They read their declaration of the Irish Republic: "We declare the right of the people of Ireland to the ownership of Ireland, and to the unfettered control of Irish destinies to be sovereign and indefeasible."

"The British attacked the position but could not dislodge them. They called in a gunboat and artillery. After five days of bombardment, the Irish patriots made a run for it. Some were killed and some were wounded and imprisoned. The general population was uninvolved in the rising.

"But the harsh treatment of the insurgents united all of Ireland against the British. A wounded James Connolly was tied to a chair and shot. Over a thousand men were rounded up and imprisoned in England. Michael Collins was one of the men locked up.

"When released, Michael began to organize. He knew pitched battles with English troops was not possible. He created a network of spies and prepared the IRA for guerrilla warfare. An assassination squad was assembled and called the twelve apostles. They were directed to kill people. The apostles decided how and when. Michael Collins picked the targets and as leader of the rebellion became the most wanted man in Ireland. He stayed mostly in Dublin, but when he did travel to other areas, he passed through checkpoints joking with the guards. Michael did not carry a gun.

"The British responded with their own death squad, a gang brought to Ireland to track down Collins and his officers. Years of spiraling violence led one man to proclaim: "It's not those who can inflict the most but those who can endure the most who will conquer." Unable to capture Collins or break the spirit of rebellion, Prime Minister Lloyd George was pressured to negotiate a treaty. They offered a free Ireland except for the six counties in the north, home to a large Protestant population loyal to England. Collins signed the treaty and returned to Ireland to convince his countrymen to accept the terms. There was an element that refused the treaty and turned their guns against their former comrades. As the British troops pulled out of southern Ireland, the Irish began a civil war. Collins used field guns provided by the British to put down the Irregulars. He decided on a trip to Cork to inspect the situation. An aide warned him of the danger in traveling. Collins' reply was, 'Surely they won't shoot me in my own country.'

"Word got out that the Collins' convoy was moving near Cork and the Irregulars planned an ambush in case he passed in that direction. The convoy reached the site fifteen minutes before sunset. A firefight broke out that lasted about seventeen minutes. They held the position until Collins' men cleared an obstruction from the roadway. They could have driven away, but instead Collins felt confident enough to step into the road to aim and fire.

"This open target was not missed by a marksman in the ambush. A bullet hit Collins in the head. He died on August 22, 1922. The civil war ended with the awful realization that former comrades shot such a man as Michael Collins. The treaty was accepted and the Irish Free State was created. All this happened because of a desperate act that seemed a gross failure at the time."

TREK 194

When IRA leader Daniel Breen died in 1969, his body still carried a bullet that hit him almost fifty years before.

As Doris and I rose one morning at dawn, Zen Jazz walked into our campsite carrying a black box.

"Where have you been Zen?" I asked. He wouldn't explain anything until he cupped his hands around a hot coffee.

"I don't blame you," Doris said giving him a hug. "I can't concentrate until after a hot cup." When the coffee was ready, he took a sip and updated us on his adventures.

"I cruised in a rented car at 69 miles-an-hour when a truck tried to occupy my lane. The truck forced me off the highway and I slammed into a tree. It is no fun to find yourself bloody and crushed by the side of the road. The only way out of that situation was to go back in time. Ten minutes before the accident I pulled off the road and read some pages from Mabel Dodge Luhan and her escape to reality on the edge of Taos desert. The time elapsed and the truck drove by changing lanes. No accident. I went back in time once to reposition myself to miss a bullet to the head. I attended my grandfather's wedding recently. It was his fifth marriage. My grandpa is 85 years old and married a woman, 65, who he met at a ballroom dance club. She had been married three times. They considered themselves used people so they went to a pawn shop to buy their rings. They were married in a corn field in Kansas. For their honeymoon they decided to hike a section of the Pacific Crest Trail."

"Your gramps sounds like a cool dude," Doris commented.

"Did you chaperon the newlyweds on their nature stroll?" I asked.

"No. After the ceremonies I joined a group in Oakland to help disseminate info on how and why to avoid the draft. Every year more potential draftees dodge the Selective Service. Zen tapped a button on his vest which read: John Wayne for Secretary of Defense.

"We have to educate people and convince them that our national security is not endangered by a civil war in a small Asian country. I want to see so many men avoid the draft that if the U.S. wants to continue the war, it will have to hire mercenaries. Maybe the Pentagon can pay the French Foreign Legion to fight for them."

"What's in the box?" Doris asked. Zen opened the box and showed us several round light-green buttons that looked like pin cushions.

"Peyote," Zen said. "I think Chaco is the perfect location for a trip. Let's have a snack and astral project."

TREK 195

In 1969 the film "Hello Dolly" brought Barbara Streisand and Louis Armstrong together in song.

Zen removed the peyote from the black box and cut them up into chewy segments.

"Before we take this leap of faith," Zen said, "I want to brief you on having an out-of-body experience. As we prepare for lift-off, you will lose control of your body. This lack of control may cause anxiety, but this will lessen as your spirit abandons the temple. On short trips a silver cord extends like a leash but that will vanish because we are going on a long trip. Your spirit body may seem useless but your senses will be on red alert. You will see colors as your spirit self takes the throttle and your physical self becomes like shedding dead skin. Don't be afraid or you may fall back into your body without venturing far afield. Maintain a bold attitude and we can fly without boundaries. No matter how much fun you have or how powerful you feel, eventually the anxiety will return from being away from your body. When this fear for the welfare of your body becomes dominant, it will trigger a speedy recoil of your spirit to your body. The trip will end suddenly and you will return here. The trip will seem like a relaxant. Is that clear?"

"Where are we going?" Doris asked.

"I don't know for sure. Since we are creative and peaceful people, I don't think we will find ourselves in the rubble of Hanoi after U.S. bombs. I feel a peaceful place but I can't say for sure."

"I'm game," I said.

"Down the hatch with the peyote." Zen prompted. "It has a bitter taste. We can mix it with fresh ginger." We opted to chew it straight and wash it down with sun tea. Zen recited hypnotic phrases as we lay down in the tent and held hands. We closed our eyes and I drifted into sleep with the sense of my other self pulling out of my body. I looked back at the three of us laying in the tent and felt myself soar over the canyon. In a short time I found myself in Sullivan County, New York. Traffic had made a four-lane road out of two lanes and the shoulders. The cars bogged down all headed in the same direction. No one honked or shouted at the people further up who were also at a standstill. I saw a man sitting on the hood of his car playing a guitar. Most people abandoned their cars and walked straight ahead with blankets and ice chests. I didn't see Zen or Doris, so I followed the stream of young people moving inexorably toward the center of the activity.

TREK 196

> In 1969 Sean Connery decided not to continue as James Bond in the sixth 007 adventure "On Her Majesty's Secret Service".

Some of the local people were unsettled by the confusion, upset at the influx of polite youngsters buying out all the groceries on the shelf. The flow of humanity continued past and emptied into a huge field shaped like a natural amphitheater. A fence went up as revelers arrived, but the area they tried to enclose was already filled with thousands of excited people.

The onslaught of more bodies trampled over the pretense of a barrier. Some folks were camped in the woods and had street signs nailed to trees. I saw some wheeling and dealing on High Street. The organizers hoped to sell tickets but the situation was out of their control.

The only option was to pass the hat. They announced from the stage that it was a free concert. With freedom comes responsibility. It seemed at first that no one was responsible. Yet everyone was responsible. As the crowd settled in, the entertainment began with Richie Havens. He played and left and came back to play some more. He reiterated the theme of the event with his song about freedom.

Country Joe kicked the concert into high gear with his "Fixin' to Die Rag". Everyone knew the song and joyously joined in. I saw a man in army fatigues who looked out of place. It was Carrington whom I had met in a campground. He was on the fringe of the festival.

"Carrington," I asked after we saluted each other. "What are you doing in your military garb?"

"It is either Vietnam or peace," he said. "I killed a few people so I can't pretend like I'm angelical."

This gathering represents one end of the polarity that tears America apart. I think Johnson threw in the towel because he realized he was wrong. But as President of a country embroiled in a war that he supported, he didn't have the guts to admit any wrong doing and end the war. All he could do was put his tail between his legs and retire to the comfort of his ranch.

He helped create the mess and then left it for someone else to clean up. He was drowned out in the chorus of "one-two-three-four, what are we fighting for? I don't know, I don't give a damn, next stop is Vietnam."

The pregnant Joan Baez sang, "We Shall Overcome".

TREK 197

In 1969 "The Madwoman of Chaillot", Katharine Hepburn says oil is bubbling up through her basement.

Beatlick Joe Speer

There was a pond in the area where revelers took time out to skinny dip. I saw Zachary and Scooter perched on a rock naked as jaybirds. I greeted them. They had arrived early and helped in the construction of the speaker towers. Their bus was parked on the rim of the bowl looking down onto the stage. He told me where free food was served by the Hog Farm from New Mexico. When I spent time in Berkeley, I knew where to catch a free meal. Good information.

Santana was the first act on Saturday. Carlos and organist Gregg Rolie were a big to-do in the Bay Area, but not many people screamed at the announcement of their set. There was a manager of a hamburger and hot dog stand who hired two hippies to tend to his business as he circulated to other parts of the festival. After he left, his help began trading food for joints.

After they had more joints than they could stuff in their pockets, they cooked the burgers and gave them away. When the food was gone, they closed the stand and rejoined the festivities.

There was a distributor of brown acid. He carried the acid in a brown bag. Somehow a hole developed in the bottom of the bag. The acid trickled out wherever he went. When it rained the moisture activated the chemicals in the acid. As people stood barefoot in the mud, the acid entered their system through their skin.

On stage they had two bands set up on large plywood with casters underneath. They would roll one band off and another one into play to save time. But when the Grateful Dead came on, the contraption broke and they had to set up again. When they finally turned on their amps, they picked up radio signals from a helicopter. The wind blew fiercely and the Dead died on stage.

It was the biggest gig of their career and they blew it. Janis was out of kilter also but it didn't matter. The event was a huge puzzle and everyone was a piece of it. Sly and the Family Stone brought the crowd to their feet.

While The Who was on stage, Abbie Hoffman decided he wanted to harangue the audience about John Sinclair busted for two joints and make everybody feel guilty because they weren't contributing to his legal fund. Pete went to town and tapped him on the back of the head with his guitar. The Jefferson Airplane flew the crowd into Sunday morning. Bonfires flickered like an inverted sky. The area was a rural metropolitan center.

Everybody was doing everything all the time. It was orchestrated chaos. I thought I saw Doris in the first-aid tent talking someone through a rough trip. "It's OK. Just relax. What is your name? What is your birthday? Did you drive here from the city?" I thought I saw Doris, but I was wrong. I was so tired that every woman looked like Doris. I returned to my tent and dreamed a dreamless sleep. I awoke to the sound of a glass bell filled with questions marks. A shadow dancing on the moon reminded me of someone I once knew.

TREK 198

> In 1969 the British film "If" pitted boarding school students against an administration ready to abro- gate individual freedom.

After the first downpour, the area in front of the stage was churned up by anxious feet into a pigsty. A swill of swell. Joe Cocker talked directly to us, and he got on fine with a little help from his friends when a second rain pelted the site. The moisture descended while bombs fell on Hanoi. We became one with na- ture. My body was back in a hot dry area so it didn't matter to me, but it was hard later when they reoccupied the stage for wet peo- ple to have fun in the dark, in the mud, in the approaching cool. Thank God they turned off the power on the amps and the towers did not fall. Many people had appointments on Monday or back to work and decided to pack it in on Sunday afternoon. Some tried to find protection in plastic. Others received the drops like inspiration and ran and played in the mud. Some people washed off in the lake and changed clothes in a tent. Get ready for extra innings.

I met a girl named Alison. She was staying in a van with her parents. We were introduced. Her dad was smoking a cigar.

"The tobacconist gives me this authority of smoke," he said. "Did you hear about the hamburger stand attacked by a gang of anti-capitalists? Freedom also means that people are free to pro- mote their products. The vendor said to 'buy and pay up or move along.' Vagrancy laws apply when standing in front of the cash register. The fractious faction responded by knocking over the stand. When the news got out, we headed a committee to reim- burse the capitalist, the seller of beef patties. Even vegetarians contributed." He passed the cigar to his wife.

"Talking about capitalists at a free event," she said, "it didn't take long for the phone company to realize they had a gold mine here in collect calls. There was a girl on the phone calling her parents to reassure them she was not starving. Everybody shared their provisions. There's a longer line for the phones than for the potty-chairs." She said and handed the cigar to me.

"As you might have heard," I said, "Abbie Hoffman has been up to no good. He has successfully extorted money from the promoters. Before the festival started, Abbie demanded money or he threatened to cause trouble. They paid him off and he has still caused trouble. He tried to sneak into where the film is stored. Maybe he thought he could steal a few reels and sell them on the black market. Pete Townshend bumped Abbie with his guitar. Abbie ended up with a bloody nose and went to the first-aid tent. No one recognized him and he had to wait his turn. He was so frustrated he left the festival alone," I reported.

TREK 199

In 1969 the film "Battle of Britain" featured a stellar cast of outnumbered Royal Air Force pilots fighting the Luftwaffe.

Every event has a spillover effect. There is a murky phase between cause and effect like fresh water mixed with brine. The three-day festival carried over into the fourth day. Some people woke up on Monday to the retroactive Sha Na Na, an energetic group who ran around the stage. They were too pepped up to confront so early in the morning without a good face wash and several cups of coffee. Hendrix's white guitar and his Band of Gypsies took over.

I heard a story that Hendrix flew in on an army helicopter. He asked the pilot questions and learned he had served in Vietnam. What did he remember about his tour of duty? The copter pilot recalled the confusing sound of guns and bombs blasting simultaneously. The horrendous sounds still caused him nightmares even though he had left Vietnam years before. During Hendrix' set, he thought of the pilot and the men still dying in Vietnam. Hendrix saw another devastated field in front of the stage. He felt the exhaustion of the musicians on stage. There was a lull in the jam like the silence before an ambush. He connected the festival with the war and updated the stars in the blood spattered banner.

Suddenly Zen appeared collecting garbage.

"Zen," I said. "Are you part of the please force?"

"No," Zen replied. "I got caught up in the spirit of participation. I wanted to contribute, so I served in the freak-out tent trying to help people over-amped on acid. One guy came in claiming he had found the Holy Grail. I asked him what his name was. He said it was Bob. I told him to just relax and the chemicals would wear off soon and he'd be hungry for a cream pie."

"After I talked him through his crisis, instead of releasing him back to the general population, I pointed to a new arrival flipped out and ranting. I suggested he become the doctor and help the next person."

Zen and I continued to work side by side picking and piling the garbage.

"Should we think about returning to our bodies?" I asked.

"I'm not going back," Zen announced.

"What? Are you serious?"

"I have seldom seen such a spirit of collective cooperation. I want my spirit to melt into this energy. From now on I will only exist as a wind of positive force."

"What about your body?"

"Burn my body in the wilderness. While it burns, chant: Let me take you higher."

"But Zen. You are my best friend. The world will be sad without you."

"I will come to you when the air moves. I will touch you with impalpable strength." I felt fear and my spirit lifted off and floated away from the site. I saw Zen as a speck standing in the middle of a huge peace sign made from garbage. I reunited instantly with my body. Doris sat in the VW. We hugged silently.

"Zen isn't coming back," I said.

TREK 200

In 1969 the film "Oh! What A Lovely War" presented the futility of World War I.

Doris Norris and I found Zen's body by the fire pit. We loaded his corpse into the '69 VW bug. She agreed to help me fulfill Zen's last request to burn his body. There was no wood in Chaco Canyon for a fire so we drove to the Los Pinos Wilderness area near Cuba, New Mexico. We found a low spot near boulders to contain the flames and decided to ignite near sunset so the smoke would dissipate in twilight gray. By 19:00 hours we wanted the embers to be on the wane. Maybe I could preserve a molar as a relic.

We collected wood and crosshatched kindling several layers deep, on top of which we laid Zen. As Doris covered him with twigs, Zen stood up. He looked just like a modern Kokopelli. I took pages from Hermann Hesse's "Siddhartha" to crumple up and place under Zen's funeral pyre. With preparations complete we had about an hour until the changing of the light so we exchanged stories about our astral trip to Woodstock.

Doris said she saw flowers and dry clothes drop from the sky. The fires at night reminded her of a vast army splayed out and alert on the night before the battle.

She remembered the assuring voice over the sound system as the storm approached and the wind put a scare into the towers. Finally they turned the power off and she took cover in the abandoned house.

Near sunset Doris struck a match and ignited Zen's bonfire. I beat on a pan with a stick while Doris read from "The Tibetan Book of the Dead". As a bed of coals developed, I threw bigger branches onto the fire. When the flames subsided, I said a prayer over the ashes. I started to rake the ashes I noticed one of his body parts was still extant. I was amazed and pointed it out to Doris.

"Look at that," she said. "Zen's penis didn't burn."

"And it is still erect after the fire," I observed. Doris took a towel and removed it from the ashes.

She placed it in the black box. We both agreed it was a sign from Zen. A whirlwind surprised us and hovered over the scorched spot. It twisted and picked up all the ashes. Zen was lifted high and dissipated in the wilderness air.

"Goodbye Zen," I shouted. Doris entered the VW to store the box. The bug suddenly took off with her feet sticking out the window.

"I can't stop," she yelled as the VW disappeared.

TREK 201

In 1969 the French film "Z" created a riveting drama about the killing of a peace movement leader in Greece.

Alone again ... circulating the sudden feeling of friendship lost ... searching for the freewheeling Volkswagen while Zen floats smoothly on hawk wing, black wing and clouds create illusions ...

Backpack Trekker: A 60's Flashback

Querida María,

You won't believe me now ... where is Doris Norris that I want you to meet? No relic of our love, no ticket from the festival or photograph to prove I was there ... I'll arrive empty-handed but not empty-headed ... I might as well start walking ... "I'm walking down the line" as Arlo sang ... I'll walk all night and at sunrise find myself on a highway .. then I'll be one ride from the Frontier Restaurant ... "In the mountains, there you feel free ..." if only Casey Stengel had started the series with Whitey Ford instead of Art Ditmar ... if that sure double play ball Bill Virdon hit at Tony Kubek in the eighth inning had stopped short of the pebble that deflected it at Tony's throat ... it's not right that the best team lost ... it's not right to be left alone in the wilderness ... only God and the Grand Canyon remain forever ... the civil rights movement is over ... flower power is over ... the dream has been deferred but they can't kill all the dreamers ... I'm alone but I feel grateful ... glory to the most high, thank you God for a singular summer ... Zen left me with a beautiful vision ... I'm no Hans Castorp disappearing in the mud and poison gas of the trenches ... I'm no Yossarian running away from the insanity of war ... I'm no Ishmael floating on a handmade coffin ... I'm not one of the forgotten dying in Calcutta in a dormitory full of the infirm with a sister of mercy holding my hand ... I see myself in a Spanish mission at the end of a long day's journey ... *una jornada* ... a born again preacher says there is only one way to salvation ... I think there are many ways ... like water running down the mountain, it will find a way along an established furrow or carve a new channel ... I think Dostoevsky found salvation through words and a love supreme ... a horde of homopterous insects cause a furious flutter outside the stained glass of the church ... the preacher ignores this pinprick of nature and reads from the book of Revelation ... "Take some laudanum and read 'Kubla Khan'," I yell from the balcony ... there is a silence like just before the lottery numbers are announced ... or the still inhalation of an assassin as he takes a bead on his target ...

Sometimes I feel like I'm almost gone ... the insects smash through the glass and carry the preacher out the front door ... I feel an upsurge of energy and know it is time to rededicate myself to the distant future ... we have to improve ourselves ... they cannot fold, spindle or mutilate the dream ... when they killed Dr. King, we created a wet dream, wet with the blood of the lamb ... Querida María ... your faith is a lifeline through the architecture of

silence ... perfection within the body of woman ... goodbye Zen ...
if I puff on a pipe on a train to Capri I will see your face in the
smoke ... I walk in the dark woods, searching for the magic
VW ... I will stand on the corner of Cornell where ... two cops on
bicycles ... both wearing helmets ... as we grow accustomed to
more armed security and searches for drugs ... one cop is writing
a ticket for a barefoot youngster on a skateboard ... the kid
breaks free ... and rolls south toward Zempoaltepec, Mexico ...
the cops snicker and enter the Frontier Restaurant ... their bikes
chained up to the front bumper of the Doris Norris '69 VW ... the
ghosts of dead writers ... sit in disarray ... I read in the newspapers about Vietnamizing the war ... let Vietnamese kill Vietnamese as we pull out the American soldiers to reduce our casual-
ties ... but keep the war going ... am I wacko or are the stripes in
our flag bending to resemble a swastika? ... it feels like I'm going
zigzag ... at a spanking pace ... there's more info every day ...
there are too many movies ... and way too many soldiers paid to
kill ... my number is called ... can I buy a lottery ticket with my
eggs and chorizo? ... in this commercial world? ... I will probably
die buying a book ... I don't want to get fleeced ... or victimized in
a health insurance scam or forfeit my social security benefits ... I
want to croak ... while I line my pockets .. what good is a college
education if you can't scrape together some moolah? ... I want to
die cutting a lucrative deal ... tomorrow there will be no mention
of this in the media ... it will be as if it never happened ...

Your son, Joe

Backpack Trekker: A 60's Flashback

SOURCES:

* "The Timetables of History – A Horizontal Linkage of People and Events" based on Werner Stein's *"Kulturfahrplan"*. English language edition; copyright 1975 Simon & Schuster/ Touchstone.
* "The Film Encyclopedia: Rating the Movies for Home Video, TV and Cable", by Ephraim Katz, 1979.
* "Encyclopedia Year Book 1970" Grollier Limited/Rock and Roll: 1955-1970, Richard Carlin.
* "Facts on File Publications", New York, 1988.
* "That Championship Feeling: The Story of the Boston Celtics" by Joe Fitzgerald.
* "At the River I Stand" by Joan Turner Beifuss, printed through Wimmer Brothers, Memphis, TN, 1985.
* "All My Octobers," by Mickey Mantle, Harper Paperbacks, NY, 1995.
* "The Illustrated Life of Michael Collins" by Colm, Connolly, Roberts, Rinehart Publishers, Boulder, CO.
* "Basketball: The American Game", by Joe Jares A. Rutledge, Book 1971.
* "Sideshow Bennie's Calendar of Wonders: A Significant Trivia Calendar 2002" Goodlettsville, TN.

Beatlick Joe Speer

ABOUT BEATLICK JOE SPEER
1948-2011

Beatlick Joe Speer, publisher of "Beatlick News: A Poetry & Arts Newsletter", came out of the great southwest. He graduated from New Mexico State University in 1970 with a degree in literature. An iconic and itinerant raconteur of the highest order, Joe loved to travel with his chauffeur/girlfriend Pamela Adams Hirst. Living out of a 1977 VW camper, they visited ancient sites, wilderness areas, remote hot springs, ghost towns and decommissioned forts from the Indian Wars.

He continuously documented his pursuit of poetry on the back roads of literature. His unique style, imagery and delivery set him apart as a performance poet. No modern media escaped his influence: community access television, radio, short film, DVD's, CD's MP3's, even YouTube. Now "Backpack Trekker: A 60's Flashback" is his final legacy as he begins his trek across the universe.

beatlick.com
facebook.com
chucksville.com

Books are like angels
moving between the living and the dead.
— Beatlick Joe

Made in the USA
Charleston, SC
18 September 2013